KU-306-704

CONTENTS

ILLUSTRATIONS

CANNIBAL CARAVAN

by

Charles "Cannibal" Miller

LONDON
MUSEUM PRESS LIMITED

First published in 1950

B51- 736

PRINTED IN GREAT BRITAIN BY
GILMOUR & DEAN LIMITED
GLASGOW AND LONDON

INTRODUCTION

CHARLES C. MILLER is still a young man, lithe, alert, vigorous, with a seeing eye and a full appreciation of life. Yet his career reads like the-dream-come-true of an adventurous small boy.

The world is his range and has been since his earliest childhood. He has fraternised with cannibals, faced wild beasts in the jungle, taken pictures of still wilder men in remote and far away places. An ace in the World War, he knows from first hand experience, the full meaning of an aerial "dog fight." He knows peace-time aviation as well. He has done barnstorm flying and has been an airplane chauffeur for a rancher. In fact, throughout his life he has known few dull moments.

Pictures have been a large part of his life. They still are. To Charlie Miller, photography is not a mere word. It couldn't be as he has been a cameraman since he was six years old. It was at this period in his life that his father gave him a camera to keep him out of mischief. It was the first of an exceedingly long line. Some of the finest instruments that have been produced have been owned or used by him. Some of the best pictures in his vast collection he has made with a camera which he had built from odds and ends gathered here and there.

It might be well to start at the beginning and just take things as they have come since Charlie Miller has done that all his life and will more than likely continue to do so until he takes his last picture.

As seems fitting, he was born in a far away place; Samarang, Java, to be explicit. His father was then a captain in the Dutch East Indian Army. When Charles was a mere toddler, orders came to his father to go to Dutch New Guinea. It was something of an assignment that the government of The Netherlands gave the captain. All he had to do was to stamp out cannibalism and head hunting. Being a good soldier, he set about his task with all possible speed.

In going to New Guinea, he took with him his wife and son. Thus, Charles Miller's mother was the first white woman to visit Dutch New Guinea. She was also the first white woman to make her home there. Charles was the first white child. The fact that there was no town in which his family could live, did not discourage Charles' father. He promptly founded one —Merauke. That was in 1902.

That there was no school was no drawback either. His mother started in to teach her son. She not only started but continued. Hence, from his mother Charles received his grammar school education.

Now get this picture. Here was a white family on a far away island. About them, the jungle, deep, almost impregnable, mysterious. In those green depths, terror in various forms. Terror both four-legged and two-legged. Men to whom other men were food. Men who ate those they slew in battle—and dried and preserved the heads of their victims as trophies.

From his very earliest memory, those green depths fascinated Charles Miller. They seemed to be calling to him. The tall trees didn't wave in the hot breath of the tropics, they beckoned. The wild men of the jungle depths were not enemies. They were attractive; something strange and new; and learning about them far more interesting knowledge than that contained between the covers of books.

How old he was when he made his first exploration, Charles Miller doesn't remember. He must have been very young because it caused a great commotion. It is easy to picture the consternation of his parents when Charlie "turned up" missing. Death lurked in the jungle. Death for grown men. And he was only a little boy.

Friendly blacks were hurriedly called in. They had no difficulty in following the trail of the little feet since a bent twig, a broken bush, the faint imprint of a foot, all were as plain to them as print. It was late in the afternoon when they found him, and brought him back. He tried to explain that he had been merely doing a little exploring. But no one seemed to understand. And so, he was sent to bed without his supper. There was no cure, however. Charles Miller is still an explorer.

Despite the many adventures of his young boyhood, adventures having to do with reptiles, animals and wild men, Charlie Miller reached high school age. That brought a temporary end to his explorations and adventures. He was shipped off to Holland for an education. When he finished high school he decided to take up engineering. So there were college years —years in which he dreamed of the wilds of his youth.

He didn't follow the calling of an engineer, however. Engineers have adventures but not enough of them. So he took up racing motor-cycles, boats and automobiles. He brushed death on many tracks in Europe but finally decided that there were still more thrills in the air. That meant becoming an aviator which he did.

Back in 1914, he was working with the Caudron airplane factory. Word reached him that the French government had need of every man with airplane knowledge. Immediately he set out to enlist. He was made a lieutenant. His duties began immediately and the fact that he had no uniform made no difference, there being no time for delay in the World War. Five months after he was commissioned, he received a uniform. Five years later, he left the service.

He is reticent concerning his war experiences. It is known, however, that he brought down many planes. In his possessions, hidden away in trunks, are medals from various nations.

After the war he did barnstorming flying. In those days, barnstorming might fairly be classified as an extra hazardous occupation. In fact, no barnstormer could obtain life insurance. The crates of those days were often merely death traps. But Miller flew them in South Africa, in the Dutch Indies, in Australia. It was there that the company backing the aerial circus went to the wall and its planes were sold to satisfy creditors.

Broke in Sidney, Miller logically enough, sought a job. A friend told him of an opening with a pie factory. As it was driving a delivery truck, he thought it right in his line. He was hired without question and the next morning started out with a full line of pies and other choice pastry, mostly of the kind containing a lot of whipped cream. It was his idea that he should make time. That the road was rough made no difference to a war time aviator.

Finally he reached his first customer and opened the back door of the truck. The sight that met his eyes caused him to drive back quickly to the bakery, slip in, get his coat and sneak right out again without the formality of resigning. In all his life, he had never seen such scrambled, mixed, blended and utterly ruined pastry.

After that, he served a rancher as an aerial chauffeur. That job gave out and then he became a tester of speed boats in Sidney Harbour. But he wasn't happy. He was thinking of Dutch New Guinea and that fascinating jungle. The thought didn't take long to be translated into action, a change hastened by the fact that his father wanted to see him.

The adventures Charles Miller had in Dutch New Guinea in his young manhood would fill several books. He learned the jungle thoroughly, the little passage ways that enable natives to travel almost at will. The tricks and the perils to be avoided. In between flying, racing and other matters, he had continued with his photography. And the jungle was well worth recording in pictures.

With a great collection of pictures and with his taste for adventure satisfied for the moment at least, he went back to Australia. Conditions didn't seem to be any better than they had been when he was there before. But money from the sale of pictures gave him a back log. He might have remained in Sidney much longer than he did had it not been for Sail-On.

Sail-On was not an order. He was a horse. A horse that was to run in the local Derby. Sail-On took Charlie Miller's eye. The price was 100 to 1 which showed that the bookmaker thought that the age of sail had been replaced by the age of steam. Nevertheless, Miller bet his entire social security on Sail-On. And Sail-On rewarded him by coming in half a length ahead of his nearest rival.

America had been beckoning to Miller. Sail-On made America possible. Soon after the race he sailed for Vancouver. He thought he was done with adventure. That he would settle down and really take pictures.

Just to make things a little more interesting, the first morning he was in Vancouver, he witnessed a hold-up. He left pronto for Seattle.

But the very first night he was in Seattle there was great commotion in his hotel. The place seemed literally full of police. When the smoke cleared away, they left with several patrol wagons loaded with prisoners. It seems that Charlie had inadvertently registered at the headquarters of a flock of bootleggers. In no time at all, he was testing airplanes and flying passengers.

From Seattle, he went on to San Francisco where he raced automobiles on the Tanforan horse race track. Next he obtained an auto of his own and instead of racing it, drove down to Los Angeles where he became a motion picture camera man. A motion picture man has a lot of adventures but after what Cannibal Charlie Miller had seen, heard and photographed, the job seemed tame.

Again, the jungle called—so he came East to lead an expedition into Dutch New Guinea for Miss Leona Jay, a society girl who craved adventure. On the expedition, Charlie proceeded to marry his charming backer, in Java.

Back in New York once again, Mr. and Mrs. Charles "Cannibal" Miller are now preparing for their next jungle trip; for once the feel of Dutch New Guinea gets in your blood—well, let Cannibal Charlie tell you, and you will understand.

L. L. STEVENSON.

CHAPTER I

CANNIBAL CARAVAN

THE miasmic mist was just lifting from the river when I gave the word to cast off. A hush fell over the throng loading the rickety dock, a hush that transferred itself to the eleven canoe-loads of Kaya-Kayas strung out in tow behind the launch. In the breathless silence that followed the only movement visible was the ceaseless cruising of the sharks as they notched the water with sun-tipped ripples of destruction.

Achmed felt the drama of the moment, felt it clear to the bottom of his black Malayan soul. With true Oriental pomp he strutted the width of the deck, paused with his hand on the whistle cord.

A cloud of steam spurted from the brass cylinder. A low, heavy note, growing in volume, shook the boat from stem to stern. From the convoy behind came two or three splashes as the weak in heart deserted with the first toot. Once more Achmed pulled. Again came the frightful blast guaranteed by the Chinese ship chandler in Java. I looked at Captain Jan Versteegh standing on the dock and I could see that at last he was impressed.

But Achmed overdid it. He gave still another jerk. For a second the note held strong and clear. Then it coughed, sputtered, and before the horrified Malay could release the cord it had died down to a hiss as impotent as steam escaping from a tenement radiator.

"Blow on it," advised Captain Versteegh.

"Don't chide him, captain," admonished the missionary who with Captain Versteegh composed the white population of Merauke. "Little boats should be seen and not heard."

Red faced, I looked for Achmed but he had already vanished into the hold. Malay curses floated out of the hatch, punctuated by the furious banging of bolt-wood as it was slammed into the fire box. In a moment clouds of smoke belched from the squat funnel and settled over the protesting Kaya-Kayas astern.

Slowly the launch began to make headway against the current. One by one the canoes behind took up the slack, and as the last one swung into line we were off. Even so, there was no immediate relief. At top speed the launch barely exceeded six miles an hour, and we were bucking the full force of a four mile current. An hour later I was still close enough to the dock to see Captain Versteegh come rushing down with a pair of old oars and wave them frantically in my direction.

I gave a short, very short, toot on the whistle, just to show I could do it. The engine faltered, but a moment later it picked up the steady throb that was already working a few of the deck planks loose.

The farewells were over but still we lingered, apparently stuck in a midstream current that matched the speed of our donkey engine. Every time Achmed threw in another stick of wood the safety valve popped. In desperation I tied down the valve and ordered Achmed to give her the works.

"Yes, tuan," he assented wildly. "I'll blow her up."

And that's what he meant to do. That stocky little Malay, after fifteen years with the Dutch Colonial Army, wasn't happy unless he was tempting death in one violent form or another. Soon sparks mingled with the smoke pouring from the funnels. Tar began bubbling in the deck seams above the fire box. Wails came from astern as the singed natives in the eleven canoes that formed our tow began batting out the smouldering embers that were showering down upon them like rain.

But we moved. A little steam leaked out around the packing of the boiler head, but in the main the rivets and bolts held. It was true the propeller was kicking up an awful pile of foam in proportion to the speed but that was just a little fault of Wah Yong, the Chinese naval architect. In designing the boat for shallow-draft navigation, he had stuck the propeller shaft straight through the lower half of the transom instead of below the keel as is customary, with the result that the blades were churning half air, half water. The boys in the first canoe of our tow were all but sprayed under before we succeeded in shifting enough cargo astern to bury the propeller.

While this shifting of ballast had the desired effect in improving the efficiency of our propeller, it created a decided list to port. That, too, was traceable to the boat designer in Java. While in Samarang, I had given Wah Yong explicit instructions on how he was to construct my yacht.

"What I want," I told him, "is a boat that will not draw more than two feet of water yet will be big enough to carry six or eight passengers, a cord of wood and half a ton of cargo. I want it steam-powered so I can refuel from the jungle and not be running out of gasoline half way up the creek. I am going to be towing a bunch of natives in their canoes so I want the stern built so it won't pull off with the first yank. The river is full of logs so I want a stout bottom. Got it?"

"Yah, sule. No tlouble atall. Velly easy." He nodded his head so convincingly I got the idea he was in the habit of turning out a boat like that every day.

I was present when the craft was launched. I thought I had seen the first and the last of it right then and there. It headed down the ways like a comet looking for a place to become a meteorite, struck the water and veered sharply to the left in a steep bank. For a moment it looked like an airplane about to slip off in a spin, then its speed was checked and it circled lazily around until it nosed back into the ways it had just left. My first impression was that somebody had left the rudder jammed hard over, but the darned boat never came out of the bank. It just lay there on its side, panting slightly but apparently well satisfied that at least it floated. Judging by the expression on Wah Yong's face, he was too.

As for the list to port, Wah Yong patiently pointed out that by piling my fire wood on the starboard side instead of in the wood bunker on the port side, I would automatically trim the ship. That sounded all right, my only experience along boating lines being in speed-boats, and a few trial runs proved that it worked out all right. The boat was accordingly paid for and loaded on the first freighter bound for Merauke, Dutch New Guinea. And now I was learning that with every stick of wood Achmed threw in the firebox, the starboard side floated that much higher. That old law of diminishing returned. With all moveable ballast needed to hold down the stern, with no room

Dema of Murder

Head hunting has its own dema which is distinguished from all others by having a preserved head worked into lavish head-dress

Cutting a Neat Figure

Tattooing is one form of adornment greatly favoured by Kaya-Kaya women

Mourning Capes

A death in a family of these women forces them to wear grass capes

for additional ballast when carrying a full load of wood, and with no way to pick up additional ballast as the wood went up in smoke, our only solution was to keep moving ourselves around on deck according to the exigencies of the situation. Refueling time always found us hanging over the starboard rail.

By us I mean first my wife, co-partner in the expedition that was taking us into Dutch New Guinea in pursuit of adventure; Achmed, our fireman; Mandoer, our headman and personal boy; Muda, Achmed's engineer, and Kitjil, Admo and Wirio. The latter five were Malays I picked up in Java. All of them had served hitches in the Dutch Colonial Army and were noted for their bravery, recklessness and faithfulness under any and all conditions. They were the backbone of our expedition, and upon them rested the responsibility of keeping the fifty or so native Kaya-Kayas who composed our carrying and fighting force in line. Even this early in the game I knew I had chosen wisely.

Our plans, always subject to change without notice, were to proceed north up the Merauke river as far as possible in the steam launch, and then to continue on up to the headwaters in the Sterren mountains by canoe, after which we were to make a few cross country jaunts, returning to the coast by way of the Digoel river that quartered off to the southwest from the same mountains in which the Oewimmerah had its source. A simple little route as easy to trace on the map as a three-months' vacation in the Maine woods. That is, it would have been if the country ever had been mapped. And it would have been mapped, too, if every mile of it wasn't over-run with cannibals.

Now there are two ways of looking at cannibals. If you are going in to New Guinea to run a survey or hunt for gold you don't want to look at them at all. But when you are going in with a camera you go looking for them on purpose. Thus upon encountering the devils your reaction is one of relief rather than of dread. No cannibals—no picture.

By high noon we had dropped the village of Merauke behind a bend and found ourselves upon a mile-wide body of water that was still more of an estuary than a fresh water river. Low banks sagging under the weight of dense vegetation bordered both sides of the stream, offering sanctuary to everything from crocodiles to sand fleas. This sanctuary extended out about a hundred yards from shore, after which the river was turned over to the sharks. Those black demons took excellent care of their charge. At no time of the day or night was the river free of their blood-thirsty patrols, and that the depths were as efficiently scoured as the surface would be evidenced when an apparently clear stretch of water would suddenly boil into foam as though shaken by a subterranean volcano.

Sharks also furnished the answer to the question of why the Kaya-Kayas, notoriously lazy, always paddled their canoes standing up. The canoes, hollowed out of teakwood trunks, were unstable enough to capsize under the weight of a fleeting thought, and as if this were not enough, the natives insisted on raising the centre of gravity several feet by standing up. They would rather run the more-than-slight chance of tipping over standing up than face the certainty of losing an arm to a shark by paddling sitting down.

Right now my natives were having the time of their lives— a free ride behind a "fire-canoe." and upstream to boot. That was why I had eleven canoes in tow instead of six. When the word spread that I wanted a crew of fifty natives and six long war canoes for the expedition, every fighting man within ten miles of Merauke headed for the dock in anything that would float. They would have come from greater distances were it not for the social custom of welcoming a stranger with his own head served on a platter. Not to mention sundry other portions of his anatomy.

I had no difficulty in selecting fifty big bucks, not one of them measuring less than six feet in height. Ten of the most intelligent Malayans were taken from the chain gang, light-hearted murderers from Java sent to serve out their sentences in New Guinea. The rest were local boys, most of whom I had known as children during my previous residence in Merauke. That many I selected, but if I thought that was the end of it, I was sadly mistaken. Another fifty or sixty, including several young women insisted upon coming along for the trip. Because they would live off the land, because they augmented our show of force, and because they would come along anyway, I told them to hook on.

In the first canoe were ten picked warriors, slightly cleaner than was their wont because of their shower bath earlier in the day but still filthy enough to survive. They were the choicest specimens of Kaya-Kaya manhood to be found on the island, everyone of them a giant of six-foot four and over. I think Wasbus, the tallest of the lot, would have topped six-foot six. His size alone would have qualified him as a leader, but in addition to bulk he had what could pass for a brain in almost any country. He further clinched his claim to fame by owning the largest canoe in Merauke, the canoe in which he and his nine compatriots were riding. It was all of thirty-five feet long, by two feet wide, and as choice a piece of boat building as has ever been dug out with a clam shell. It was further distinguished by having the two eyes in the bow painted a brilliant red and emphazised by circles of white.

My Javanese cut-throats occupied the second canoe. The chain gang was still close enough behind them to keep them together out of a feeling of mutual sympathy, but as we progressed and their sense of freedom increased, they gradually lost their clannishness. In considering them it must be remembered that their only crime was that of murder, and up to the arrival of the Dutch, murder in Java was no crime. It was a necessary pleasure.

The other nine canoes, trailing along like a string of logs, were filled with a heterogeneous collection of warriors and their female admirers. The women were not there by permission of any sense of gallantry. If they wanted to be there, they would have to work and work harder than the men. When the time came, they'd have to paddle, cut fire wood, cook, and otherwise make themselves useful. This latter included assuaging any sudden biological urges on the part of the bucks.

But for the moment, at least, all thoughts of work were forgotten. Shrieks of sheer animal delight at thus easily ascending the river made a bedlam out of our party. Every now and then a warrior would let fly with an arrow at some shark cruising dangerously close, and then everyone would watch in fascinated enjoyment as the other sharks closed in to devour their wounded companion. Cannibalism was a trait the natives could always admire, even in sharks.

The current in the river at this point had picked up considerably because of ebb tide, and to avoid the brunt of it I swung closer to shore. Here the water was sluggish, but so was my boat. The wild life along the bank which at first showed signs of alarm at our approach soon grew resigned to our presence and eventually accepted us as a permanent part of the landscape.

It hurt my pride to see a crocodile rear up prepared to dash into the water at a second's notice, then gradually settle back and finally drop off in a prolonged slumber. I shot one out of pure malice for doing nothing more than that.

That was a mistake. The echo of my shot had hardly ceased reverberating from one jungle wall to the other than every canoe in the fleet was free of the tow line and the natives were paddling for shore like mad. The crocodile, in the meantime, was making a shambles out of everything less than two feet in diameter. Twice he stood on his tail, to come crashing down like a thirty-foot flail. In the two minutes between the time I killed him and the time he realised he was dead, the crock had wiped out nearly thirty feet of jungle, making an ideal landing place for the canoes.

Immediately a frightful row went up. Everybody claimed the crock or at least half of him. Stone axes were about to take part in the argument before I could make myself heard. Even then I had to fire my pistol to command attention.

"The river is full of *Kiws*, is it not so?"

They agreed the river was full of crocodiles.

"I have many bullets for my gun, is it not so?"

They agreed on this point also.

"Well then, stop fighting. I will shoot many more crocodiles for you when you work hard for me. Yes?"

"Yes, tuan. Eeeyah—eeyah—" and with wild shrieks they fell upon the crocodile still twitching on the ground.

By this time Achmed was on deck with six gleaming axes under his arm. He didn't say anything, just stood there.

One by one the natives hovering around the crock caught sight of Achmed and came sidling over.

They eyed the axes enviously. Bright gleaming metal—metal, not stone—sharp—cut off a head in jig time—what they would give for one of those axes. Achmed surveyed the wild crew with insolent superiority. Despite the fact that he was smaller even than their women, he knew he could handle any ten that wanted to fight. Didn't he carry a gun? Wasn't he in charge of the toolchest—that treasure load of genuine metal that would cut? Wasn't he my Number one boy? With the air of a king bestowing knighthood on half a dozen vassals, he summoned six stalwarts to paddle out for the axes.

"Cut wood for the fire canoe—this long, so," he ordered, indicating the desired length on the axe handle. "Rush it along."

Howling with delight, the six selected wood-choppers plunged into the jungle. For a minute I thought I had seen the last of them. Natives will do anything for metal. In the stone-age land of Dutch New Guinea so phenomenal a thing as iron or steel that will hold an edge and cut is valued more than life itself. And these boys, armed with not one but six magic axes, might well varnish into the jungle to hew out an empire of their own. They probably could have done it, too, and might have tried weren't they followed by every jealous citizen on the shore. Everyone wanted to watch the axes sink into hard wood like a bamboo knife into soft flesh. White men tackling a dead teak or ebony tree swear the wood is hard enough to turn an axe, but to these natives, accustomed to wearing out a tree with a stone club, the wood melted away in glorious fashion. Then too, these giants of mine swung an axe as though resolved that if they couldn't cut a tree down with one stroke at least they could knock it over.

While the work of cutting wood and butchering the crock was getting under way, Achmed was getting the boat ready to take on cargo. Leery of the ebbing tide, he backed out into the stream, and then directed a few of the boys to line up the canoes end to end to form a narrow bridge between the launch and shore. I was doubtful about this, but pretty soon a stream of natives began crossing the primitive pontoon bridge like so many ants, each one loaded down with wood. Several, in the hope that next time they would be remembered when the axes were passed around, came aboard loaded down with brush, twigs and even dry grass.

Leona and I used this interlude for our dinner hour. I was starved, practically famished in fact, and as the dinner progressed under the skilled hands of Admo, whose fame as a chef extended from one end of the Dutch East Indies to the other, I ate until I had to move my chair back from the table to make room for my stomach. Then remembering there were tough days on the trail ahead, I plunged into a second helping of curry. Along about this time I was slowed down enough to notice my wife wasn't eating much more than you could stuff into a parrot. Once I had noticed this much, I suddenly recalled that we were on our honeymoon.

"What's the matter?" I asked solicitously. "Aren't you hungry?"

"I guess not," she said, looking at me in a peculiar way and laying down her fork. "I feel hungry, but I don't feel like eating."

We were sitting under an awning on the forward deck, me with my back to the shore and my wife facing me. A disturbance of some kind caused me to turn around, and then, for the first time, I caught the full significance of the scene upon which my wife had been gazing during the dinner.

Clustered about the gutted remnants of a once mighty crocodile were eighteen to twenty natives, bloody from head to foot and fighting loudly for the choicest morsels. A couple were sawing away at the claws with their bamboo knives, the claws being valuable both as arrow points and as necklace beads. Three or four other were gently pounding out the teeth with their stone clubs, the teeth being as highly valued as the claws and for the same purposes. More were engaged in cleaning off patches of hide with which to make drum heads, and still others were salvaging the more edible chunks of flesh. All in all, it was a pretty rough sight for a girl brought up on Park Avenue in New York City. If that weren't enough, there was the smell of the natives engaged in loading wood.

Now the smell of a little native is something to conjure with. Some say it is strong enough to cut into small bricks and use as the foundation of a house. Others claim that a polecat caught in the rain smells like fried chicken to a hungry tramp in comparison. My own interpretation of the smell, and the more accurate one, I think, is that it resembles the odour of a barrel of rancid butter left in the sun so long it has finally blown the head off. That goes for the little natives. Mine were the big ones. Full of apologies at my carelessness, I hastily changed places with her, but her appetite was gone.

The taxidermists engaged on the crock having finished their ghoulish task, and the boat once more floating on an even keel, thanks to the fresh load of wood, Achmed firmly retrieved the axes and locked them up in their chest. The concentrated gaze of a hundred pairs of eyes followed them into their resting place.

In less time than it takes to tell, the natives were in their canoes and lined up expectantly in back of us. Achmed tooted the whistle defiantly, a thousand parrots screeched in terror, flocks of waterfowl hydroplaned across the river, and even the pink flamingoes on the far shore got tangled up with themselves in fright. When we moved, we did it in style.

By dusk that evening we had covered all of ten miles in approximately the same number of hours. At that rate it would take us ten days to reach Bupul instead of five as I had originally estimated. Then I recalled that we were back in the stone-age, and time no longer meant anything. My impatience subsided at once. It was good to be back in the jungle.

That night we tied up in midstream to avoid the mosquitos and flies as much as possible. The natives, however, camped on shore. I use the word "camped" advisedly. They simply pulled their canoes up on shore, crawled out on the mud and flopped. My five Malays distributed themselves about on the deck, their rifles cuddled up to their bosoms like so many mistresses, and were prepared to take on all comers. I never had to worry about appointing a night watch as long as I had those boys around. One of them always stood guard, but this really wasn't necessary. The other four, asleep, were no more dead to the world than hungry police dogs.

Like the Malays, my wife and I slept on deck. We could have had more privacy, but in the jungle privacy is a dangerous thing. One is seldom beheaded in the middle of camp, but it is amazing how the mortality rate increased around the edges.

A couple of hundred yards from the centre of camp and it goes up to a hundred per cent. Leona was completely exhausted but she couldn't go to sleep. She just lay on the deck, tense and listening, nor did she have to strain her ears to hear what was going on. Somewhere on shore, and not very far off, a bull crock was coughing heavily as though he had just choked on a wild boar. Night birds, one of them with a voice like a train going over a trestle, were reviewing the events of the week, while from the river itself came a frightful splashing and carrying carrying-on. Sharks were patrolling the depths, crocodiles and savages stalked the shore, squadrons of mosquitos droned through the heavy air.

The first day in the jungle was over, and all was well.

CHAPTER II

DEMAS AND DEMONS

SOMEWHERE on the river ahead of us was the most incredible figure in Dutch New Guinea, Captain Gustav Schultz, retired, of the Dutch Colonial Army. To say that he is retired is a mild exaggeration. The army retired him and then waited for him to retire the army. He is a one-man expedition, and the only man who can travel the jungles of Dutch New Guinea protected solely by his reputation.

Behind Schultz is a record second only to the one hung up by my father, dean of the tropical empire builders. It was my father who was in the vanguard when the Dutch moved into their East Indies possessions and Schultz was my father's right hand man. Tall, gaunt, raw-boned, Schultz is so deeply tanned by an equatorial sun he has no more chance of becoming white again than an old saddle. Against this dark background his blue eyes gleam like ice, so cold and piercing they can stop a head hunter in his tracks. He is a jungle man, and he can't leave. Part of his time he is wandering around in the jungle, exploring unmapped streams, noting strange customs of hostile natives, and going his own way, impervious to hardship and danger. I had an appointment to meet him in Bupul, but if I knew Schultz he would be heading down stream to meet us. Anything was better than waiting.

Four days out and forty miles up from Merauke and we ran into him. When I first caught sight of him he was being regally propelled down the river by his ten stalwart boys, convicted Javanese murderers all. He sat in the middle of the canoe, his feet propped up on a case of cartridges, his head pillowed comfortably on the carcass of a fresh-killed kangaroo. He was dressed in what was once a suit of tropic whites of army issue, and thrust back on his head was a thick pith helmet, a chunk missing from the side. His ten boys, paddling standing up native-fashion, towered way above him but so completely did he dominate the scene from his prone position the paddlers formed nothing more than an appropriate background for his personality.

"Hi, Charlie," he shouted as soon as he was within hailing distance. "Eeyah—Eeyah—Eeyah!"

His bellow sent the sharks patrolling the surface scurrying for deep water. The only answer to equal a hail like that was a blast on the whistle. I gave her a toot that staggered the engine. Then with a few prodigious strokes Schultz's crew swept their hollowed log along side and I was greeting my old friend for the first time in ten years.

"My God, Charlie, it's good to see you," he bellowed in Dutch, leaping over the low rail with the agility of a kangaroo despite his sixty years.

"Have a drink," I shouted in return, knowing full well that any time I wasted on greetings when there was Holland gin on board would be held against me.

Over trays of gin-splits served by the efficient Wirio, greetings introductions and minor gossip flowed like water. Suddenly Schultz turned to me, a wide grin on his face. "I say, Charles," he said in his formal English. "Have you seen any cassowaries?"

I knew instantly to what he was referring, but tried to head him off. "You were going to tell us about the Imo," I said pointedly.

Schultz turned to Leona, the grin still on his face. "Would you know, Charles was the damnedest kid for pets I have ever seen," he said. "When he was a kid in Merauke he had pet kangaroos, pet crocodiles, pet boars, pet crown pigeons, everything until one day one of the soldiers gave him a pet cassowary. You know cassowaries, no?"

Leona nodded. We had seen several of the giant birds in the meadows that occasionally bordered the river.

"Well, cassowaries are peculiar birds. They can kick like a mule. That is very bad, but worse than that they have another habit. You know how it is with skunks—a lift of the tail when bothered—pssst—and such terrible results. Cassowaries are very much like that except that they don' t have a tail to hist, and they don't 'pssst,' they 'phoooot.' Fifteen feet in a straight line like a bullet. Now you can imagine what would happen when

Charlie's cassowary got off the rope and Charlie started chasing it. Or can't you?"

I was relieved when Wirio begged us to eat the supper of fresh kangaroo meat he had prepared. I quickly hurried aft and gave orders to camp for the night. The anchor was dropped and the natives paddled for shore to start their own cooking fires.

After supper we sat on deck, protected from the onslaughts of droves of mosquitos by smudge pots, by Captain Schultz's vicious pipe, and by Leona's Siamese citronella, a weird combination of Oriental perfumes and tear gas.

"How does it look up in the jungle?" I asked, getting down to business.

Schultz puffed deeply two or three times on his terrible mixture of Turkish tobacco and half-cured native stuff. "I'd say things were about average," he spoke at last. "The Imo is active again, but so far they have been taking it out on raids against each other or in Digoel territory. Nobody has been bothering me."

Knowing Schultz, and knowing the Imo, I didn't expect they would be bothering him. Schultz knew I was a member of the Imo, because I was a native even though my parents were white, and as such was entitled to all the rights and honours of a warrior. That I was a warrior I had proven to the satisfaction of the natives on expeditions with my father.

The Imo as an organisation was the most powerful influence in the Dutch New Guinea jungle. What it amounted to was a bloody brotherhood composed of warriors from all the villages within the boundaries of the land claimed by the Jei-Anim and Marind-Anim tribes. Far back in the jungle but within the boundaries of the Jei and Marind tribes were lesser tribes, all bound together by the intangible threads of the dread brotherhood. To become a member a young buck had to prove his courage by taking a head, after which he was initiated into the inner circle and no questions asked. That the head might have belonged to a fellow-member of the Imo was more of a tribute than a reflection on the applicant's courage. Thus, the Imo was a combination fraternal and military order that, aroused, might summon hundreds of tested warriors to unite in a wave of avenging fury against a common foe. On the other hand, with no common enemy in sight, the various locals, might engage in a little intra-fraternal strife with murderous results but without affecting the unity of the whole. It was a secret order without secrets, a brotherhood without brotherly love, and a military machine as accustomed to fighting against each other as with each other. The one thing all branches of the Imo had in common was a love of rituals. They liked to paint their faces with grey clay, put on their elaborate head-dresses of rare bird plumes, and pound the drums. On one other thing they were united, their hatred of the Majo, the rival organisation of the Imo over in the territory controlled by the Digoel tribes. But of this much one could be certain, if the Imo was for you in one section of the country, there was no guarantee that you would be welcomed in another, but if the Imo was against you anywhere, it was against you everywhere. And that would be just too bad.

"There's one thing I would recommend," said Schultz after we had worn out the Imo as a topic of conversation. "At low tide to-morrow, put all your boys to digging clams and picking up shells. The last time I was way inland I found the natives ready to sell their souls for shells. You can buy more with a dozen clam shells than you can with the whole Dutch mint. When you were here last the coastal natives used to trade with the inlanders, buying bows and arrows with clam shells, but now the coastal tribes are getting all their stuff from white traders, and the boys back in the hills are running low on decorations."

Schultz was using the term decorations in its most delicate sense. The most striking adornment on a male Kaya-Kaya, a term used to designate any native of Dutch New Guinea regardless of tribe, was the pubic shell, worn as protection in place of a breech cloth. A single string of rattan around the waist supporting a shell to protect the genitals constituted a full dress uniform. Some of the wealthier sported necklaces of crocodile teeth and claws and a few boar's tusks in addition, but all sported pubic shells except in the poorest tribes where a wide belt of rattan was made to do the work. If the inlanders were low on such vital garments, by all means we would supply them.

As the evening wore on and Wirio continued to keep the glasses filled, it was only natural that the conversation turn to the demas, ruling spirits of Dutch New Guinea. According to native belief, demas are half man, half spirit, and each dema has his particular function to perform. Like the gods of the Greeks, these demas are prodigious powers, working miracles on a colossal scale. Floods, droughts, fevers, famines, abundance, and war all have their respective demas. There is the coconut dema, represented at festivals by a witch-doctor whose fantastic head-dress is woven to resemble a palm tree about three feet high. The leaves are beautifully covered with red clay, and hanging to the fronds are several rudely carved coconuts. The roots of the symbolic palm are long straws woven into the hair, a bit of realism based on the grim belief that coconut palms grow out of human heads. The coconut dema is chief of the friendly spirits, closely followed by the sago dema, the kangaroo dema, the banana, sweet potato and tobacco demas, all represented by more or less recognisable head-dresses at the dema festivals. These towering structures sometimes weigh as much as a hundred pounds, and more than once I have seen the bearers pass out under the weight of their burdens. This is easily understandable when one realises that a festival might last for days, with the demas taking a highly active part for the first ten or twelve hours, after which the natives are sufficiently worked up to carry on their orgies under their own momentum.

Schultz told of an interesting ceremony he had encountered over on the Koembe river about forty miles west of us. An entire village had been stricken by fever, and the fever dema had been taking some frightful abuse at the hands of his worshippers. That is one thing about the Kaya-Kaya. If he doesn't like a dema he has no reluctance about insulting him. Dozens of men were laid out, and wrapped in palm fronds, row on row. Some were already dead, some on the verge of dying. Schultz dosed the survivors up with quinine, but just to make the cure certain, they had a dema drive. Tremendous fires were started at both ends of the village, and then two warriors, completely concealed beneath layers of red leaves and gorgeous feathers, entered at one end of the village brandishing red spears and bows and arrows. They danced into each hut, making threatening gestures with their weapons to frighten out the fever dema. In the meantime young bucks were busy throwing stalks of green bamboo into the huge fires, the hollow stalks filling with steam and exploding with tremendous reports. Demas frightened out of the huts were scared clear out of the village by these explosions, and by the frightful din set up by all who were able to howl.

The two warriors who did the scaring were not completely satisfied with their work however. After they completed their rounds, they eased off to the river where they stood in water up to their neck. Then and not until then they removed their robes of leaves and feathers that concealed them so that upon their return to the village they would not be recognised by the fever demas they had molested.

As a general rule, however, dema festivals are gay affairs, with a parade of the demas, and the performers' bodies shiny with coconut oil or brilliant with red clay. Very often, when their head-dresses reach skyscraper proportions, or consist of a whole stuffed kangaroo or crocodile they are accompanied by small boys suitably dolled up who assist the balancing act with long poles. The parade is officially opened by the Diwa-Zib, the great dema of the head hunt. The principal part of his head-dress is a human head worked into a great design of plumes and coloured leaves six to eight feet high. He steps to the top of a bamboo platform decorated with colourful feathers and daubed with red clay where he begins a slow solemn dance that sometimes lasts all night. The other demas now enter the village and go through their acts in pantomime, after which the general public is free to join in the brawl. And a drunken brawl it turns out to be. Only the Diwa-Zib, dema of the head hunt, stays sober. He is the one god no one curses, whom all respect.

The natives have many theories concerning the origin of their land, the rivers, fire and themselves. In the first place the demas are to blame for everything. Once a long time back the island was a nice place to live, but the demas started to play with fire and pretty soon they had burned up everything. Even the mountains caught fire and trembled and shook. The earth wrinkled and cracked, and when the rains finally came, all the water ran into the cracks and became rivers. Where the rains came from nobody knows, but they do know the island was caused when Darvi, the colossal dema of the demas, suddenly became angry and threw a piece of earth out into the sea. Kangaroos, pigs, reptiles, and plants were on the earth, so they just kept right on living in their new location. The natives believe their ancestors are descendants of these original plants and animals. Hence various family groups are divided into clans according to the species from which they originated. There are snake people, sago and kangaroo people, etc., all of which makes them at least partly related to their respective demas. Asked how they know they are kangaroo people they reply that only their forefathers who were born from the kangaroos could answer that, and they have long since been dead. However, they take no chances on offending their ancestors. Should a pig man be dining on pork, it is not at all uncommon to hear him remark, "Grandfather, you must have been a great man. You do taste so good."

It is fire and not the flood that plays the predominant part in their beliefs. Almost every creature bears some mark as the result of the carelessness of the dema who set the island on fire. Herons legs turned red and have remained so ever since. Cassowaries lost all their feathers and now have only a few quills. Their necks were scorched bare, and they carry their toasted red flabs to this day. Crabs still sizzle, and all bald men are relatives of the first men singed by the fire. As conclusive evidence of all their beliefs, they claim that way in the interior remains of the great fire can still be found smouldering underground. As far as I have been able to determine, and Schultz bears me out on this, the same stories exist with very few minor alterations in every tribe in Dutch New Guinea. Even the ferocious Digoels trace their ancestry to beasts and plants, and mention the great fire in their folk-lore.

Schultz and I probably would have talked all night had not Leona finally convinced us there was ample time to talk in the next few days.

The next day we were cruising along in regal luxury, our feet cocked up on the starboard rail, our wood pile being slightly reduced and our weight needed on that side to trim the ship, when a sudden exclamation from Schultz caused me to look around.

"I say, did you ever see such a crocodile in your life? If that isn't the damnedest bastard I have ever seen, I'll eat it." Schultz's formal English included army terminology, picked up from British officers in India.

The crock he indicated had raised up on shore about two hundred yards ahead of us. It stood three feet high if it stood an inch, and the tip of its tail was some thirty feet back in the jungle from its snout. The captain worked the bolt of his rifle, raised his sights and without taking his feet from the rail, fired one shot. The crock went down as though slapped with a pile driver. The launch lunged forward a good mile an hour faster as our flotilla of canoes dropped the tow line as one unit.

"Go to it, boys," exulted Captain Schultz as his crew of convicts gained the lead in the race to the still threshing crocodile. But Wasbus was right in there with his crew of giants. They were handling their eight-foot paddles like so much matchwood, scooping out gaping holes in the water as they sizzled towards shore. Lord how they could manhandle a boat. But for some reason they never closed the gap between them and Schultz's crew. The captain had his men trained to within a hair of their lives, and they darn well knew their business or they didn't last long.

"My boys are soft,' I apologised as I saw Schultz's crew swarm over the dying monster. "Wait until I get back. Then we'll take your boys in tow seven days a week."

"I 'll be waiting," said Schultz confidently.

Relieved of our drag, we were surging along at a tremendous pace, the launch shaking like an empty freight car on a down grade. For the first time I noticed a faint indication of foam as the bow slugged through the water at eight miles an hour.

We continued an animated conversation for another hour, by which time the boys who had stayed for the autopsy on the crocodile had overtaken us. Without straining any muscles either. Achmed pulled into shore for another timber cutting expedition. Almost instantly we were besieged by swarms of vicious black flies.

The flies were particularly hard on Leona. They seemed to take a particular delight in drilling into any exposed portion they could find in her. In torment she asked Captain Schultz what she should do.

"Do? Don't do anything. Get a couple of boys to do it. Hasn't Charlie trained you to get work out of these natives? Hey, come here, you black devil. Can't you see the flies are bothering the white lady? Jump!"

After one startled look the native thus addressed jumped. A palm leaf fan appeared as if by magic, swirling whirlwinds in the air. The flies vanished. A few minutes later I looked over and saw Leona was still far from comfortable. At last she whispered to me: "Bring back the flies. I can't stand the smell."

I sniffed the native. He was a little ripe. But that was one thing about which neither Schultz nor I could do anything. The smell of a native is as unchangeable as the proverbial spots on a leopard. It was either that or the flies, and no two ways about it. Leona took the flies. Fortunately, about that time Achmed deemed the wood supply sufficient, and as soon as we got underway the flies thinned out enough to make life endurable.

A few hours later I heard a low throbbing that was not a loose bearing in the propeller shaft. Captain Schultz heard it too.

"Listen," he said, suddenly intent. From far back in the jungle I heard the old familiar "chunka-chunk, chunka-chunk, chunka-chunk," of a war drum. It was the first time I had heard the sound for years, but the hair from the back of my head to the base of my spine began to crawl.

Leona couldn't hear it.

"You don't hear it," Schultz protested. "You feel it. It throbs in you here—in your chest. You feel it long before you hear it."

I think Schultz is right about that. Many is the time I have felt the drums throbbing, but when I have strained my ears to pick up the sound I have heard nothing. Then when I have given up straining, dismissing it as a trick of the imagination, I have picked up the throbbing as definitely as though someone were thumping me on the chest. It is an eerie sensation, but then nothing about jungle drums savours of anything earthly.

For an hour the distant booming continued, now loud enough for Leona to hear, and at other times fading away to a menacing whisper. Conversation was at a virtual standstill. The hundred natives behind were as silent as snakes for the first time since we left Merauke. I noticed that the war bows, previously concealed in the bottoms of the canoes, were now plainly in evidence, and each warrior fairly bristled with arrows. We were getting into head hunter land.

That night the drums began again, this time the unearthly booming pulsating from both sides of the river. From the stern deck came the mighty snoring of Captain Schultz. The drums were his lullaby. From my cot I listened with keen enjoyment as the broken, barbaric rhythms came rolling through the night. I wondered dreamily if the obliging drummers were bothered with mosquitos. But Leona, from her cot, caught none of these soothing sensations. To her the drums dripped menace with every beat. Their staggered rhythms were the dance of death pounded out in monotone. She spent another sleepless night.

CHAPTER III

TWENTIETH CENTURY STONE AGE

BUPUL is a stinking little city of some 200 souls all black in colour and intent. It is located on the Merauke river, 100 miles above the village of Merauke, and it marks the head of steam navigation. At least it is as far as we could get with the steam launch.

We pulled up to the village on the evening of our tenth day out from Merauke. The entire population was on shore to welcome us, somewhat enviously to be sure, for some of our bucks were nice and fat from long days of idleness and good food.

Leona insisted on going ashore, it being her first opportunity to inspect a genuine native village at first hand. Well, she was going to have to face the facts of life sooner or later, so I took her on a tour of inspection.

The first thing to be noticed was that the natives were not just nude, they were plumb stark naked. The males were indisputably males, and there was no mistaking the other sex either. A few of the important city fathers wore decorated pubic shells, but the rest wore theirs straight. Somehow I do not feel it is a style calculated to spread. The shells cannot be very comfortable.

Though naked, the natives were none-the-less clothed in the latest fashion. Considering the primitive dress-making, there was not much danger that the fashions would change from year to year. To prevent wear and tear on costumes, the women had their styles carved on. When Leona encountered one woman in the process of whittling out a new mode, she almost fainted.

The woman, little more than a girl, was about as ghastly a sight as one would care to meet. Her body was slashed from head to foot. Her plump breasts looked as though they had been cut to ribbons. As a sample, one cut began between the eyes, curved up over the forehead, then down beneath the eye and around the cheek to the back of the jawbone. From there it writhed down her throat to her right breast, around which it spiralled to the tip like a coiled snake. A corresponding cut seared down the other side of her body. To complete the design other gashes covered her lower limbs and abdomen. In spite of her pain she was plainly proud of the job, and stolidly rubbed the ashes of alang-alang grass into the gaping wounds. This was to prevent their healing too fast to leave a substantial welt. As blood and pus forced out the caked ashes, she patiently spread the wound and packed in more. Flies surrounded her in a cloud.

"And I used to think it was torture to get a permanent wave," said Leona.

"It's pretty bad," I admitted, "except that it is all over now. You should have seen her getting cut up. If that work was done with a razor it would have been bad enough, but she had nothing as easy as that. She had to lie still while the witch doctor bore down on a clam shell so dull it took half his strength to cut into her at all. Hour after hour."

"No thank you," said Leona with a shudder.

Some of the completed designs sported by the other women were enough to make Leona blush. Where every one is naked even of pubic hair, sex has lost an awful lot of allure unless something is done about it. The women used tattooing for this effect. Raised designs, some a half inch high and an inch wide on the abdomen and legs were intended to direct attention only one way. That there weren't more children in the village was not the fault of the tattooing so much as the high infant mortality rate.

Some men, too, resorted to tattoo work to emphasise their charms, and in their case some of the designs became even more pointed. As a rule, however, the men were seldom as heavily scarred as the women.

Like our own boys, the villagers were members of the Marind-Anim tribe. In Dutch New Guinea tribes spread up and down a river, a natural course to take as the river offers easy communication between villages. In all the thousands of years of continuous warfare, no tribe has managed to grow beyond its own river, and probably wouldn't know what to do if it did. It works like this: On the Merauke River live the Jei-Anims; on the Digoel River live the Digoels. The Digoels haven't got anything on their river that the Jei-Anims don't have on theirs except Digoel heads. And vice versa. When the Jei-Anims raid, they aren't out to acquire new territory. All they want is heads. Getting these without losing their own, they scurry for home where they can show them off to advantage. This serves two purposes: it gives the successful warrior an admiring audience before which to display his trophies, and it leaves a ransacked village to which the Digoels can return and raise more heads. On the other hand, if the victorious warriors were to occupy the conquered village for any length of time, either avenging Digoel tribesmen might sweep down on them, or their own brothers, figuring they were gone long enough to be fairly considered Digoels, would jump over some night to add their heads to the home town collection. As a result, expansion has been slow.

Bupul, for instance, could be considered as a New Guinea metropolis. The villagers sell a few baskets of copra at least once a year to the traders who stop at Merauke. Several villagers have beads or cotton dress goods, and the chief and one or two of the head men even have knives. In other words, they are a comparatively cultured and well-travelled lot. They are a stalwart lot, too. Not a weakling is to be found in the village, nor are any doddering old men to be found occupying the sunny side of the huts. They have long since contributed to the support of the village. They were eaten up.

Bupul evidences its advancement in other ways. The sanitation department is one of the best in the jungle. Of necessity there are no outhouses. A native enjoying a few minutes of solitary confinement in an outhouse would be picked off like a ripe plum by some raiding party. Not every time, maybe, but enough so to make outhouses extremely unpopular, always supposing, of course, that the village went in for this adjunct of civilisation, which it doesn't. No, they use dogs. The dogs and tamed boars clean up human waste and the waste from meals, and the flies clean up what the dogs leave. If the flies could only be put to some use, the cycle would be complete.

These dogs are frightful beasts. Probably descended from the vicious Australian dingo, the breed has since been adopting the worst traits of German police dogs, English bulls, airedales and any other dog that could be stolen from its white owner. They are highly valued by their owners, not only for their scavenging properties but for their hunting ability and downright uncontrollable meanness, and their edibility.

While the dogs can dispose of a tremendous amount of offal, they cannot dispose of the smell. A village that can be smelled five miles away on a calm night is bound to be a mite on the strong side when you get right on the main drag. And Bupul can be smelled five miles away upwind. There are a lot of reasons for this. One reason is fit to print. That is the copra pile. Copra is the meat of the coconut, dried in the sun until there is nothing left but oil-saturated pieces. If left too long the pile gets rancid, and when it gets rancid it gets terrible. Just as musk is the carrying agent for fine perfumes, the copra pile is the carrying agent for the foul odours of Bupul. Considering the limited toilet facilities, what these odours consist of is best left to the imagination.

As soon as Leona became sufficiently accustomed to the smell so that her eyes stopped watering, we entered one of the thatched huts. After the first awful gasp, the olfactory nerves were sufficiently stunned to remain in a stupor for the rest of the visit. A half a dozen natives followed us in and stood about in the dim shadows ogling every move we made. There was little inside of note except the fleas. A pile of leaves on the floor indicated the sleeping quarters. A dirty pile of gourds marked the pantry department, and three heads, rather moth-eaten, marked the trophy room. The walls of the hut were made from alang-alang grass, bound into bundles about six inches in diameter, and these bundles stood upright and lashed together about three bundles thick, formed the walls. The roof was made of palm fronds, overlapped to a depth of a foot or more and supported by bamboo poles meeting at a common centre. The huts are waterproof in that what rain they don't shed they absorb up to a certain point. At the end of a long wet spell the thatch is soggy enough to sprout mushrooms. This smells too.

A furious yapping of dogs, followed by a shot, popped me out of the hut as though I had been stung. It was Captain Schultz. A long, low-slung mutt had sunk its fangs into Schultz's leg up to the gums, receiving in return a bullet between the eyes. Schultz was now engaged in shaking the corpse loose, in the meantime standing on one foot and cursing like a fiend, in twelve languages.

A wound of any kind can be a serious thing in the jungle but it was not that that bothered Schultz so much as the loss to his dignity. The natives were only too well aware of this. Two minutes after the shot there was not a dog to be seen in the village. The natives had corralled their mutts and spirited them into every available hiding place.

Leona came rushing up then, and between us we managed to steer Captain Schultz toward the boat instead of on the tour of dog extermination he was intent on making. In spite of this, we had no sooner dressed his four punctures, than he was on deck with his rifle.

"An insult to the white race," he growled, squinting down the sights and knocking off a mangy cur that slid out from behind a hut.

"Listen, you blood-thirsty old reprobate," I warned, "I've got to get some pictures of this mob. If you go shooting all their flea bags, I won't be able to get them out for any shots of my own."

"Oh, all right," he growled. "Hurry to shoot fast, so. Udderwise I forget like and shoot maybe a dog by mistake. For the goddam." His formal English wasn't up to handling so strained a situation.

From time to time coming up the river I had stopped to shoot a few close-ups of the tree-climbing fish, mangrove hens, pelicans, and flamingoes which would let us come within a few feet. I had also canned a few hundred feet of crocodiles, and one sequence showing a dozen of my boys capturing a big crock alive by the simple expedient of wedging a hard wood stick in the reptile's throat when it opened its mouth to attack. This is easier than it sounds. A crocodile has a big mouth, making it a simple matter to slam a stick of wood into its throat as a yard-long row of teeth flashes by your face. Any bull fighter could do it with just a little practice, as soon as he got used to standing up to his knees in solid mud.

That was all good action stuff, coupled with the usual amount of scenic atmosphere. But I wanted more than that. I wanted to come home with the Stone-Age preserved on film. Bupul was the gateway to the Stone-Age.

After the "dog bite's man" episode, I had considerable trouble getting my cast of characters out in the sunlight. They seemed perfectly content to remain within their huts, out of range of the watchful eye of Schultz. However, aided by Wasbus, who ejected a few by the simple expedient of throwing them outside bodily, and Achmed and his crew of Malays, who prodded them out with their gun barrels, I soon had them assembled.

I had my standard camera set up in the centre of the village, and after panning the sorry looking lot, I had them proceed with their everyday tasks. These seemed to consist of falling asleep, each one working at it in his or her own way.

Prompted by Wasbus, they were quick to overcome this lethargy. Wasbus was a dynamo, or more aptly, a whole power-house of energy. He was the kind of a director many a Hollywood producer would like to turn loose among his own casts. He packed his diplomacy in his war club, did not hesitate to argue with it, and when his arguments were concluded he herded together a new cast to carry out the old.

What I wanted to get more than anything else were close-ups. I had the one big heavy standard camera unexcelled for close-up work but too cumbersome to lug around in the jungle. I was going to have to leave that on the launch to be returned to Merauke by Captain Schultz while Leona and I went on into the jungle equipped with light hand cameras. In the meantime, however, I wanted to get as many close-ups out of the way as I could while I still had the standard. It would save us a lot of detail work later on when the facilities ranged from "not so good," to downright "bad."

There were such typical shots as a group of natives wearing down a teakwood tree with their stone hatchets. Each blow struck crushed a limited amount of wood. After so many blows the natives would stop to pull away the broken fibres, exposing new wood to be pounded at. On ebony I would have needed a micropscopic camera to record the progress. As it was I would have had to wait all week for the tree to get tired and fall down, so I had Wasbus lop it off with an axe. This put me in solid with the villagers, so much so that when I wanted a shot of a couple of them scooping out a canoe I had difficulty in keeping the whole tribe from pitching in.

A canoe is made by selecting a thirty to forty foot section of teak wood and pounding it into shape on the outside. Fire judiciously applied facilitates the work of rounding out the ends. For the rest, the outside of the canoe follows pretty well the shape of the tree. Fires are then started all along the top of the log and allowed to burn their way down. From time to time the fires are moved along and the charred wood scraped out with shells, after which the fire is rekindled. This process is continued until the trunk consists of a shell about two inches thick. To prevent the fire from burning completely through, thin portions are covered with wet clay while the glowing embers eat through the thick spots. A canoe can be made in this fashion within the short space of three months, if one is in a hurry. Few natives are.

By the time I had all I wanted of wood chopping and boat building, the sun was too low to make further shooting advisable. Accordingly we knocked off for the day, and returned to the boat.

We found our invalided captain half way through a quart jug of gin, which he was carrying in one hand as he limped around the deck supervising the activities of Admo. Crown pigeon was on the menu, and Schultz was seeing to it that Admo did the noble bird justice. Then, just to see that we didn't starve to death, he had ordered Admo to prepare plenty of rice and gravy, sweet potatoes, baked bananas, oysters and a couple of dozen baking powder biscuits. The poor chef had every burner on the gasoline stove loaded down with victuals, and was doing his baking in the fire box of the steam engine.

Our own natives had taken advantage of the lay-over in Bupul to do a little hunting of their own. We could see them on shore clustered around their fires as they roasted huge chunks of kangaroo, wild boar, and crocodile. To augment the meat diet they had coconuts, yams, bananas and sago. Food is the least of one's worries in the Dutch New Guinea jungle.

The villagers had practically the same menu, with the addition of a couple of dogs.

The next day I resumed my close-up work. Craftsmanship this time. The manufacture of bows and arrows by scraping down the selected material with shells. The making of fire by rubbing an ebony rod on an ebony block over a handful of coconut fibre tinder. The making of knives by splitting bamboo and peeling down the edge a fibre at a time until it was almost as keen as steel. Home building, cooking, tattooing, mat weaving, all these occupied my camera for most of the day. In all, about three thousand feet of film.

How simple to get was that footage. Just focus the camera and grind away. No headhunters waiting for a break, no cannibals sizing up my spare ribs. No hostile arrows whishing between the legs of my tripod. No snakes, no leeches, only a few flies.

Not that my subjects weren't the genuine article when it came to lopping off a few skulls or broiling up a human haunch now and then. But they were house broken. They knew better than to practice their arts when white men were around.

From now on it would be different. Up the creek white men were no better than bleached-out natives, and the cannibals had an overpowering yen to know if the bleaching process had impaired the quality of the steaks. I have been informed by those who ought to know that it has, but this hasn't discouraged them from hoping that the next one might taste better.

It was with these thoughts on my mind that I ordered the boys to transfer cargo from the steam launch to the canoes in readiness for an early start in the morning. Captain Schultz watched the preparations with a gloomy eye, not because he was pessimistic about the future, he had too much contempt for the natives for that, but because he wasn't coming along.

"Charlie," he said, speaking in Dutch, "When you get up there in the mountains where no white man has ever been before, you're going to wish you had me along."

This wasn't the first time he had made the same observation.

"Now listen, Schultz," I pleaded, "I can make out all right up there. What I need is a man who can take the steam launch down the Merauke, along the coast to the Digoel River, and up the Digoel to Assike. Now there's only one man in ten thousand that can do that, and you're the man."

"Granted," agreed Captain Schultz, and he wasn't boasting either. "But just the same, you are going to run into lots of trouble."

"I'm expecting it," I said.

"Dot's all that's necessary," replied Captain Schultz in English as Leona came up. "When you expect it, then it isn't trouble, it's just part of the job. It's when you don't expect it that trouble comes up on horseback."

"Now who's talking trouble?" asked Leona doubtfully.

"Captain Schultz was just saying there is no such thing as trouble," I explained. "Come on, we've got to get a good night's sleep. Tomorrow we really start slumming."

That night we heard the drums again.

CHAPTER IV

TWO HEADS ARE BETTER THAN ONE

WASBUS was raring to go the next morning, an unusual condition for him or any other native to be in. But far be it from me to argue when the wind is right, the tide is right, or the natives are right. I just took advantage of the abnormal circumstance, hustled Leona into her canoe and gave the order to shove off. Captain Schultz bellowed a startled farewell from the deck of the steam launch, the villagers shrieked a lament, and we shot out into the stream.

A quarter of a mile out and we were overtaken by a frightful blast of rage that nearly over-turned the hindmost canoe. Wasbus, setting the pace in my canoe, really settled down and dug. I looked back, puzzled. I couldn't see anything amiss until I turned my field glasses on the launch. Then I saw the trouble—the propeller was churning idly in mid-air.

Let it be said to my credit that I had nothing to do with it. Wasbus had supervised the loading of the launch with firewood the evening before, and if, in his savage ignorance, he had the load stacked so far forward as to raise the stern out of water, whose fault was it? And who could prove that Wasbus deliberately misplaced the deck load to get even with Schultz's crew for beating him out of the crocodile? Certainly not me.

Wasbus flashed one glance over his shoulder, grinned fit to split his skull, and settled down to a steady, tremendous stroke. I can still feel a surge across my back every time I think of Wasbus bending a paddle.

Now that our expedition was really under way, it stacked up like this: There were ten canoes averaging ten occupants in each. One Malay, armed with a rifle, held down the bow of each canoe except mine. Achmed, because he was the best shot, rode in the bow of my wife's canoe. My ten chain gangers, sixty warriors and about twenty women furnished the power. Because I wanted to be able to move around in a hurry if the need arose, I rode in the canoe manhandled by Wasbus and his nine giants. What a crew they were. We never got stuck on top of a sandbar, we just knocked the top off.

Our equipment, including four hand cameras, fifty thousand feet of film, ammunition, tool chest, and elaborate medicine cabinet, canned hams, sausages, corned beef, soups, boullion cubes, biscuits, cooking oil, butter, tea and coffee, sacks of rice, boxes of gifts, and our clothes, were distributed equally among the ten canoes. All told, there must have been a ton and a half of junk to keep track of, which isn't much when you figure it amounts to less than forty pounds to the paddler. The natives were weighted down with their bows and arrows and a pubic shell for Sunday best. That was all.

We were rapidly approaching that strange stretch of river where the salt water meets the fresh. Now the simplest way would be for the fresh water to just drizzle in, getting saltier as it went along, but no, it couldn't do it that way. Not and still be a part of that exaggerated island called New Guinea. There had to be theatricals.

We pulled up on shore, way up, to let the theatricals go by.

Lots of estuaries have bores, most of them, in fact but they are respectable, self-controlled bores. The bore on the Ganges in India gets a little out of hand at times and wrecks a few ships, but the Merauke does it twice a day.

Sitting up on a muddy knoll with the leeches dripping down our necks, we had a clear view of the impressive spectacle. It was announced by a roar as of thunder. Then around the bend rushed the incoming tide in a wall of water eight feet high. The poor old river, unaware of its impending doom, just kept slogging along.

But there was a lot of power in that sluggish water. Once it got the idea that its territory was being invaded by the salty tidal wave, it reared up and fought back. Water boiled and churned in a titanic struggle. For a moment the tidal wall was stopped in its tracks. Then like repressed flood waters suddenly breaking through a dam, it surged forward again. Once more the river reared up to check its stride. Again the furious struggle between opposing forces, the jungle walls echoing to the roars of the foam-flecked contestants. Time after time this was repeated, the destructive wave forming, collapsing and reforming as the tide called in all its reserves. For thousands of years the river had been going down to ignominious defeat twice a day, but it kept right on pitching. Some day it might win, but not to-day. In half an hour all was calm and serene. The mud flats were covered to the high-tide mark with placid, coffee-coloured water, in repose after its hard-earned victory. A few islands of foam circled idly, uncertain of where to go. Water reeds stood motionless as though exhausted by the tremendous struggle that had rolled over them a few minutes before. Then out of the murky depths rose collossal remnants of the Tertiary Period to haunt the twentieth century, giant turtles five feet across the beam. Those living relics of a period best known for its fossils are to be found only in Dutch New Guinea, and there in only two or three rivers.

According to paleontologists, these monstrosities were fairly common in all parts of the globe during the Tertiary Period, having survived the Mesozoic Period in pretty good shape. For some reason not easy to explain the species has dwindled until now it is holding out only in Dutch New Guinea, last stronghold of the Stone-Age. I am sure of this much: the turtles weren't killed off. They are the toughest babies to kill I have ever encountered, and even after they had been dead for a day or so they don't know it. The natives prize them for food but can't do anything about it. The boys go out and kill one, but it just keeps right on heading for deep water, and when it gets there it might go for miles before it decides it's dead enough to kick the bucket.

Coupled with its tenacious grip on life the giant turtle displays all the suspicion of a gun-shy stag. It is impossible to approach one sunning itself on the bank if there is so much as a single movement on board a canoe. The only way to get within rifle range is to pick one out downstream and then drift down like a floating log. In this manner I managed to knock one cold enough for purposes of inspection. A lucky shot straight through the cast-iron skull nailed it to the shore.

Wasbus and his cohorts instantly sprang to life. One minute they were lying flat and the next second they were standing upright with flailing paddles and nary a list to the canoe. I was hurtled to shore so fast I barely had time to ram home another shell. Almost instantly they were all over the turtle, bouncing their stone clubs off its armour-plated body. And their clubs really bounced.

The monster measured eight feet from the tip of its rock-crusher beak to the tip of its crocodile-like tail. Its shell, shaped like a porridge bowl, was a good five feet overall and four feet across the beam. Greenish black in colour, its armour plates were two inches thick at the edges, and must have been four inches thick along the back. We never got it open to find out. Without ever apparently regaining consciousness, the monster suddenly began to work its powerful, crocodile-shaped legs convulsively. Deeper and deeper they plowed into the mud, Wasbus and his boys clinging to the lip of the shell like demons. Any second I expected them to tear the shell clear off. Instead, they began to yield ground. Slowly, ponderously, like a stone boat getting under way on a greased skid, the turtle began to slide toward the water, gaining momentum with each lunge of its powerful legs. It was a juggernaut. There was no stopping it. Reaching the water, it swept the straining natives aside and vanished in a whirlpool of its own making.

By watching these turtles cruise lazily around like floating islands wasn't getting us any farther up the creek. Leona wanted to move anyway. She couldn't appreciate the leeches. Instead of being grateful that they weren't painful or itch-provoking, she resented their slimy presence at all. Not that I favour them. They are found everywhere, in the water, on the ground, and up in the trees. Before they drill for blood they are just little worm-like things built on the lines of a soft-shell snail. Brush one off a leaf and it will slide under a tight collar as easily as an angle worm slipping through a crack in the rain barrel. Once it has slected its pasture you will note a slight stinging sensation, little more painful than a mosquito bite, that lasts but a second. The initial nip is the only discomfort. After that the leech swells up peacefully on your blood. When full it slips off, probably under your belt or into your shoe where a little pressure bursts it like a balloon.

If you try to pick one before it is ripe, you'll soon learn you can't pry it off with a crow bar. The only way to remove the pest is to cut it in half with a sharp knife. After awhile the head gets tired of sucking blood into a missing stomach and lets go. In the meantime, of course, your shirt or pants or whatever clothing happens to bear the leech when it parts company with its head is soaked with blood. After a day with the leeches one looks bloodier than a headhunter after a successful call on his neighbours.

When it came to leeches the natives were one up on us. A leech had no place of concealment on a native. I was still engaged in slicing them off my belt line when our canoes slid into a tunnel of gloom. Fresh water! The jungle closed over our heads like a screen, shutting off light and air, confining the heat.

All the while we had been cruising up the open stretches of tide-water; we had air and sun to evaporate the perspiration and keep us cool in the process. Out there the heat was that of an oven, now it was that of a steam bath. Where before we had perspired, now we sweated. Where before the natives had smelled awful, now they stunk with an all-pervading stench. Where before we had travelled in mid-stream, out of arrow range of either shore, we now paddled in midstream within range of both shores. We were in the Rain Forest!

We weren't alone either. Lots of life goes on in the Rain Forest, and lots of death too. It's the old law of supply and demand. Where life is plentiful, death comes cheap. This applies not only to the game but to humans as well. Waste on a tremendous scale is the law of the land, modified, but slightly by the second major law, the survival of the fittest. Under the law of waste, however, many of the fittest fail to survive. Equipped with modern rifles, backed up by the pick of the Merauke warriors, were were unquestionably the fittest outfit in the jungle. Yet some idiot squatting in the mud behind a mangrove tree could put an arrow through anyone of us any time he felt like committing suicide. Oh, we were the might of the Twentieth Century striding through the Stone-Age, all right, but an arrow, a snake bite, a sudden slip in crocodile waters, and that old common denominator of all ages, death, would knock us off as easily as an oily native. In the face of such unflattering lack of discrimination, I laid down a rule

Wasbus

Clown, headman and all round goat was Wasbus

Cannibal Retinue

Surrounded by cannabalistic members of his crew, ' Cannibal ' Miller sourly inspects another wet camp-site. Note bedroom slippers.

Barber Shop

Weaving a warrior's head-dress is a three-man job

that no one, under any circumstances, was to leave the main party. Hunters, wood cutters and fruit pickers had to travel in groups of five or more.

This rule was enforced the first night, and I didn't have anything to do with the enforcement.

For camp that night I had selected a dry knoll screened from the river by a curtain of wading mangrove trees. Two or three mighty teakwood trees rising sixty feet or more had starved out the underbrush and carried the lianas up so high the knarled vine trunks were scattered in a wide circle like guy ropes for the tent-like canopy above.

As soon as the canoes were pulled up and the duffle stowed, I lighted the firewood that had been prepared for me. This was a sort of ceremony, the natives always delighting in the magic of a match. Within five minutes a dozen fires were going and supper was under way. The smoke from the fires, held down by the dome of leaves above, soon ridded the place of mosquitos. An ideal spot, if there ever was one, in all respects but one. The mass of jungle crowding around the little park offered perfect concealment for any sneaking headhunter anxious to add to his collection.

Here was a case in which the department of sanitation was in direct opposition· to the department of safety. For my comfort and peace of mind I preferred that the natives do their business well away from our sleeping quarters. They were apt to be careless about little matters like that, with resulting distress to both Leona and myself, me because it was my habit to stroll around in Oriental bedroom slippers. On the other hand it was seldom that five of them were moved at the same time. Under the circumstances, the only thing I could do was to have a trench dug to serve as the company latrine. The natives were sheepish about using such a modern convenience. It was too much like making a ceremony out of a necessary nuisance, dignifying it in such a way. Still, by threats and example I managed to get the idea across that it was to be used. And if I caught anyone sneaking into the jungle, or worse yet, violating the camp site, so help me, there would be another black skin hanging up to dry.

Leona got out her bottle of citronella and swabbed it on so

thick I had to back her away from an open fire so the fumes wouldn't explode. She was then ready for bed. Except that there wasn't any bed.

"Where do we sleep?" she asked.

I shrugged. "Anywhere your little heart desires."

"But my tent? And where is the cot?"

She didn't feel the poetry in it when I told her the sky was her canopy, and that she was to sleep cuddled in the bosom of old Mother Earth herself.

"You mean sleep like a native?" she gasped.

"Sure, Sleep is still the same old sleep it was a million years ago. You just close your eyes and drop unconscious. The ground is like a bed of silk. At least it is after you drop unconscious."

She was doubtful. Even after Admo spread out a sleeping mat and a blanket she didn't consider that her bed had been made. It didn't look complete. But she tried it. I don't know if it was because she was worn out or if the citronella fumes got her, but a minute later she was asleep.

Without a word of direction on my part the five Malays took up their positions around her. Not even a leech could get by that vigilant ring.

I took a final turn around camp to satisfy myself that all was well on this, our first night away from the steam launch. Groups of natives, men and women alike, lay in grotesque heaps on the ground, lost in sleep. Others still clustered around the cooking fires, tossing in chunks of dried kangaroo meat every now and then to satisfy their boracious, never satiated appetites. Their meal time lasted twenty-four hours a day, as though the very labour of eating worked up their appetites. Even while paddling they carried their dried meat strung on armlets around the biceps, where a quick yank would detach a chunk just in time to ward off starvation between strokes.

Everything was in order. I was just about to turn back when I heard a faint "squush." Instantly my pistol was out. The sound was much like that made when a soft tomato is hit squarely with a well-swung golf driver. It was not repeated. I was about to dismiss it as an over-ripe mango plopping to the ground when I noticed the group of natives around the fire closest to the sound had stopped chattering and were listening intently.

"What was it?" I asked sharply.

"Tuan, I don't know," a particularly hideous native replied. In the firelight I recognised him as Sekoa, one of my boat crew, by the two boar tusks he had thrust up through his nostrils. They curved outward below the bridge of his nose, flaring in terrifying fashion beneath his eyes.

"It wasn't a ripe fruit?"

"Yes, tuan, that was it." But I could see that neither he nor anyone else believed it.

"Come on," I ordered abruptly. "We'll find out. It sounded to me as though one of the boys disobeyed me and went outside the camp alone."

Wide-eyed but willing, they fitted their powerful bows with arrows. I went in advance, my flashlight cutting a tunnel of white ahead of us. For purposes of intimidation the flashlight was a better weapon than a gun. The natives worshipped it as a god in its own right.

Right away I discovered no ripe fruit had made the sound. There wasn't a fruit tree within fifty yards of the place. Finding what did make it was a different problem. Three times we scoured the area, peering into clumps of brush, forcing our way into thickets to see what they might conceal. It was Sekoa who found the head of the stone war club. So heavily had it been wielded its stout handle had snapped as though cut with an axe. A few feet away my flashlight picked out a matted spot in a small clearing where a body had crushed a scattering of pale fungus to earth.

That was all Sekoa and the rest of the natives, now increased in number to about twenty—needed. They were off on the trail like a shot. Not noisily, but like phantoms. I'm not going to say they followed tracks in a thick jungle after dark. But they knew their woodcraft. Given a certain situation, such as a tangle of brush, a fallen tree, a swamp, and they would know instinctively which route their quarry took to avoid the obstacle.

In this case we had not far to go. Less than a hundred yards from the edge of camp we found what we sought. Directly in the beam of my flashlight so that there was no missing it, so that every eye was of necessity focussed directly upon it, was the headless corpse of a native. The decapitation was not a clean job, having been performed with a bamboo knife. Steeling myself, I knelt over the body. Pointing to the tattoo marks, I asked who it was.

"I know, tuan," volunteered a native, beaming proudly when I flashed my light on him. "It is Avazere."

Avazere. One of the paddlers in my wife's canoe. I hoped she wouldn't notice his absence in the morning.

Well, there was nothing to be done for him now. Leading the way back to camp, I detailed ten men to shovel a grave and bury the first victim who thought it was safe to wander beyond the limits of camp. I flopped on my sleeping mat beside Leona. After long service in the jungle, you reach a point when you can force your mind to exclude all undesirable thoughts. I thought I could, but when I lay down I found I was seething with an inward rage against whomever had murdered my native. I was soft, I told myself. Too much civilisation had made me squeamish. Cursing my softness, I fell asleep.

The ungodly cackling of parrots and birds of paradise routed me off my mat a half hour before sunrise. The Malays were all awake and squatting on his haunches just beyond them was Sekoa. Catching my eye, he beckoned hopefully.

"What is it, Sekoa?" I asked, moving softly so as not to disturb Leona.

"Oh, tuan, come." He was practically hugging himself with delight, squirming around like a petted puppy.

He led me over to a cluster of natives who were gathered around something on the ground. Sekoa pushed them aside roughly, with a "make-way-for-the-king" attitude.

"Look, tuan!"

Staring up at me was the head I recognised with a sickening shock as having once belonged to Avazere. Beside it was another head, crowned by long unkempt hair into which was woven a matting of dry grass arranged in a style unfamiliar to me.

Sekoa raised this second head proudly. "Look, tuan," he said, indicating the neck. "Smooth!"

It was indeed smooth, as though lopped off by a guillotine. Sekoa was all grins at the excellence of the job. Figuring I was sufficiently impressed, the big buck could keep his secret no longer. Picking up the shovel I had given him for grave digging he raised it up and brought it down edgeways suggestively. "Thwish," he said, mimicking the sound and bursting into a high pitched giggle that jarred my spine like chalk on slate.

By dint of much questioning, I got the whole story. The ten men I had detailed for grave digging couldn't see much point in all that work when the jungle was full of ants for just that purpose. On the other hand, the shovel had a blade of steel. Too bad to waste steel digging in the ground, with steel so scarce, and so good for cutting off heads. Better to use it for what it was intended. A little scouting around, by the aid of a late rising moon, showed that only one man had killed Avazere. And he had lost his stone club. One man and unarmed. And they were ten, with a steel shovel. Not to get him under circumstances like that was a sin against nature. They got him. "Thwish!"

"Very well," I said, inwardly glad they did get him. The story, thanks to the jungle grapevine, would go ahead of us that we were a good bunch to leave alone. "Now you can take Avazere's head and bury it with the body."

Instantly a silence fell over the gibbering group. "But, tuan, the head, it is a good one."

To waste so valuable a trophy was inconceivable. Not only that, it was downright disrespectful to take good old Avazere's head and plant it in the ground like a seed. It wouldn't grow. But if they cured it they might be able to get many presents for it farther up the line. A handsome gift it would make, worth many gifts in return. Was it not true, tuan, that two heads were better than one?

There is a point in discipline when you cease being a good leader and become a slave driver. I had reached one of those points now. I could adhere to my standards and have the head buried, or I could yield to the standards of the Stone-Age and let them preserve the head of their former comrade for the future enrichment of all concerned, including the victim. Dead and buried, he was not only gone and forgotten, he was also useless. This way he was dead and forgotten, but still useful. After all, as they pointed out, two heads were better than one.

CHAPTER V

BOW AND TORCH HUNT CLUB

LEONA never missed her paddler. She was still at the stage when all natives look alike, and the substitution of another boy in the stern was not detected. From her position in the canoe the natives towering above her were best recognised by their posteriors anyway.

We were bowling along at a great rate now. Though the river was flowing faster the farther we went, my huskies were hitting six and even seven miles a day. Often, on clear straight stretches, we skimmed along at better than a mile an hour. As a driver of racing boats, this speed would have been unendurable were I not a jungle man long before I ever jazzed up a motor. To me there is more thrill in the surge of power packed by a crew of paddlers than in the roar of a super-engine. In defence of my boys, I also will point out that we were bucking an eight-mile current. Downstream under the same power we would have careened along at seventeen miles an hour, a respectable gait in any country.

Lolling at ease in the canoe with nothing to do for hours at a stretch, time would have hung heavy on our hands were it not for the variety of entertainment provided by the jungle. Old man jungle crams more plants into a square inch than any floriculturist could hope to raise in a square foot. Parasitic growths of unrivalled beauty, fatal to any hot-house tree, flourish from nearly every limb. Of course, they kill the trees in the jungle, too, but more will grow. Orchids of all hues including the black, splash gleaming colour through the waxy green of the foliage. Lilies of a score of varieties wade out into the stream to pay floral tribute to our passing. Even the sinister death-lily, eater of insects, wafts its heavy breath across the steaming water.

We had our aviary, too. Birds of paradise more fantastic than any dyed plumage ever seen on a woman's hat seared their brilliant way across the river like irridescent flames. Not that they were often igniting the air with their presence. Far too often they were heard rather than seen, and when they were heard a lot of illusions were shattered. A convention of birds of paradise sounds like a carload of live crows crossing a trestle of loose ties on a flat-wheeled gondola. And that's a mild description.

Parrots chattered all over the place. White parrots and parakeets, green parrots, red-headed parrots, pink parrots, all kinds of parrots. And herons, cassowaries, frog-voiced hornbills, crows, snipes, ducks, birds were everywhere. Some sang, but most of them just hollered.

There was another dweller of the airways not so pleasant. Bats. Vampire bats, fruit bats, insectivorous bats, giant bats, dwarf bats and just plain bats. Of all the repulsive creatures to be found, these are the worst, and I am not referring just to personal appearances, which are bad enough.

All day the bats hang from the lower limbs of high crowned trees. Especially do they favour trees leaning over the river. There the heat waves rising from the water keep them in a perpetual steam-bath. These moist cloisters are natural incubators for parasites, and when it comes to parasites, bats have them. The bats hang upside down in huge clusters like poisonous fruit, thousands of them, and each bat is homesteaded by fleas, millions of them. The fleas are so thick, in fact, that they are constantly jumping each other's claims, the dispossessed victims dropping like fine rain whenever a bat moves in its sleep.

I tried my shotgun to clear the trees so we could pass beneath without a flea bath, but it didn't work. The squealing pests flew blindly in black clouds after each shot, shedding their repulsive passengers all over us. So thick were the bats that at each shot from my twelve gauge shotgun a dozen or more dropped into the river, dead or crippled. The natives gathered them up eagerly. Later they would be tossed whole into the fire, the fleas seared off, and the rest eaten like chicken.

The ones I shot were the giant fruit bats, spanning four feet, and armed with fangs nearly an inch long that thrust their way up past blunt, sneering nostrils. Some jungle men call them vampire bats, but if they are blood suckers they don't work at it very hard. Take five mosquitos within a mile of camp and you'll get bit five times. But with five thousand vampires within half-a-mile of camp, not one will molest you. And the chances are that if one of them does, you will find upon investigation it is just an over-size mosquito after all.

Just the same, I don't like them. Leona never tried to find out if she like them or not. At the first glimpse of one she disappeared inside her huge, floppy combination sunshade and hat, emerging only after repeated assurances that the air was clear.

As sociable as the bats but far more pleasing to the eye were the parrots. They, too, congregated in droves, preferring to roost in solitary jungle giants bordering the stream. They would perch thickly on the crown branches, climbing back and forth, sometimes right side up and sometimes upside down, like animated blossoms. Because of their enormous appetites, their penchant for fruits, and their healthy digestive tracts it was necessary for me to clear them out of their favoured haunts before we could pass safely beneath. A gunshot or two, fired at random, usually did the trick.

We had our choice of birds for dinner. Ducks were so plentiful. One shot would kill as many as half-a-dozen. Snipe crowded the sand bars and beaches, offering the most delicious of morsels. I didn't shoot them. The natives had their own method of knocking them off. Armed with a slender bamboo pole some twenty feet long, a native would take his stand on the beach, waiting patiently until he was entirely surrounded by the plump runners. Then with a single swish of the pole across the sand he would mow them down, breaking legs or neck indiscriminately. As many as twenty would fall before a single sweep. Fried as only Admo knew how to fry them they made a meal without parallel.

Still, we couldn't live on birds. Three days up from Bupul I found it necessary to replenish the larder with fresh meat. The natives were also low on their second staple, sago. To kill two birds with one stone, I pitched camp that night on a high bank overgrown with sago palm directly across the river from a huge prairie of alang-alang grass. To move in I had but to oust a family of crocodiles on the shore, kill a fifteen-foot python and fumigate a mosquito cloud of hurricane proportions. After that the camp was comparatively free of pests. We went to sleep to the lullaby of a war drum booming out less than a mile away. Either the mosquitos were interfering with the drummer's work or he was a lousy amateur. The rhythm was terrible.

The next morning I split my crew, half staying in camp to prepare sago, the other half crossing the river to prepare for the hunt. I left Leona with the sago pulpers under the watchful eye of Achmed and Admo while I took the best bowmen on the hunt. I wanted to record it on film so I wanted good subjects to work on. Wasbus was already showing signs of camera consciousness. For the occasion he had dandified himself until he was one of the most hideous objects I had ever gazed upon. His skin, normally as scaly as an aggravated case of dandruff, was oiled until he gleamed like a greasy pot. He had cut two new plugs for his nose out of bamboo, both large enough to stop a gallon jug. His bored ears were adorned with crocodile teeth, pulled the evening before and with considerable flesh still adhering to them. Flies followed him in swarms. He was, beyond all shadow of a doubt, in his glory.

The first step in the hunt was the erection of a barricade. This was a V-shaped fence about a quarter-mile long, the point resting on the water's edge and the two sides flaring out into the meadow until they were a couple of hundred yards apart at the mouth of the trap. The idea was that game, forced into the primitive corral, would follow the fence to the water and there halt in terror, giving the bowmen plenty of time to work. Crocodiles have instilled a healthy respect for the river in most of the animals of Dutch New Guinea, and there isn't much they wouldn't rather do than jump in.

The barricades were built out of dry brush, dead limbs, palm leaves, driftwood, anything with bulk to it. Because we had axes, the natives even went so far as to lop down a small grove of bamboo, not so much because we needed the bamboo as because they liked to see steel cut into the stuff. By noon the barricades were built. The rest was easy.

The rest consisted of sending a dozen beaters to the far side of the alang-alang meadow armed with drums and torches. The meadow at this point was about a mile wide, pinched off on the southern side by the jungle, but on the northern side it just kept right on going. The grass, from six to eight feet high, is as dry as tinder and as inflammable as gunpowder. It is also as sharp-edged as a razor, with saw teeth that will cut leather. It is always in this state, the green stalks forcing their way up through the thatch of the old, going to seed and dying in an unending cycle that knows no season.

A wind from the south-east was just strong enough to billow the field in as fine a panorama as I have ever registered on film. Tall grass or grain fields are much more responsive to the wind than water anyway, dipping and bowing with every passing zephyr in a manner to delight the heart of a cameraman. I stood on a high platform of bamboo and panned the whole field. In spite of the fact that twenty natives were forcing their way through the saw-toothed grass, disturbing countless forms of wild game, not a sign of life was to be seen from my platform. Everything was submerged in the yellow sea. Just so my action wouldn't be submerged too, I had the natives remaining with me knock down the grass for a wide area surrounding the platform.

In a short time billows of smoke on the far side of the meadow announced that the drive was on. I heard the roll of drums from the beaters, a roll that started out strong and ominous but a moment later was lost in a roar far more terrifying than anything emanating from a man-made instrument. The roar of a prairie fire.

As if that were the signal, the wind suddenly doubled in intensity. Flames leaped up, consuming even the smoke in the completeness of their fierce attack. Visibility beyond the wall of fire was wiped out by a sheet of heat waves. No flames, no smoke, just solid heat as material as concrete. High overhead, ash-laden whirlwinds formed out of nothing, lowered spinning vortexes to suck on the flames like inverted bellows. Birds drawn into the heat traps shrilled feebly and plummetted to their deaths like smoking meteors, feathers singed off before they struck the ground, It suddenly dawned on me that my platform was a tough place to be with a camera.

I had no time to think further on the situation. Game began

popping out of the thick grass like grasshoppers out of a hay-field. First came the kangaroos. Giant fellows six feet tall not counting the tail. Reaching the clearing I had prepared they got up flying speed in three prodigious jumps and took off over the barricade like scouting planes leaving a short field. Cursing softly I shifted my camera into high speed for slow motion, but it was like trying to stop bullets. The best I could get were some grey streaks.

I had better luck with the smaller kangaroos. They were a distinct species about three feet tall, and geared for half-speed. They were limited to about twenty-five feet to the jump and were fast while in the air but were slower on the uptake. Some cleared the barricade, but scores were diverted, milling against the fence in wild-eyed frenzy before they broke for the point of the V.

Then came the wild boars. Blowing and foaming in desperate terror, they burst from cover like vengeful torpedoes. Straight for the fence they charged. Wham! If there wasn't a hole where one hit, there was where he left. They had the long-legged body of a Great Dane, the head of an Arkansas razor-back, and the sock of a locomotive. They had speed to burn, and when last seen were burning it. Any crocodiles waiting for them at the river just got themselves run over.

As a fleeting bit of action I saw Wasbus plant himself in front of a charging boar, snap back his eighty-five-pound-pull war bow and drive a five foot arrow clear through the beast from stem to stern. It didn't stop until it hit a stump in the barricade.

Action was building up at the point of the V. Switching over to a telephoto lens, I began picking up the slaughter. The crew I had left there was augmented by warriors from the sago detail who were unable to resist the excitement. They had gone mad, to put it mildly. The bloodlust was running at such heat they were grappling with kangaroos with bare hands, tearing out the throats of the beasts with their teeth. Arrows were being discharged with such fury and abandon it was just a matter of luck that they struck no human targets. So thick were the kangaroos and wild boars that it was impossible to shoot into the mass without killing one or more.

Smaller game was pouring into the trap now. Cassowaries

half the size of ostriches rushed into the bloody vortex, their rudimentary wings, flailing, and their sharp-toed feet packing death in every kick. I saw one native go down, nearly split in two, when a bird caught him full on. The natives prize the cassowary, not only for eating but also because the toe nails make fine arrow heads. They went after them with poles, swinging at the long, snake-like necks. Dead cassowaries began to pile up on the heap of butchered kangaroos and boars.

But the parade of delicacies was not through. After the cassowaries came the choicest bird in New Guinea—the crown pigeon. This bird is another of those curious survivals of a former age. In shape it resembles the pigeon after which it is named. In size it corresponds closely to a big turkey. It is short-legged like its predecessor, the dodo, and like the dodo it cannot fly. Its head is crowned with a ridiculous tuft of feathers that bobs furiously as the bird churns its stubby legs and flaps its atrophied wings in land-locked flight. They, too, went down beneath the flailing poles of the natives.

Jungle rats the size of fox-terriers, midget kangaroos, even snakes, swarmed through the grass in droves. Just as I began to think they were pretty small stuff to catch with the camera, a shower of sparks descended upon me. For the first time I noticed that I was soaked with perspiration, that the heat was terrible. For a moment I stared about me blankly, unaware of the cause. So intent had I been in catching the action I had completely forgotten the fire.

But I can take a hint. When the very grass beneath the platform exploded into flame as though hit with an incendiary bomb, I left. I was running long before I hit, and when my feet finally touched I was three jumps away before my full weight rested on the ground. A camera under each arm, I made tracks for the water, but not many tracks. I think most of my running was done in mid-air.

Twice masses of terrified animals nearly swept me off my feet. Kicking and cursing, I ploughed my way through, still clutching my cameras.

Wasbus and his boys were waiting for me in the canoe. So vividly had I impressed upon Wasbus the necessity of waiting that I think he would have turned into a charred corpse rather than pull out without me. Loyalty in natives is a great thing, when you back it up with fear of a thousand devils. And then some.

Some of the black boys, drunk on blood, were staging an orgy of kill-crazy lust in the midst of the first scattered flames, but the majority had paddled out to mid-stream, their canoes loaded down with a choice assortment of meat. The water was full of struggling animals, making paddling precarious. Just before the solid heat-wall rolled down to the river, the few remaining natives suddenly sobered enough to run shrieking to the shore. Upon my shouted instructions, enforced with a pistol shot fired into the air, a canoe dashed in and picked them up. Just in time, too. Although a native will take a canoe through any kind of water, I think he would rather face fire than enter a river bodily. They fear crocodiles too much to even think of learning to swim.

We retreated to the far shore before the fierce heat, but intense as it was it couldn't surpass the stench of burning hair and feathers. The smoke was terrific. I wanted to film the wild sight, the river full of lunging kangaroos, flapping land birds, boars, and snakes, all set against a raging backdrop of the infernal regions, but I couldn't get it. The smoke couldn't be cut with a knife let alone a lens. Away from the river the fire had burned dry and clear, but here, where it was waging its death struggle, there was too much green stuff mixed with the cinder. Green stuff and corpses.

With one final burst of flame thirty feet high, the fire swept itself into a hissing death in the river. The end came as suddenly as if the fire had rushed up to the water and jumped in. One minute a hell on earth, the next minute a prairie of black ashes as dead as the charred pile that marked the V of our barricade.

At least as far as we were concerned it was dead. Flames still roared on the northern side of the meadow, swiftly eating their way into the vast expanse of alang-alang that extended, broken only by a few trees, to the northern horizon. Waste, waste on a prodigious, New Guinea scale. Enough waste here to destroy the heart of a conservationist. Yet it was waste such as had been carried on in New Guinea ever since the land had broken away from Mother Asia and drifted out to sea. Every hunt of any proportions whatsoever is carried on just as I have described it here. If the natives ever think about it at all they reason that there is always another meadow to set on fire. And so far they have been right.

CHAPTER VI

FESTIVAL OF THE PUNCTURED SCHNOZZLES

WE could tell we were approaching Bara while still two days away by the smell, an acrid odour cutting through the river mists like smoke from a bonfire of rubber boots. Distance loaned enchantment. As we came closer, the smell intensified until it attained the proportions of an explosion in an ammonia plant.

We weren't setting any speed records either. Our boys were still suffering from the feast that followed the hunt. Heavy with solid food and bloated by wind, they were much in the same condition as a python after swallowing a pig. Except that a python doesn't burp or cause other disturbances.

To make matters worse, we were constantly running aground. Twenty feet of water under the canoe one minute, and solid sand the next. But there was no capsizing. Word had leaked out that the white tuan might be a little put out if a canoe tipped over and some of his duffle got wet. If the rumours were as strong as when I started them out, the natives probably suspected that drowning was infinitely preferable to capsizing. I do know that a canoe had but to scrape bottom and half the paddlers would be in the creek, steadying the sides for dear life. And I mean dear life.

In one of those stretches we had to pull the canoes over a forty-foot spit of sand flowing less than three inches of water. Great care had to be taken with those hollow trees as a little strain in the wrong places would split one wide open. Half the men were loaded down with equipment while the other half nursed their crafts over the riffles.

Without warning an arrow thunged through the side of a canoe and buried itself in the other side.

My .45 was out and bellowing a reply almost instantly. I thought my draw would have done credit to a movie cowboy, but fast as it was, Achmed was faster. And where I was firing blindly for effect, Achmed was putting lead where it would do some good. His years of jungle fighting with the Dutch Colonial Army had trained him to make every shot count, and count fast.

Right then and there the jungle began shedding arrows like a porcupine sheds quills. All but one were hopelessly short. Those bush-whacking head-hunters just shot and ran, but above all they ran. They didn't bother to pull back their bows. They didn't bother to aim. They just let fly from whatever position they happened to be in and ran. Our fusilage caught them with their bow strings down, and a good thing it was for us, too. Another second and we would have bristled with enough kindling wood to cook a twelve-course dinner.

One native was floundering in the water with an arrow through his leg. Others were muscling the heavy canoes over the sand in frantic lunges. Still others were shedding their duffle into canoes and grabbing up weapons, hell bent for retaliation. The raiders were fleeing, and that was the signal for pursuit. I cast a quick glance about for Leona.

She was down in the water spluttering furiously, with Admo, Wirio, Muda and Kitjal, four of her Malay bodyguards, keeping her there. They had their rifles at the ready, aching for a chance to use them but not deserting Leona no matter how tempting the provocation. She was not appreciating their earnest efforts. I just let her sit while I broke up what was threatening to develop into a riot of our own.

Wasbus, aided and abetted by the blood-thirsty Sekoa, was all for standing the country on end to shake out the ambushers who had tried to lift our heads. The two of them, with about a dozen others, were already scrambling through the barricade of lianas along the shore before I got out a bellow that halted them in their tracks.

"Come back here," I shouted. Wasbus hesitated looked longingly into the jungle like a half-trained pup called off a chicken. "Come on," I demanded sternly. "Get back here."

Wasbus came, head down, feet shuffling through the ripples. Stopping, he picked up a fresh-water clam on which he had stubbed his foot. This he proffered to me gravely.

"Good eating, tuan," he mumbled placatively.

Split-Ear

This Kaya-Kaya lost his ear rings the hard way, by yanking

Dressed to Kill

The bird of paradise furnishes the favourite head-dress of the Kaya-Kayas. This chap carries his nose plugs to extremes to off-set his mild-appearance

What can you do with a savage like that? One minute filled with a lust for blood, the next bringing in a dripping clam as a peace offering. The rest of his crew of killers stood about apprehensively first on one foot and then on the other. I laughed. The natives grinned delightedly. I laughed louder and they broke into high-pitched giggles. The tension was broken.

"All right," I said. "Get more clams. We'll have a clam feast."

So instead of having a vicious head-hunt on my hands, I had a spirited clam hunt, with a score of potential murderers sliding their feet along in the sand like small boys imitating the choo-choo trains. Whenever one slid his foot into a clam there was a whoop of delight. Even Leona, dripping water and indignation, had to laugh at the ludicrousness of the situation. For a girl emerging from her first brush with jungle death, she was doing all right.

I turned my attention to the boy wounded in the leg. The five-foot arrow had gone completely through the long muscle at the back of the leg about eight inches above the knee. About fifteen inches projected beyond the wound, leaving more than three feet to be pulled through unless I cut off the head and backed it out. This the black boy refused to permit.

"See, tuan," he said, rubbing the blood off the arrow head, "Metal. Sharp metal. Arrow too good to cut."

I shrugged. If he wanted the arrow that bad, it wasn't my leg that would be sore after five feet of scalloped bamboo shaft had been pulled through. I gave a tentative yank on the blood-lubricated stick. It was surprisingly firm, as hard to pull out as a butcher's peg from a round roast. The native grinned reassuringly.

"I'm a warrior," he said, pointing to his scars. "I'm Imo."

By this time we were surrounded by a circle of appreciative natives. Under the circumstances the only thing I could do was give my patient as big a play as he deserved. With suitable gestures and passes, I grasped the shaft firmly, gave a swift jerk and out it came, followed by a spurt of blood.

The audience "Oohed!" in admiration. My patient beamed.

Leona had been rummaging for the medicine chest. Finding

E

it at the bottom of a pile of duffle, she came over with bandages and iodine. Here was further glory.

While I held the wound open, Leona swabbed in iodine. The pain must have been terrific but the leg I was holding scarcely quivered. The next step was the bandaging. Leona used about two yards of double-folded gauze, binding it fast with adhesive tape. Our patient was turned over to his admiring fans.

While everybody in the crew was engaged in examining the bandage, I washed off the arrow. The metal point intrigued me and I wanted to know where it came from. There was no difficulty in determining its source. The point was a three-inch metal cross of the type given out by coastal missionaries to the natives who deserted their heathen gods in favour of Christianity.

The foot of the cross had been ground to needle sharpness, and the arms were gound until they were keen as razor blades. A more perfect arrow head has never been invented. One of those things going through the mid-riff would cut loose the works. After estimating its effectiveness I was surprised that not all of the natives on the island had become Christians.

An investigation of the ambush site revealed a few blood stains, proving the effectiveness of Achmed's sharp-shooting. But there were no bodies. If any one had been mortally wounded, the survivors had carted off the meat for their own cook fires. Our boys sniffed the fresh blood regretfully, but came away promptly enough at my orders. The fact that there were more than twenty in the ambushing party may have accounted for the willingness of my boys to leave. Twenty warriors make a good sized chunk of fighting material.

A half hour later, when we were once more ready to get under way, our wounded boy was a comparatively rich man In addition to possessing an arrow with a metal point, he had a new bamboo knife, a couple of boar's tusks, some alligator claws, a stone axe and a choice assortment of arrow shafts. In exchange he had given strips of bandage and a few patches of adhesive tape. At least twenty of the crew sported blood-stained gauze hair ribbons or gory patches of tape on their already hideous faces. That kind of stuff was too valuable to waste on punctures when the whole shore was lined with mud. Our patient was resting comfortably, nay regally, with a couple of slimy mud packs hermetically sealing his wound. So much for hospitalisation.

By mid-afternoon we reached kampong Bara, capital village of the Rain Forest. The welcome signs were out. Women rushed for the shore to roll in the mud in what looked like the last stages of a royal fit. Like their civilised sisters receiving company, they did not want to be caught in an old dress so they were busy applying a fresh pack of mud to cover the old dirt. The men were no more dignified. They were hopping up and down on the shore like monkeys afflicted with fleas in vital areas. Huge clusters of feathers and bright coloured flowers decorated their posteriors. With wild shrieks they would leap into the air, turn their bottoms up and wave their dazzling feathery welcome at us. Truly it was wonderful to look upon.

Although we had sent no runners ahead—the mortality rate on runners is one hundred per cent—we were expected. A new thatched hut had been prepared for Leona and me. The bachelors' lodge had been enlarged to take care of my boys, and plenty of bucks were around to take care of the women in my party. Willing hads assisted us in unloading. In fact if we hadn't resisted mightily we would have been stripped of our very clothing within fifteen minutes. This acquisitiveness is not limited to the Baranites. It is a general rule all over the island. Anything not nailed down, padlocked, and mounted guard over is common property.

Because Bara is so ideally typical of all villages of the Marind Anim tribe, I'll go into a little detail describing it. Just how old it is, is impossible to say. Raids one hundred per cent successful have levelled it countless times, but the site has been occupied by villages of one kind or another for thousands of years. The rubble, however, does not accumulate from century to century. The absence of stone work and pottery eliminates any possibility of tracing the history of the village from its ruins or ash piles. Everything is built out of palm, bamboo and grass, stuff that rots away without leaving a trace. After a century of continuous occupancy a good fire would put the village right back where it started from as far as ruins were concerned.

Just as the rubble does not increase, neither does the population. About 250 natives were living there when we arrived, and there is no indication that there ever were more than that. The village was oval in shape with about thirty huts surrounding the central plaza. One end of the oval reached the river, the bank at this point being about four feet high and worn down by constant travel to and from the combination boat landing and water supply. The other end of the oval was left open for the benefit of the occupants of the bachelor lodge, set about fifty yards back from the village proper, and to provide access to the ceremonial lodge, likewise set apart from the huts and opposite the opening from the bachelor lodge. From the bachelor lodge to the river was a distince of about 250 yards, while in width the village measured less than 100 yards from jungle wall to jungle wall.

The huts were marvels of simplicity and inefficiency. They were of light bamboo construction capable of withstanding hurricanes because of an ingenious engineering novelty. Bracing the huts on the side opposite the last wind storm were a series of bamboo poles. Should the next hurricane come from another direction, the natives scurried around to collect the poles and prop up their huts on the menaced side. You could always tell the direction of the prevailing winds by the list of the huts and the location of the flying buttresses. Of course the roofs might blow off, but that was all right. They weren't keeping out any rain anyway.

The hut built for Leona and me was typical of all of them save that it was new and hence unpopulated by fleas. In size it was almost twenty feet wide by a good thirty feet long. In shape it resembled an ordinary wood shed except that one side of the peaked roof was higher than the other by a foot, and overlapped it about three feet. This was to provide a vent for smoke and an entrance for mosquitos running the full length of the house. The side walls were about five feet high, the front and rear walls about eight feet at the peak. There were no windows, and only the one square doorway opening on the plaza. Of course, in case you wanted to leave in a hurry you could always make your own door by diving through the wall.

So much for the architecture. The construction was more complicated. The frame-work, as I have mentioned before, was of bamboo, chewed to appropriate lengths by stone axes. Four large trunks furnished the corner posts to which the cross-members were lashed with rattan. Poles every three feet supported the beams, and the beams in turn supported the rafters spaced a little closer together. Once the bamboo skeleton was erected and lashed firmly enough to support a man's weight, the thatchers went to work with palm fronds, over-lapping them like shingles. The first fronds are always carefully placed, but after a while the carpenters get tired of the work. They usually end up by placing the thatch on upside down— it's easier to do that way—so that the top half of the roof sheds water, the lower half diverts it into the interior. The walls show the same careful technique. With a tropical storm mumbling in the offing, I had my tent set up in the middle of the hut as a precautionary measure. After the storm broke I wished I had set it up outside. Two holes in the roof directly above the tent cataracted so much water on us we couldn't sleep because of the roar.

The storm was gone by morning, leaving the village smelling fresh and sweet and pure for a couple of hours. Most of the villagers had been washed to a limited extent by the shower baths built into their roofs, and others had been rinsed off by little brooklets meandering through their beds on the floors of their huts.

The chief, a bull of a fellow named Birgzi, informed me that in our honour they would hold their *karapau*, or nose-boring festival the next day. I was glad to hear that. A nose-boring festival was one of the things I wanted to catch for my picture. I assured him I appreciated the honour, and in return I would change his name to Bertie. I couldn't have done more. His appreciation was so touching I wished I had gone ahead and given him the full name of Bertram. A new name is the highest honour that can be bestowed on one of those boys, and all the while we were there he strutted around the village referring to himself in the third person as Bertie. The Napoleonic complex is not new in the scale of civilisation.

The nose-boring festival is a splendid example of how to eliminate nuisances by honouring them. Each year about a dozen boys of the village reach the age of puberty but not the age of discretion. They have the free run of the village, and consort regularly and oftener with all the girls, eating with them, sleeping with them and otherwise making pests of themselves as far as their elders are concerned.

If the boys were permitted to continue their happy existence, family life would soon become unendurable. So the boys are promoted. They become bachelors with great pomp and ceremony, the principal part of which is having their noses bored and in keeping with their new-found dignity they are shoved into the bachelor lodge where they are out of the way and forgotten. No longer can they sleep with their girl friends. They can come into the village for their meals, but each night they must return to the lodge. If they wish to continue their love affairs, they must do so on the sly. At least they are no longer promiscuously underfoot.

The first step in the nose-boring festival is in catching the noses. The boys seemed to sense that their freedom was in danger. All morning they were scarce, but our presence created too much excitement in the village. They couldn't sit out in the jungle, when right in their own town was a white man and a wonderful white woman who smelled like a bouquet though she wore no flowers (Citronella). It was as if a circus had come to town. One by one they seeped in to stare at us round-eyed. Then from behind huts would creep warriors and zing—another boy would be in the corral.

The corral in this case was the ceremonial lodge, the sagging roof patched up with fresh fronds, and bolstered with more poles. There were no sides to the structure, a labour-saving convenience which permitted free movement of the spirits. The interior was divided into bamboo stalls for this occasion, one stall for each eligible victim. The furnishings of the stall were of the simplest, one platform about a foot square upon which the initiate had to squat from the time he was caught until his nose was bored. In the cases of the boys caught in the morning this meant all afternoon and night, an ordeal calculated to purify the soul and paralyse the muscles so they couldn't kick so much when the time came. Guards saw that the boys stayed where they were put.

The Marind-Anims are an ancestor worshipping race. They

pay tribute to the departed as long as they can remember them, which in some cases is as long as three months. By that time somebody else has died, so they pay tribute to him. However, for so great a ceremony as the *karapau*, they dig back to antiquity to resurrect the memory of all who have died since the previous festival, which may have been held as long as a year ago, or just a few months back, depending upon the number of eligibles for bachelorhood. They don't want any of the ghosts to miss the fun.

Portraits of the departed are carved upon the trunk of a soft tree, called the *oemitroe*, and the pole is then stuck up in front of the ceremonial lodge. It resembles the totem pole of the Canadian-Pacific Indians only in that the figures are on a pole. The carving is of the crudest, and in most cases is even worse than that. By stretching the imagination, one is able to visualise a human outline among the scratches, but even a strong imagination cannot stand up to the strain of figuring out a personality in each batch of scratches. In Bara five men and four women had died since the last *karapau*, and the artist, an under-study of the witch-doctor, wore out half a dozen clam shells scratching their figures in the soft wood. The only thing you could be sure of in his figures was the sex, but at least he got them all on the pole. In some cases where a head-hunt has wiped out half a village, one figure is made to do the work of all the departed.

After the artist had worked his fingers to the bone, the witch-doctor, a pretty decent sort of a chap whom I called Fritz, supervised the erection of the pole on a spot where the figures could have a clear view of the festivities. With suitable gestures and incantations, he presented the figures with sight, saw that they had food, and thereafter forgot about them. For the rest of the ceremony we had to wait until morning.

The dawn was heralded with the beating of drums. The musicians were cold and stiff, their rhythm more so, but even at that the noise was pretty awful. The dozen boys in the stalls must have thought so too, for as I stuck my head out the door I saw one of them scoot for the tall timber. His muscles were too cramped to make the grade, however, and he was dragged squealing back to his place. Apparently the futility of his break discouraged the rest of them, for none followed.

Under normal conditions, the nose-boring would have begun at once, but the light was not yet bright enough for good pictures. I had them hold off for a couple of hours until the sun was higher. The delay was not too well received. Here this was a gala day, and I was holding up the parade. To make amends I put on a show of my own. A little rummaging around in my gift box yielded a few packages of Chinese fire crackers, a phonograph with records, a Santa Claus mask and some coloured crayons. The crayons I used to enhance the carvings on the pole as high as I could reach, winning the undying gratitude of the bereaved. The fire crackers I tossed around here and there as evidence that the dead were arriving upon the scene and thus explosively announcing their presence. Then donning the Santa Claus mask, I turned on the phonograph. The mask was bad enough, but when the first strains of Tiger Rag blared into the jungle, I lost my audience.

Only the strongest sense of duty kept the guards at the ceremonial lodge in their places. The boys were already too terrified by what was to come to pay much attention to any additional horrors. By the time order was once more restored, the sun was in an ideal position for shooting. The drums resumed their booming, timorously at first, if a war drum can ever be timorous, but with growing confidence. The first boy was yanked squealing from his perch.

Nose boring means just that. The instrument of torture is no little stick to be thrust through the vomer, that thin partition of flesh and cartilage between the nostrils. It is a ten to fifteen foot length of rattan a little better than the thickness of a pencil, and though the bark has been removed it is not much smoother than a rat-tail file.

The boy is brought into the circle of warriors—no women are permitted to witness the ordeal—the drums pound in rising fury to drown out any screams of pain, and the stage is set. I focussed my camera and waved them on. Two warriors grasped the first victim, the witch-doctor and his understudy grasped the rattan rod. With his fore-finger thrust up the boy's right nostril to back up the vomer, the witch-doctor placed the pointed end of the rod against the thin partition and pushed. The boy howled. The drums drowned him out. Fritz pushed again, and this time the rod went through. By this time the boy was jerking up and down like a puppet on a string. The warriors holding him were vastly amused. They hadn't had so much fun since the last head-hunt.

With the hole made, the idea now was to pull the whole length of rattan through the wound without ripping out the partition at the tip. To this end Fritz held the vomer firm while his understudy pulled on the pliable rod hand over hand, like a sailor coiling rope. Any knots and irregularities of the rod went right on through. You just had to yank a little harder, that was all. The boy would live.

He did live, too. When the last foot of the rod had passed through his nose, he took a bamboo plug a half inch in diameter and with his own hands thrust it through the opening. This was to prevent its closing together while healing. Every day he would remove the plug, wrap a fresh leaf around it and thrust it back in. When the wound was entirely healed, he might let the hole remain its natural size or he might stretch it, depending upon the strength of his vanity.

But right now he wasn't interested in that. After inserting the plug, he tottered through the laughing, hand-clapping bunch of black yokels surrounding him, wobbled uncertainly across an open space of ground and passed out cold. But he was forgotten. Another boy was having his nose pierced.

For more than an hour the nose-boring proceeded, the excitement and the sight of blood working the warriors into a frenzy. The whole thing was a success. Of the dozen boys operated upon, only one jerked so savagely as to break loose from the rod, tearing out the tip of his nose. A couple passed out and had to be operated on while unconscious, but this was to be expected. If I had had to squat upon a platform for hours on end, and then listen to those drums and the shrieks of agony from my playmates, I think I could have done something big in the way of passing out myself.

Leona thought the whole thing outrageous and barbaric, which it was. She hovered around the edges, as close as the women were permitted to come, and as soon as a boy staggered in her direction she caught him up and poured iodine on his schnozzle. She would have put on bandages, except that the iodine shocked them into a new frenzy of pain and she couldn't catch them again.

When the last boy staggered away the warriors could no longer control themselves. They leaped, they shrieked, they rolled on the ground in paroxysms of frenzy so primitive as to be neither religious nor even human. One man squatted on his haunches, battering out great gouges of earth with his stone club, pausing every now and then to raise his head and howl. Another spun madly like a whirling dervish, meanwhile shooting arrows into the air until they seemed to be hurled from him by centrifugal force. Others pawed the earth like mad bulls, then spurted around in circles hurling everyone in their path out of the way. One of them tried to run over me, but a right to the jaw changed his mind and his tracks. After that any particularly vicious attacks of frenzy always took place well removed from my presence. None of the natives in his right mind would deliberately attack a white man but he would deliberately dance himself out of his right mind so he could attack him. Schultz is the boy who had an answer for that. When he is alone and the natives start going crazy, he goes just three times crazier three times faster than they can. One pass at him means three passes back, and at that rate there is no fun in it for the natives. They respect his insanity.

The nose boring that started the riot was forgotten. So were the boys who were the victims. They were left to nurse their wounds, and those who had dropped unconscious were left to revive as best as they could. The show must go on.

The women were in on the fiesta now. The noon hour came and went. New drummers replaced those that were worn out. Men and women too old to take a vigorous part in the dance kept the cooking fires going, with a plentiful supply of meat and sago always charring on the red-hot cooking stones. Exhausted dancers flopped near the fires to recover, grabbing off chunks of food to speed their revival. All this in a temperature of well over a hundred degrees.

By nightfall, instead of being worn out, the natives were just getting ready to go to town. Sex now reared its ugly head.

There is nothing pleasant or sentimental about jungle sex. An exhausted female dancer falling to the ground would be promptly attacked by the closest male. His act would incite the rest, and as many as a dozen would attack the same woman before she could crawl away out of sight and out of mind. Under normal circumstances the male would then be through for the night, but these were not normal circumstances. On every side were acts of violence to further stimulate his lust.

After a hasty visit to the fire for food and drink, he would rejoin the leaping mob, a lusty beast from head to toe. The drink had something to do with it. Brewed from *wati* root well chewed up by the women and expectorated into a bowl, the liquid had been left in the hot sun to ferment all day. In taste it was more bitter than quinine, and in effect it was more powerful than rubbing alcohol. Judging by the reaction it produced on the natives, it must have contained aphrodisiacal properties as well.

Leona had long since been sent to her tent under the protection of her five Malays, not only because the sights were too repulsive for her to gaze upon, but because it wasn't safe for her to be about. It wasn't safe for me either, but outside with the natives I was in a better position to stop anything before it got started than I would be in the tent. Once anything got started there would be no stopping it anyway so it was up to me not to let it start.

The scene had now boiled down to pure savagery. My own boys and women were doing nothing to contribute to the moral tone. They were right in there with the rest, if anything even more barbaric for having cast off their restraining shackles of civilisation. Flames fifteen to twenty feet high doubled and tripled the number of dancers by adding black, grotesque shadows to the whirling mob. Twenty or more drummers pounded away on taut crocodile skins, each one working on a separate rhythm and no two rythms alike. Everywhere couples were sprawled on the ground in carnal embrace. No one paid any attention to them other than to leap over them that the dance might continue uninterrupted. The cameraman in me regretted that the light was too dim for photography, but I wouldn't have been able to release such a film anyway so it was all right.

Some psychologists claim that these orgies are a necessary part of primitive life, that otherwise the males would never be sufficiently stimulated to keep the birth rate on par with the death rate. This is true to a limited extent, but in a different way. In their youth the natives indulge in intercourse so frequently, often several times a day, that in maturity they seldom feel the urge. If left to the elders, there might not be many babies. However, the youths pay all the attention to the birth rate that is necessary and the population of the tribe is perfectly safe without any sex orgies.

The best way to account for a festival such as the *karapau* is to put it down as nothing more than animal fun. The bright flames, the blood-stirring drums, the leaping dancers, the licentious brawls in which every man's wife is your own—that is enough reason for an orgy.

It was dawn again before the flames began to die down, before the dancers who fell to earth stayed there. When a tired drummer quit, there were no more shuffling hands to replace his own. Somewhere a boy moaned in agony as his torn face touched the ground. The festival of the bored noses was about over. It was safe to go to bed.

As I approached my hut I was suddenly aware that I had been on the go for twenty-four hours. So had Achmed, Admo and the other Malays but there was no trace of sleep in their eyes. They were as alert in the dim dawn as they had been on the previous morning. No wonder Leona could sleep soundly while all hell was breaking loose outside, knowing she was safe as long as her bodyguard had bullets for their rifles. It was good to have somebody you could trust in a land where trust was reposed only in a stone club. And it was good to sleep knowing that the chances were pretty good that you would wake up.

CHAPTER VII

THROUGH THE RAIN FOREST

THE day following the *karapau* the whole village had a hang-over.

If they were half as sick as they looked, they should have been dead, and I think if they could have smelled themselves as others smelled them they would have died. A sorrier looking lot would be hard to imagine this side of a nightmare. Most of the boys spent the day lying where they had fallen the night before, afraid to move because of the spirits who were wandering around with stone clubs, banging away at anybody who raised a head. Being savages they had one solace denied the civilised man. When they got sick they didn't have to rush for the bath room.

There was, however, one sober native in camp, a woman about to swell the Kaya-Kaya population by one. Leona discovered her moaning in her little doghouse set a few yards back into the jungle from the village. Her husband lay alongside the hut moaning in sympathy. He was sick too, from too much *wati*. At a word from Leona, Achmed threw him out.

It didn't take Leona long to find that the woman, named Mabol, had laboured thus in torment for three days without any assistance even from her husband. She was *tabu*. That was why she was isolated from the village in the tiny thatched hut, a hut scarcely larger than a dog house, and so poorly constructed it didn't even keep out the sun, let alone rain. The deluge on the evening of our arrival had formed a pond in her accouchement bed, and her tossing around during the hours of travail had worked it into a mud wallow. But the rain had its advantages too. It gave her some muddy water to drink and that was something.

Leona's horror at discovering Mabol's condition was no less than Mabol's horror at being thus discovered. Nothing short of death for all concerned could follow such reckless flouting of the tabus. And she did so want to see her little baby, the little fellow who was causing her so much agony. After forty eight hours in the mud, now she was going to die, the baby was going to die, and the beautiful white lady, so like a white cloud was going to die too. She drew in a shuddering sob, folded her quivering hands, and settled back into the mud to wait for death.

Thinking the woman had fainted, Leona sent Wirio on the run to find me while she and her inseparable Malays pulled the dog house out of the way. Then tabu or no tabu, she moved Mabol's inert body to a soft bed of leaves, Achmed protesting but helping just the same. He knew he would be cursed, but he was relying upon my medicine to get him out of it.

Fritz, the witch-doctor, was in no condition to summon any evil spirits when, for the psychological effect it would produce on the natives, I asked him to lift some of the tabus surrounding birth. He scowled weakly and mumbled something about bad medicine. Raising my voice and my pistol at the same time I shouted, "Evil Demas, leave this place!"

Then I fired the pistol.

To those poor natives suffering from the horrible after-effects of a twenty-four hour spree on *wati* and sex, the report must have sounded like the end of the world. A howl of terror and anguish rocked the village. Poor Fritz recoiled as though I had slapped his face with a stone axe. If he had had any thoughts of enforcing the tabus, or if he was thinking of challenging the superiority of my medicine, those thoughts were gone now. There was no room for them in his throbbing brain. He waved his hand weakly and collapsed on the ground, careful, however, that his aching head floated gently to rest without unnecessary shock.

By the time I reached the birthday party, everything was over. On the ground a wrinkled, reddish-brown baby "waaan-waaaned" every time it could get enough wind into itself to "waaan." Mabol was stretched out as rigid as a board. The baby had been born in one mighty convulsion following the report of my pistol. Poor Mabol thought it was one of the demas come to claim her life.

Leona borrowed my knife to complete her mid-wifery chores

while I set to work restoring the mother. A little massaging of her arms and legs helped her relax. A gentle belly rub followed by a mild application of artificial respiration brought her around. It wasn't the treatment that did it, it was the idea that somebody was working over her, trying to help her that roused her from her resignation to death. Even then I doubt if she would have completely revived had she not heard the bellowing of her child. Once she got the idea that not only was she alive but the baby too, she sat right up.

A half hour later Mabol wobbled unsteadily for the shore of the river, her little boy in her arms. Leona tried to intercept her, but to no avail. Straight into the water she went, dumped the baby in and gave him a thorough scouring. The baby's first and only bath. If she had come out then, Leona could have forgiven her, but a washing was not enough. Right at the water's edge was a nice puddle of yellow, goeey mud. Into this the baby was dumped. Over and over he was rolled until he looked more like a butter ball than a human being. Not that he looked an awful lot like one in the first place. When he was thoroughly plastered with yellow mud from head to foot, the mother kneaded up a ball of clay with which to seal the umbilical cord. The baby was now launched on the way to manhood, safe from preying ghosts who would never recognise in that lump of mud a potential warrior. That was Mabol's first thought, to disguise her off-spring so the evil spirits wouldn't recognise it. And having accomplished this, she calmly sat down and discharged the placenta.

The husband came wandering around about then wondering just how much all the broken tabus were going to kick back on his head. I reassured him on this point and complimented him on beong the father of so fine a *hon-a-hon*. This raised a baffling point which has been a subject of speculation for centuries. Does a baby grow in a woman like a mango on a tree, or does the male have something to do with it? Any native favouring the latter theory is confronted with still another problem ; which male? For the peace of mind of all concerned the questions are best left unasked and unanswered.

One tabu was creating concern all through the village. It is a rigid rule that the path made by the mother in carrying her *hon-a-hon*, as all new-born babies of either sex are called, from the birth-hut to the water is not to be crossed by anyone under any circumstances for at least seven days. Anyone crossing the path breaks a hole in it, admitting the evil spirits who promptly take up their abode in the baby. But Mabol, in her excitement, had wandered all over the place, practically cutting off the village from the river.

My stock as a witch doctor would have taken a sharp slump if I hadn't been able to fix that. I did it up right with a package of fire crackers with which I bombed spirits right and left. If there were any left after I got through blasting, they were a badly singed lot. Everyone was happy, including Fritz, after I let him light some fire crackers himself. He was hard to get started in view of his hang-over, and he didn't like the idea of playing with fire crackers anyway. They scared him. But once I routed out an audience of his own boys he couldn't back down. And after I got him started I had a hard time stopping him. Not content with bombing spirits, he insisted on bombing some of his personal enemies as well.

Never before had a baby been so explosively ushered into Bara. With such a start he was already ordained for great things, so I gave him a name in keeping with his prospects. I called him Archibald. When the awed natives couldn't get the pronounciation I shortened it to Archie. After that everything was lovely. So proud was Mabol that if Leona hadn't taken her sharply in hand she would have carried her son all over the village that those still unable to walk might see the wonder child with the wonder name given it by the white sombe-onim (chief).

While on the subject of babies this is a good time to outline the stages through which one passes to reach manhood. As soon as the baby emerges from the suckling stage it is stuffed with bananas. The mother takes a ripe fruit, sticks one end in the baby's mouth and pushes. The soft pulp is gradually forced down the infant's throat, and if it doesn't like it, at least it can't squawk. When the end is reached, the mother shoves it down with her thumb. The baby is fed for another hour.

When and if the youngster turns five his first important

birthday is reached. The family holds a big celebration, the old man get drunk and the boy is doused from head to foot with a frightful smelling mixture of soot and coconut oil. This is to blacken him up even darker than his natural colour. Pot-bellied and spindly-shanked, the little back boy spends the next five to seven years in splendid idleness, getting under-foot when anything exciting is going on, and clearing out when any work is to be done. His games are usually childish versions of adult sports. He and his playmates stage mimic wars that sometimes produce fatal results, they capture small game, trap birds, rob bird's nests, practice love-making, steal, and other-wise have a high old time. All the while he runs around clothed only in soot and coconut oil.

At the age of puberty he goes through the nose-boring ceremony just described, after which he changes from black to red. The soot and oil with which he has been impregnated over a period of years is allowed to wear out under successive applications of red clay. He begins to sport arm bands, nose plugs, ear rings, necklaces of boar's tusks or crocodile claws, and doctor up his bushy hair by weaving in dry grass and soaking the whole mess in rancid oil. During his childhood oil has kept his skin fairly smooth, but the red clay soon drys it up. He becomes scaly. His skin cracks until it resembles the chapped hands of a small boy during snowball season. His feet become tough, with pads on the heels and toes thicker than those on a bear. He practices constantly with bow and arrows. He learns how to make and use war clubs and spears. Gradually he is preparing for that great day when he will take part in a head-hunt and come home with the grisly trophy that will permit him to take a bride. But above all he is building up his smell.

His official social life is limited pretty much to the males who share the bachelor lodge with him. He gets along fine, fights among the occupants being almost unknown. In spite of the handicaps placed on his love-making, his sexual urges seldom go long unsatisfied. The jungle is a big place, offering many trysting nooks where obliging maidens can frequently be encountered. His life has its darker side too. He has to work.

Once a week he has to go hunting, which means that at the

F

end of the day he has to collect whatever game he has killed and carry it home. Then every month or so he might be called upon to wear down a sago palm for the women to cut up. As if this were not enough work, the thatch on the bachelor lodge needs repair from time to time. Usually, however, the lodge is large enough so that he can keep moving around to dry corners as leaks develop in the roof. Not until there are no dry spots left do the occupants have to patch the roof.

When the great day comes that he bags a human head he can wash off the red clay, go into the village and set up housekeeping with a wife of his own. If he is especially capable he is inducted into the secret society of the Imo, and thereafter he daubs his face with grey clay whenever taking part in a raid. White clay is used as a sign of mourning. Upon the death of any member of the family he smears himself white, and upon his own death he is covered with white clay. Thus from birth to death he passes through four colour stages: yellow clay at birth, black soot for childhood, red clay for puberty, then his natural black again for maturity, and white clay for death.

Bara was just representative enough for me to catch the four stages and colours of man on my film. And having accomplished this, there was nothing to do but push on into the Rain Forest, this time on foot.

On the map, there is a large blank space between the headwaters of the Merauke River at Bara and the junction of the Oewimmerah and Digoel Rivers. It is only seventy miles across there, but it took us just twenty-eight days to make the trip. In New Guinea distances are best measured in terms of time anyway. If I had had to depend upon my original crew, it would have taken us two months, but thanks to the attractions of my magic, I was able to line up about forty more carriers from Bara. They were willing to act as carriers just for the fun of seeing what would happen next.

At daybreak we ferried all my junk across the river, gave each carrier about twenty pounds of equipment and started out. There was a general fight to carry the canned stuff, the natives figuring that if they toted the cans when full they could have the tins when empty. Heavy stuff, like five gallon cans of kerosene for the lanterns were carried in rattan slings strung on poles with a native at each end. Smaller stuff was carried in gunny sacks. The idea was not so much one of comfort in carrying as ease in shedding. This was jungle travel, with no open prairies calling for long marches. Should a snake snap out of the lianas, the natives wanted to be free to jump right out from under their loads. If fitted out with pack sacks and knapsacks, they might have been able to carry things a lot easier, but their jumps for safety would have been a lot shorter.

Five miles a day was a tremendous speed. I can still hear the wind whistling by my ears whenever I think of it. It would take a full half-hour for my cannibal caravan to pass a given spot. On the march I had a cutting crew, armed with machetes, hacking a tunnel through the lianas, brambles, brush and fallen limbs. This tunnel was no wider than the edge of a machete. It was a slit through which you forced your way about as easily as you could carry a step ladder through a barbed wire entanglement.

Until someone tries it he has no idea of the splendid exercise to be found in swinging a machete at a bunch of lianas. The machete, or *klewang* as the Malays call it, is a heavy bladed instrument about thirty inches long that resembles a cross between a meat cleaver and a broad sword. On the backswing it tangles with every available twig and vine. Freed of encumbrances, you can begin the down-swing. Then just as you are building up momentum to slice through a liana as thick as your wrist, the klewang catches on something over your head and yanks out an arm at the socket. Of course all the while you are doing this you are standing on slippery moss or slimy mud, your ribs massaged by the sharp, severed edges of the stuff you just cut through. But there are always pretty flowers you can look at.

Just to keep my boys together, and incidently any equipment they happened to be carrying, I arranged my caravan so that every third or fourth man was either a Malay or a trusted murderer from the Merauke chain gang. These men I armed with rifles. Their pride in my confidence in them was the best insurance I could have. Any native developing an overwhelming attachment for his burden had no opportunity to run off with it as long as my Malays and Javanese killers were on the job. I want to emphasise again that the natives are not to be trusted any further than you can broad-jump in a bag. They don't steal in our meaning of the word. They just walk off with the stuff and never come back. They have about the same sense of right and wrong as a magpie. They mean no particular harm, they are just following the only law they know; take what you can get while you can get it, and beat it while the beating is good.

New Guinea considerately offers no tigers, lions, jaguars, wolves, bears or other mammalian varmints calculated to make life miserable and uncertain. About the only carnivorous creatures you have to watch out for are the cannibals. To compensate for the lack of varmints, New Guinea places at your disposal five kinds of cobra, and countless other breeds and varieties of poisonous reptiles. Some pack a venom that kills in fifteen seconds, others discharge a poison so mild it rarely proves fatal under two hours. Seven varieties of non-poisonous, bone-crushing python are also included in the lot.

Other problems arise to take a lot of comfort out of jungle travel in spite of my best efforts to cater to my natural laziness. These can be best illustrated by lifting a day from our itinerary while in the Rain Forest.

All night the drums had been rolling with a steady throb that meant nothing. Towards dawn the drumming died out, partly because the swingsters were sleepy and partly because the dank mists took all the tautness out of their drum heads. But silence did not descend over the jungle. The birds of paradise began squawking to high heaven that a new day was on the way. I can sleep through a native jam session but I defy anybody to sleep through a conclave of birds of paradise. When they begin, the camp wakes up.

The gasoline storm lantern I keep going all night while in the jungle cast a brilliant white glare over the camp, but even as I looked it seemed to fade away into nothingness. Abruptly the sun was up. I couldn't see it, you never can see it in the Rain Forest, but the light was there. At least enough of it to dwarf the storm lantern. All around the natives lying on the bare ground were coming to life, stretching stiffly and urinating as they stretched. Every one was drugged with sleep save the five Malays stationed around our tent. If they ever slept, I was too sound asleep myself to catch them at it.

In a few minutes the campfires had been kicked into life, the boys were clustered around warming themselves up and frying up a few chunks of dried meat or sago. Leona and I had breakfast in style—cereal, condensed milk, sugar, coffee, fresh coconut milk, and an omelet of duck eggs, followed by cigarettes from a freshly opened tin. While we sat back in luxury on canvas camp stools, a hundred men and women picked out their loads from the tarpaulin-protected pile in the centre of camp. Each knew what he or she was to carry, and no attempt was made to dodge responsibility. Wasbus, being the largest and strongest in the crew, carried the least.

Achmed supervised the packing of our personal effects, Admo looked after the food and cooking utensils, and Wirio, Kitjil and Mudo took charge of the cameras and film. Each of them had a boy to do the work under their supervision. As my personal boys, and Leona's body-guard, they were far too exalted to do any work themselves. When everything was in readiness, Achmed rationed out the machetes to the chopping crew (never trust a head-hunter with a machete overnight) I slipped on my bedroom slippers, and away we went.

It was just 7 a.m. Being practically on the equator, the days and nights were evenly divided, the sun disappearing promptly at 6 p.m. and popping up at the same hour in the morning. Everything was soaking wet. Water stood in huge drops on every leaf, and dripped from the trees in a downpour that gave the jungle its name of Rain Forest.

For the first three hours we had easy going, following a native trail about 12 inches wide, which is just $11\frac{1}{2}$ inches wider than than a trail cut with a machete. Then the Kaya-Kaya trail jogged casually off to the west for no reason whatever, and we were confronted with a solid wall of lianas. There was a chance that the trail might resume its northward course a little farther on, but once you let yourself be lured off on the easiest course you are done for. Trails never go where you think they are going, and when at last you come to this realisation you are so hopelessly lost you can't even trust your compass anymore.

The choppers swung into action, cutting down the creepers

and stomping them underfoot. Hack, chop, pull, tromp. In two hours we cut our way down into a valley and up into a clearing on top of a slight ridge, As the crow flies, we had made less than a quarter of a mile in two hours, but had piled up the impressive total of three miles in five hours, thanks to the ready-made trail we had followed earlier. I called a halt for lunch.

While the boys were preparing the noon meal, Leona and I went over each other for leeches. There were twenty-two on me and seventeen on Leona. I remember the figures because they were still horrifying objects to Leona and she counted them. She cut each one in half with a grimace of loathing, and when the tails came off spurting blood in her hand she would flick them away with a small shriek. Before we got back to civilisation she was shaving them off as casually as I shaved my whiskers, but it was weeks before she could stifle the shriek that marked the decapitation of each leech.

Now that we were away from fast-flowing water, we fell back upon coconuts for our drinking water. The milk of a green coconut is delicious, stimulating and when freshly cut is always cool. And it goes through you like a dose of salts impregnated with dynamite. Of course you get used to it after a while, but for the first couple of weeks it's nip and tuck between you and your belt buckle.

For emergency purposes, just in case coconuts were too far away, every member of our party was supplied with a canteen of fresh water. Every noon I held canteen inspection to make sure that all were filled, and filled with water, not *wati*, kerosene or some other liquid delicacy. If any were empty I made the boys fill up a five-gallon tin at the closest creek or swamp, bring the water to a boil, remove the scum and filter out the sediment. Then I refilled the canteens, dropping a chlorine tablet in each. The water was pure, but the taste was not of the best. The natives preferred to lie down beside a green pond, brush away the scum, and lap up their typhoid straight. No one sticks his head in the water for this purpose. A crocodile might grab it. He holds his head about a foot above the surface where he can see what is going on, and with his right hand shoots a jet of water toward his mouth. When he gets good at it he can create a high-class bubble fountain about a foot high.

It was intensely hot in the clearing. Our clothing, soaking wet all morning, dried out so rapidly you could see the moisture evaporate. Although we had worked hard, the heat killed our appetites. We ate lightly, a little hard tack, some boiled rice, and a can of sardines. For dessert we had bananas and *djamboes*, a delicious fruit a little larger than a crab apple, pink in colour, and with a taste reminiscent of pears. It is peculiar in that the seed grows above the fruit itself, giving you a juicy morsel a hundred per cent edible.

One of the boys who had picked coconuts from the cluster of palms at the edge of the clearing reported seeing a break in the jungle about two miles north. With that as our objective, we once more attacked the jungle

It was good to get back in the shade. Although the temperature must have been well into the nineties, it actually felt cold and clammy in there. The sun was completely blocked out by the foliage overhead. No grass of any kind was to be seen, only moss, soft and springy underfoot. Here and there pallid toadstools, some of them a foot across the crown, were splashed on the jungle floor like white cow chips. Huge ferns fifteen to twenty feet high spread regal fronds in majestic banks as though arranged by a master gardener. Flies and mosquitos droning through the oppressive silence sounded like bombing planes. Not that there actually was a silence with a hundred natives forcing their way through the brush. But they didn't talk or laugh. You could hear them slither and crush their way past creepers, but after awhile you forget that noise and found yourself listening to nothing but the silence. I was used to it, but Leona found it unnerving, especially when all of a sudden she came to the realisation that it wasn't a complete silence, that somewhere a drum was throbbing — just the suggestion of a drum, barely enough to emphasise the silence. Then she stayed close to me, fingering her pearl-handled revolver, once more aware that the weapon was not just part of a costume to make her look like a girl explorer for a jungle movie.

A ghastly shriek practically lifted the topee from my head.

It came from the head of the column, and without asking, I knew what it was. Snake bite!

Leaving Leona in charge of the Malays, I dashed forward. No matter what the outcome, the sight of a man suffering from snake bite would not be a pleasant one for her. But I was wrong. There was no suffering. The man was dead. He had time for but one shriek before he collapsed, apparently dead before he hit the ground. Beside him lay the writhing halves of an *oelar bisa*. I was glad one of the boys had been able to get his machete in there in time to kill the snake. At least it sort of evened the score.

The corpse was a horrible example of jungle death. One terrible paroxysm of pain had racked the native before death froze him in the midst of his first and only convulsion. His eyes were starting from their sockets. His teeth had bitten through his lower lip. His arms and legs were grotesquely twisted and drawn up beneath his body. When I first touched the body it was rigid, but as I tugged at a contorted arm to locate the wound, the corpse went limp as a rag doll. Only after a minute examination was I able to locate the twin punctures on the back of the right hand. Little tiny holes, no larger than pin pricks. The snake had apparently caught him as his right arm was straining to free his machete from a deep bite into a liana.

Had we been in a village, there would have been a period of mourning, but on the trail the natives waive all formality. Corpses don't keep well. We carried the body into a cleared spot and left it wrapped in leaves. The ants would take care of the embalming.

An hour later we were down in the bottoms where the jungle really gets tough. Bamboo barricades weren't helping matters much. Bamboo grows like bunch grass magnified a hundred times. There is no trespassing through a clump. Old stalks which have fallen leave jagged splinters as hard as flint and sharp as razors thrust helter-skelter through the mess. Young shoots just beneath the dead leaves are capped with needle-pointed spear heads that will go through bare feet or shoe leather like a spindle goes through paper. And if you still want to go through, there is a coating of fuzz on the stalks that burns like itching powder, only worse. This fuzz causes an irritation known to the Malays as bamboo *buloo*. If neglected buloo can become as serious as poison ivy. The only way to get rid of the stuff is to strip to the skin and rub the whole body with soil. If you really get into it bad, there is no saving your clothes. The fuzz can't be washed out. Some bamboo has another pleasant trick up its stalk. At each joint is a ring of three-inch needles that would do justice to a Texas prickly pear. So when you aren't rubbing off itching powder, you are impaling yourself on spiked collars. These are the annoyances. Bamboo also houses some real dangers. Snakes. The clumps are alive with snakes, all poisonous. Always damp, always warm, always impenetrable to anything but reptiles, the clumps are perfect incubators for the deadly little wrigglers. All this on one bundle of raw fish poles.

In skirting the bamboo bog we ran into another jungle nuisance. This time it was a network of *pohon-oepas* vines, the cobras of the liana family. It makes a beautiful arbor, this stuff, for funerals. The elm-shaped leaves are tinted a delicate green, but the welts they raise when brushed across the skin are a brilliant scarlet. The poison burns like sulphuric acid, and two minutes after you tangle with the vines you feel like every red corpuscle in your body has caught fire. Your veins seem to swell up with steam and threaten to pop like safety valves. The vine bears a grey berry resembling nothing more than a raw oyster. A few drops of berry juice on any part of the body will produce a lump as painful and long-lasting as a serious bruise. If the juice touches an open wound, it's all over. Some interior tribes use *pohon-oepas* juice to poison their arrows. They don't need anything better, or worse.

Choosing between the two evils, I took the bamboo. Scouting around, we found a passage between two clumps through which we would have to cut our way less than thirty feet. Thirty feet. Pace it off. Ten steps.

We hadn't worked at it five minutes before I heard the nightmarish howl that announces a snake bite. This time I was on that native so fast I practically scared the poison out of him. Fortunately Wasbus was in the cutting crew too. Between us we yanked the stricken boy out of the bamboo. It was like dragging him through a hedge of broken bottles, but we had no time to worry about that. Once in the clear we threw him on the ground, Wasbus on top of him to stop his writhing. Yanking out my pocket knife. I made two incisions an inch long and about a quarter of an inch deep across the punctures in the fore-arm. Wasting no time I yanked out a .45 cartridge, extracted the bullet with my teeth and heaped the powder in a cirdle around the wound. A touch of a match —whoof—a shriek of agony, and the boy was on the way to recovery.

He didn't know it yet. He still thought he was dead. Patiently I explained that my magic was greater than the black magic of the snake, that he was not dead, that in fact he would not die. This was too much for the boys clustered around us. It was all right for my magic to work miracles, but this business of bringing the dead back to life was stretching my power a little too far. I was putting a strain on it that was bound to break it. And when it snapped back, where would we be?

But it didn't break. I had caught the boy in time. The burning powder had cauterised the wound, literally broiling the poison in its own juice. A faint look of hope appeared in the boy's eyes. The natives began to jabber like hens. He was coming to life. In a half hour his recovery was assured. The snake *dema* had been cheated.

Oh, boy, did I rate with those natives. After that they would have stacked me up against any ten *demas* any medicine man could dig up and give me odds of ten-to-one. I was it. And when I gave instructions that the sick boy was to be carried on a litter, my hold on their affections was assured. Such consideration from a man of my power was a demonstration of kindness they would never forget. For two days they didn't steal a thing.

It took us another hour to cut through that thirty feet of bamboo, and during that time we encountered seven snakes, all bright and shiny, members of the cobra family. I heaved a sigh of relief when we were through. I burned like fire from the bamboo fuzz stuck all over my perspiring body but a quick rub-down with soil, and mud, followed by a rinse in eight ounces of water, fixed me up. A change of clothes helped. Leona coming through at the tail end of the parade, when most of the fuzz had been rubbed off, escaped the most of it but even she got enough to necessitate a rub-down and a change of clothing.

After that it was merely a repetition of what had gone before. First masses of lianas to be cut through, then dark, park-like areas of teak-wood, eucalyptus, ebony and sandalwood, reaching up so high the underbrush starved to death for lack of light. Here broad avenues between the trunks enabled us to make good time. The soil, moss covered for the most part, was soft and buoyant, a pleasure to walk upon. Though plenty of dead limbs and fallen trees littered the ground, the heat and moisture soon reduces them to mouldering mounds that offer little interference. The lianas were still there, but their network of creepers was high up in the crowns of the trees. Only a few knotted trunks as thick as my leg reached the ground, and they were easily avoided.

A few minutes before five o'clock we reached the clearing spotted at noon. Total distance from dawn to dusk, five miles. One dead and one wounded. Everybody else scratched on vines, cut on bamboo and irritated by buloo, flies, mosquitos and leeches. And then there were the runs, induced by coconut milk. There were no complaints when I gave the order to make camp.

By the time the sun set our tent was up, the cooking fires were going, and the odour of cooking was in the moist air. In the centre of the camp circle about thirty natives were clustered around one proud black boy named Kewab, the boy I trusted with the gasoline lantern. He pumped up the lantern, making a ceremony of each stroke. Then he applied the generating torch, mumbling incantations all the while. When at last it caught hold there was a gasp of awe, followed by a shout of delight as the lantern was hoisted high on a bamboo pole. Immediately there was a crowding beneath the light as each native took up a position best suited for catching the hundreds of scorched beetles and insects fatally attracted to the light. They dropped half-cooked from the hot reflector and were promptly devoured like peanuts. Kewab, because he was the engineer, had the choice of positions.

After we had eaten and smoked we were ready for bed.

Achmed took his position before the door, the other four Malays took up their posts, one at each corner of the tent. It was bed time, but it wasn't lights out. Instead, we distributed the kerosene lanterns to be placed in a circle around the camp. Drums were rolling again in the distance, and if we had visitors, we wanted to see who they were.

And so it went for twenty-eight days. Every day was like the one described here, except that I cut down on the mortality rate on snake bite, losing only four boys for that reason on the whole trip. Every day was like the day described here except when it rained. Then it was worse.

CHAPTER VIII

CONDENSED CANNIBALS

FOR several hours we knew we were being watched. Our boys were becoming uneasy. Several times we caught faint rustlings in the underbrush paralleling our trail, but try as we would we never caught sight of any moving object. It was all very mysterious, except that there was no mystery. It was just those human jack rabbits, the pigmies, taking stock of the situation.

We had reached the slimy shores of the dark brown Oewimmerah river and were two days upstream, near the Ingevakkee river, when we first detected the presence of the black midgets. Then just before I was about to give orders to camp for the night, we stumbled upon a small garden. The sight of such agricultural activity in the midst of the jungle and in the midst of the Stone Age was an anachronism about as absurd as having Columbus beginning his voyage of discovery in an airplane. Schultz had told me I could expect to find farmers in the interior, but I wasn't prepared for the scale of operations. There must have been twenty sweet potato plants in the patch before us.

A few paces away we came upon another garden, this one devoted to the raising of calabashes. The tangled vines showed every indication of loving care, each long, banana-shaped gourd being tenderly bedded down upon a mat of leaves. Some of them were as long as two feet, and reached a maximum diameter in the middle of two inches. I picked one and found it as hard as cast iron. Certainly it was not edible, nor was its capacity great enough to serve any culinary purposes. Just what the gourds were used for I was to learn later. So was a shocked Leona.

Almost before we knew it we were in the centre of a deserted village. All around us, skilfully blended into the jungle, were the thimble shaped huts of the pigmies. They looked like bee hives but they smelled like pig-sties. It was the smell that betrayed the immediate presence of the inhabitants. No deserted village could preserve so ripe an odour for any length of time.

I gave the boys the order to prepare camp. In a few minutes all the duffle was stowed away under the tarpaulin in the centre of the village and the work of preparing supper was under way. I kept watching the jungle intently, and soon I was rewarded by seeing a head pop into sight and then snap back behind a mango tree. Having seen one, I was able to pick out others, but never did I get more than a fleeting glimpse. I set out to lure the darting shadows back into their village by displaying tempting shells.

It was like sitting on a log in the middle of a forest trying to entice wild rabbits into your hands by dangling a carrot between your knees. I could tell by the frequency with which shadows popped up that I was using the right bait. It was just a question of matching my patience against their instinctive wariness. A more suspicious, jittery, timid race it would be difficult to find.

After two hours during which I used up all my gestures of peace, a tiny form emerged from behind a bush so small I would have sworn it could conceal nothing larger than a chipmunk. After my start of surprise I tossed a shell toward him. Instantly he was gone. Not even a cloud of smoke to show where he had been. And then I noticed that the shell was gone too. Those little devils were fast. I tossed out another shell and sat back to await developments. This time they were not so long in coming. Within fifteen minutes I had a procession of dwarfed phantoms materialising out of nothing and departing into an invisible limbo richer by one shell. After witnessing this phenomenon I could understand the Hindu rope trick. But eventually I won. I got one to stay by me long enough so I could explain that we were friendly, that we had no intention of eating anybody, and that we were such swell fellows we were even willing to pay out invaluable shells for every minor favour.

It took quite a long time for this to sink in. In fact, it was dawn before all the pigmies had filtered in from the jungle to sleep in their own huts. After looking them over in broad daylight I was surprised that they got the idea at all. They were the acme of dumbness in human form.

Kini was about as smart a pigmy as I ever encountered, and in describing him, I describe the race in better terms than it deserves. Kini was about four feet five inches tall, but he looked as though he had once been a six-footer caught in a barrel of alum solution and shrunk. Everything about him was weazened except his arms. They were long, reaching nearly to his knees. His brain had suffered most in the shrinking process. There were times when I wondered if it hadn't vanished completely. A half-wit was an intellectual giant in comparison.

The pigmy dialect was a bastard off-shoot of the Marind-Anim language in which I was fluent. By couching my speech in the simplest terms and repeating myself a half dozen times, Kini would get the idea. His mouth would drop open in gaping wonder at his own brilliance, a flicker of intelligence would flit across his dull eyes, and he would burst into a torrent of eloquence consisting of the word " Huh." repeated time and again. Then he would stop while an open-mouthed grin spread across his vacant face, his gaze, meanwhile, darting hither and yon searching out avenues of escape should the occasion warrant.

On Kini I found the use to which calabash shells were put by the pigmies. Just as my natives favoured the pubic shell over the loin cloth, so did the pigmies favour the calabash. Shells were scarce in the Ingevakkee river, and the tiny fellows were too timid to barter for them with the natives down stream. So they raised their own in the form of calabashes. A calabash two feet long is an awe-inspiring spectacle when worn by a pigmy only four feet five inches tall.

As phallic symbolism the calabash has got it all over anything I have ever seen. No stretch of the imagination is required to catch the significance. And if there was, the method of wearing it would destroy any lingering doubts. The top end of the gourd is cut off, the edges ground smooth, and the article of formal attire is then fastened on by a single strand of rattan around the waist. Some stick out straight in front, some twist to left or right, but the more preferred, such as was worn by

Kini, curve gently upward to chest level, ending in a small bulb. Kini, being more inventive than the average, had lopped off the top end of his calabash, using it as a repository for his betel nut and tobacco. A tuft of coconut fibre tinder sticking out at the end gave it a final flourish. I suspect him of being a dude.

We stayed with the pigmies for three days, during which I added a couple of thousand feet of film to my travelogue. It was exhausting work luring the wily midgets out into the sunlight where I could get clear shots. Leona came to my rescue by completely winning over both the men and women of the tribe. With her directing, they would do anything I wanted.

She did this by taking over the children in wholesale lots. They were not exactly prepossessing. All those kids needed was a fringe of hair around the face to pass themselves off as monkeys. With their preternaturally long arms, their short legs, and their weazened, prematurely aged faces, the youngsters scurried around like grounded gibbons. Those of toddling age waddled on their spindly legs like mechanical dolls in which all the saw-dust stuffing had settled in their bulging stomachs. The babes-on-hips clung to their miniature mothers with a clutch far more simian than human. In spite of this Leona thought they were cute.

She made friends with the youngsters by giving them a shell apiece. At first the little fellows were as wary as wild rabbits, but soon she was surrounded five deep by a shrill, chittering crowd. Smaller children tried to crowd in, and were promptly batted down. Then came the youths and adults. They lost no time in forcibly removing the shells from the hands of their juniors, all the while clamouring for gifts of their own. This multi-millionairess was something the likes of which they had never seen before, and they were going to collect while she was still insane. In the end I had to come to her rescue, but she was definitely established in their minds as a fairy god-mother. When she wanted them to do something she had only to convey her wishes through her interpreter, and it was as good as done. That is, it was if it wasn't something too complicated or something that took too long. Their memories were only good for about five minutes, and not too reliable after the first three.

It was Leona who persuaded the warriors to pose for me while I took pictures of them shooting at targets, making bows, hoeing their gardens and hunting small kangaroos. I wanted to make the film as enlightening and educational as possible, but somehow, no matter what the natives were doing, the predominant part of the scene seemed to be those ridiculous calabashes. I remember one sequence in which I showed a pigmy craftsman cleverly working a bow out of a stalk of bamboo. In spite of his dumbness he was an artisan to the bottom of his soul, and the way he shaved down the hard stalk with a boar's tusk was a miracle of workmanship. Yet when I ran off the scene in London before a group of movie moguls I had to repeat it twice before they saw the bow. They thought it was a piece of pornographic photography.

There was one thing in which the pigmies excelled and that was in the catching of butterflies. Leona was wild about the gorgeous insects, some of them with a wing-span of more than a foot. They came in all shapes and colours, some with long streamers trailing behind their flashing, iridescent wings, others more conservative in shape but of hues that would put a peacock or even a bird of paradise to shame. As soon as the pigmies learned Leona would pay cold shell for choice specimens, the fragile beauties had no rest. Armed with slender wands tipped with a sticky tree gum, the little fellows stalked their prey with infinite cunning and patience. Squatting down beside a flower favoured by the butterflies, a pigmy would sit for hours on end until one came within reach. Out would flash the wand with a deft delicacy that seldom dislodged more than a few scales, and the victim would be stuck on the gum. I don't know how they did it, but any expedition in search of choice butterflies could not do better than to take along a few Dutch New Guinea pigmies.

This patience was an outgrowth of the fear under which the pigmies dwelled. Just as any hunted animal will freeze to the ground and remain in that position as long as danger threatens so would the pigmies. The reason they had gardens was because they were afraid to go alone into the jungle to hunt for the wild vegetables. Even after we had been living amongst them for three days, they were constantly darting behind trees or popping off into the brush at the slightest provocation. This timidity was only apparent as long as we were there in superior force. There is no question in my mind that had any of our boys gone into the jungle in less than groups of five they would never have come back. I saw too many dried heads hanging within the foul smelling huts to doubt the blood-thirsty nature of our midget hosts.

The pigmies cannot hope to cope with their larger brethren in open warfare so they resort to guile. Poison is their favourite method of murder, this in spite of the fact that a poisoned arrow spoils the victim for eating purposes. Unable to pull a bow heavy enough to drive an arrow through a man, they tip their little arrows with the juice of the *pohon-oepas* berry, making up with poison for the lack of penetrating power. They have another little trick that sometimes makes me suspect they are not as dumb as they look.

Learning by some mysterious means of a hunting or raiding party in their vicinity, they will prepare bundles of needle-pointed bamboo splinters soaked in *pohon-oepas* juice. Then in the dead of night they will surround the camp like shadows, planting the poisoned splinters point upwards in all the trails leading out of the camp. The next day the hapless party will walk over the fatal points in their bare feet, dying miserably within a few hours. Trails leading into pigmy villages are often thus guarded. I learned this by accident when one of my boys overheard two pigmies discussing a fresh batch of splinters for the protection of their own village. After that I always shunned their trails and cut my own while in pigmy land.

There is no headman or single witch-doctor in a pigmy village. No one man has enough intelligence to act as leader. Instead they have a sort of village council with half a dozen of the ablest warriors settling all questions of civic and religious administration. By pooling their brains, they scare up enough authority to preserve as much peace as their primitive lives require. On civil and domestic questions, however, their authority seldom includes the women. These hell-cats fight amongst themselves like demons, never settling a dispute without resorting to mayhem. They 'll belabour each other with clubs, teeth and nails. And when they get through hair and blood are all over the place.

Wasbus found the pigmies intensely amusing. He amounted to a Gulliver in Lilliputia, and he enjoyed the situation to the full. Nothing delighted him more than to pick up a couple of squabbling females by the neck and let them continue the fight in mid-air. Then when the two would turn their fury on him, flailing him desperately with bamboo canes he would drop them and howl with laughter.

This aroused the indignation of one of the head men whose wife was thus manhandled. Instantly Wasbus was surrounded by a dozen warriors, all with their tiny bows drawn back. For a moment things looked serious. Then to my amazement, and Wasbus', a pigmy sprang to defense with flailing war club. A furious altercation ensued, in which the lone defender seemed to be getting the worse of it. Suddenly the offended husband sprang forward and knocked our defence attorney cold with a blow on the head. My .45 was out, but there was no call to use it. The fight was over. Everybody was happy except our staunch defender. Leona put some liniment on his head, and pretty soon he was happy too. The liniment smelled good.

It took quite a bit of questioning on my part before I finally learned the whyfore of the happy truce. Realising the hopelessness of trying to whip a giant the size of Wasbus, who was backed up by a party the size of mine, they appointed one of their own men to defend us and whipped him. Thus they were victorious, we were defeated, and it was a great day for all concerned. They apply the same rationalisation in cases of raids. After their village has been half wiped out by a raiding party, they appoint one of the survivors to represent the raiders and wipe him out. Thus is defeat converted into victory.

I was glad when I got all the footage I needed. The village was too foul to endure for another day. While all natives make water with complete abandon and careless disregard of surroundings, most of them will at least scoop out a hole for their more serious business. Not so the pigmies. Anyplace, anytime is their motto. They even violate the floors of their huts. As for burying the offensive matter, what need with all the flies around?

The morning of the fourth day found us once more on the trail. We were still in the jungle, but as we ascended ever higher, there was a perceptible thinning out of the underbrush. We were leaving the fringe of the Rain Forest. Ahead lay the foothills of the Sterren mountains. I had heard strange rumours about those mountains, rumours of a strange race, of a lost civilisation, of a country terrorised by a dragon thirty feet long. I wanted to see what was going on up there.

CHAPTER IX

FOUND—A LOST RACE

IT was great to be in the open forest again. No more hacking and clawing at lianas. No more leaving half my pants hanging on a clump of brambles. No more crashing snake infested thickets. Instead we had open, park-like stretches through which we could often see as much as a hundred yards ahead. Once more it was evident that the trees were supported by trunks and not suspended by net-works of vines. Firm soil and soft grass replaced the spongy peat and moss floor of the Rain Forest. There were still a lot of dead limbs and fallen trees to break our necks on, but at least it wasn't overgrown with barbed vine entanglements. We even could breathe air instead of stagnant exhalations of the heavy vegetation. The sense of spacious freedom was glorious, especially for my feet. As I have mentioned before, I wear bedroom slippers while in the jungle. Once I affected stout boots scientifically designed for jungle travel. Within a week I was suffering from sweat-softened feet, blistered heels, chafed ham-strings, swollen veins and heat rash. The boots were water-logged after the first ten minutes of bog-hopping, and thereafter I walked around in my personal, self-contained swamp. At night, if I placed my boots close enough to the fire to dry, they petrified on the spot. If I moved them back from the fire for a gradual dehydration, certain types of fungus flourished on the moist heat, and by morning my boots were rooted to the ground by toad stools. Keeping them oiled, soft, and free of fungus was a full-time job for two boys.

In delightful contrast were my bedroom slippers. Soft as an Indian's moccasins, comfortably padded and light, they gave my feet all the freedom they needed. In swampy country I could remove them, bail them out and wring them dry in one motion. They never came off, no matter how adhesive the muck, after I had mastered the art of hanging onto them with my toes.

I got so I could beat a barefoot native in a race through a quagmire and never cast a shoe. There 's a trick to it, but it 's easily mastered and worth the effort.

If stony country were to be encountered, that would be a different question. Blistered heels are much to be preferred over stone bruises. But Dutch New Guinea offers nary a stone in the wild state between Merauke and the cliffs of the Sterren mountains. In fact, rocks are so rare they have become articles of commerce, and such stones as are used for axes, clubs and cooking utensils are reverently passed from generation to generation.

But even leather bedroom slippers offer a certain amount of confinement. That was why I was glad when we cleared the Rain Forest and reached the foothills. I could then dispense with the leather slippers and don straw sandals equipped with nothing more binding than a toe strap. They are really comfortable.

Leona never could see eye-to-eye with me on the sandal business. She tried it, but her feet were so small she couldn 't get enough of a toe-hold to keep them on. So she continued in sturdy high shoes where the going was tough, and low-heeled oxfords in the open stretches. And, my theories to the contrary, remaining quite comfortable through it all.

We were making good time now, better than ten miles a day on an up-hill grade. Each night the temperature dropped a little lower, the boys moved a little closer to the fire, and the mosquitos became a little more energetic. Then came the day when we broke through the last barrier of forest to stand in the clear upon a high plateau. Behind us, stretching 300 miles to the coast, was a sea of green. Ahead, rising out of a jumbled world of barren grey, was a fairyland of pink and white peaks, strangely unreal and translucent in the brilliant glare of the sun. The snow-capped backbone of New Guinea! We had reached the Sterren mountains.

For an hour we waded through knee-deep grass, glorying in the crisp freshness of a breeze that swept down from the glaciers. The natives, I noticed, were not sharing our enthusiasm. They sniffed the breeze apprehensively until kangaroos, smaller than those to be found in the Rain Forest, flashed ahead of us, followed by wildly fluttering crowned pigeons. Then they forgot the cold in the lure of the hunt. They bagged enough game to keep our small army in meat for another week. To give the boys time to prepare the additions to the larder I ordered camp pitched on the bank of a small wash containing a plentiful supply of dry, heather-like wood.

It was my intention to press on to the snow line. Not that I had any particular business up there, but it is one of the rules of the exploring profession to go where you have no particular business to be. By dawn, however, I realised that if I was going to roll any snowballs, I was going to have to do it prac-tically alone. My boys were nearly frozen to death. It was not cold in the wash in which we camped, and roaring fires twenty feet high would have dispelled any lingering chill in the air, but the boys had seen the snow and felt the cool breeze, and that was enough for them. They were resigned to die on the spot, mentally frozen to death.

I snapped them out of it in the morning with gallons of hot tea, a real luxury. Right after breakfast, loaded down with kangaroo and crowned pigeon in addition to our regular luggage, we beat a hasty retreat for the tropics, ten miles down the slope. In spite of heavy loads and a rapid pace, the natives didn't warm up until we were once more surrounded by banana palms, coconuts and leeches. Even then the thawing out process was gradual. I think it took two or three days before their brains were entirely free of chillblains.

But having been within sight of the snow, I was not to be turned back now. Besides, I had figured out an excuse for going up there. If I could get the right angles and the right backgrounds, I could shoot some snow scenes that would prove remarkably effective as contrast for my jungle stuff. I already had plenty of long-range shots to use for this purpose, but when you want to go some place it doesn't take much of an excuse.

To Wasbus' horror, I picked him for one of the ten boys who would accompany me on my dash for the peaks. For the rest I took Achmed and Wirio and two members of the chain gang for rifle-bearers, and five members of my paddling crew armed with bows and arrows. It was plain to see they regarded the honour as a dubious one. Wasbus spent a full hour girding his loins with a string of rattan and adjusting his pubic shell for the maximum of warmth.

I left Leona in camp, guarded by the remaining three Malays and the rest of the Javanese chain gang, any one of whom would have gladly given her his life. The rest of the natives would have fought for her too, if they remembered her before they got too far away from the scene of battle. They mean well, maybe, but their instinct is limited to self-preservation. The Malays and Javanese, being on an infinitely higher scale, are fiercely loyal, and when treated right will battle in your defence to the last drop of blood. I treated them right, but Leona pampered them. Thus while they respected me, they worshipped her, and where they would battle for me, for her they would wade in and really go to town.

It didn't take the eleven of us long to get where we wanted to go. To anyone familiar with mountain climbing, the ascent up the Sterren range would have been as strange as a climb up a crater on the moon. Millions of years ago the foothills over which we scrambled might have been solid rock, but they had waited so long for discovery they finally crumbled into dust. If it weren't for the frequent rains they would have blown away. Mighty cliffs were reduced to rolling mounds, dusty corpses of a majestic splendour. Not until we assaulted the snow-capped peaks themselves did we run into anything resembling rock, and then it was soft sandstone that disintegrated underfoot. It was as hard on the bare feet of my boys as sandpaper.

Twice we forded mountain streams as icy cold as the snow that fed them. Wasbus got in the middle of the first one and couldn't go on. He thought he had lost his legs at the knees until I convinced him they were just a little numb from the cold. After that he bolted across like a skipped stone, howling like an orphaned pup.

Little timber was to be found on the upper slopes. There were patches of grey-green brush that converted parts of the landscape into heather-covered Scottish highlands, and a few groves of a small, hardy evergreen with long plumy needles that seemed to be natives of the country, but for the most part such trees as we did encounter were stunted outcasts of the jungle, Eucalyptus, ebony and teakwood shivered in the biting breeze, cursing the unkind wind that had carried their seed up in the snows when the tropics were just a few miles away and down hill to boot. Still, they could like it or lump it. Most of them had apparently lumped it.

By nightfall we were within striking range of the snow. I spent most of the night playing nurse-maid to my boys. Each of them was supplied with a woollen blanket, brought along on the expedition for bundling up malaria victims. They didn't know what to do with them. None had ever slept in a blanket before. I rolled them up like cocoons, and then wandered around seeing that they didn't unroll. The way they wriggled around you would have thought they were sleeping inside rolls of barbed wire. It was cold. A fierce, bitter, penetrating cold all the worse for not being below freezing. I've never spent a more miserable night in my life. Long before dawn I had resolved to leave the exploration of New Guinea's mountains to the Arctic boys with their parkas and dog teams.

I didn't have any trouble getting my boys awake in the morning, but I did have trouble getting them up. It wasn't so bad with those who slept stretched out. They could be hauled to their feet and propped up, but those who spent the night in a ball had to be straightened, a joint at a time. I poured hot tea into them as though they were so many cold motors, and eventually we got started. By that time, of course, the sun was well up, turning the south slope into a frying pan. In the thin, non-heat-conducting air, everything in the shade froze, and everything exposed to the sun fried. If it isn't one thing, it's another.

Alternately freezing while labouring through the dark shadows of a deep gulch, and roasting while crossing the high ridges, we reached the first fingers of snow groping blindly down eroded canyons of their own making. The ground was like a ploughed field during the first spring thaw, frozen underneath and wet and slippery on top. My boys skidded around on it as gingerly as cats on a hot stove. For the sake of the record I lined them up on the hard, frozen snow and shot a couple of hundred feet of their frantic efforts to keep both feet and their bodies off the icy crust at the same time. They played tragedy and I shot comedy. I doubt if they appreciated the awe-inspiring manifestations of nature. My feet were wet and cold and I didn't either. The view was beautiful, but was best appreciated from a warm projection booth. We got out of there without stopping for lunch.

Whooping it up on the way down, my boys were like kids playing hookey when we entered the mile-wide temperate zone separating the Arctic circle from the equator. They went bounding over a knoll in high spirits, suddenly to stop practically in mid-air as though confronted by a truant officer. They stood on the crest as rigid as fence posts.

Flanked by Achmed and Wirio with their rifles at the ready, I hurried up to see what was wrong. A couple more men on the other side and we would have been spared the trouble. As it was, I found a group of six hunters in the gulch below as badly scared and just as petrified as my boys on the ridge. The unexpected presence of the hunting party in the midst of this mountainous isolation wasn't exactly soothing on my nerves, but at least I wasn't paralysed.

Quickly stepping to the fore, my pistol pointed straight at them in a gesture of peace. I spoke reassuringly in the Marind tongue. The only response to my friendly speech was from my own boys. They thought it was a fine overture to lull the suspicions of the enemy until we could get close enough to wipe them out in one swoop.

I tried two or three other dialects without result. It was evident that the hunters spoke a language with which I was not familiar. Then I didn't know what to do. Neither did they. I finally settled the problem by taking them captive. At least in that way I could make peace on my own terms.

Capturing them was an easy matter. I simply fired my pistol into the air. Their bowels gave a tremendous start, and they were through. My boys took over their weapons while they stood vibrating like Model T's missing on a couple of cylinders. Capturing them alive was so easy my boys wanted to celebrate by killing them on the spot. For a minute it was nip and tuck between my authority and their instinct to kill, but I finally won with the only phrase that carried any weight—"God damn the goddam son-of-a-bitch that makes the first

goddam move." That held them. Schultz had some more
phrases that paralysed them. They might not know what the
words meant but there was no mistaking the implication. No
nation has been able to produce an oath so mouth-filling, so
impressive and so universally satisfactory. Even mules get the
drift.

When peace was thus profanely restored, I was at liberty to
inspect my captives. They were a handsome lot, of average
height and aristocratic bearing. In colour they resembled the
American Indian more than any other race I have ever run
across. They even had the high cheek bones and sharp, im-
perious noses of the Indian. In fact, the only way they resembled
the other natives of Dutch New Guinea was in their smell.
Their odour was strong enough to resist the most cutting breeze,
leaving them absolutely impervious to the cold. That's the
only way I can account for their hardihood. They were completely nude, yet lying at their feet were a couple of dozen
white, plump ptarmigan-like birds found only in the snow
country. The sextet must have spent at least half the day
stalking the birds over the icy drifts dressed only in their smell.

When it came to weapons their craftsmanship was a
revelation. First to attract my attention were their knives.
Instead of being made of bamboo they were worked out of
human thigh bones. The knob at the end of each one had been
cleverly worked into a grim caricature of a human head.
Below this was a grip some four inches long, after which the
bone was scraped down so that just the flat side furnished the
long, slender blade. As instruments of murder, they were the
choicest native weapons I had seen in Dutch New Guinea.

The arrows, too, were marvels of workmanship. In the first
place they were straight. This was enough in itself to set them
apart from all other New Guinea arrows. Most natives just
lop off a slender bamboo shoot, stick a point on the end, and
let the other fellow worry about the straightness of the arrow
that kills him. But these boys showed infinite pains in their
selection of straight bamboo stock, and still more pains in
smoothing down the joints so that the whole shaft varied not
more than an eighth of an inch in diameter. The points, for
the most part, were of small crocodile teeth, filed down on

stone and inserted in the hollow end of the shaft. They were then bound fast with green rattan which shrinks tight as it dries. There was no notch to take the bow string, the arrows having a perfectly flat butt. The bows were carefully designed and balanced to give an even pull top and bottom. This, too, was an innovation. Most native bows consist of a length of split bamboo, tapered top and bottom, and let the centre of pull fall where it may. After looking over the efficient weapons, I was more than glad our party outnumbered them. Those bows weren't playthings.

My captives were not at all sure they wanted to come with us when I started them down the slope. Adults are taken captive for only one purpose in New Guinea, and if we were too lazy to kill them on the spot and cart their carcasses into camp, they were darned if they were going to walk them in for us. They just stood there, as stolid and silent as rocks. Wasbus wrapped his fingers around the necks of a couple and thereafter they were more easily persuaded. This in spite of the fact that they were positive they were being kept alive because we had no refrigeration with which to keep them dead. Wasbus had this power. I don't know if it could be attributed to his giant size, the tremendous boar's tusks he had thrust through his nose, the hideous tattooing across his face, or his smell, but I had only to turn him loose and peace would reign. If not immediately, at least presently.

When we stopped to eat the strangers refused to join us. No use getting fat just to make a better feast for us. Again I called upon diplomat Wasbus. Seizing a haunch of kangaroo, the giant proceeded to ram chunks of it into the faces of his wards, just as a native mother would ram banana pulp into the mouth of her offspring. Rather than have their teeth shoved down their throats along with the meat the captives fell to with more eagerness than their appetites warranted. But they still spoke nary a word.

By the time we reached camp the next day my captives were convinced their end was near. Their presence created tremendous excitement. Like the captives themselves, my boys could see in their presence only another item on the menu, and they were all for starting the feast at once. Howling dancers surrounded the new arrivals, indicating by whirling war clubs and mouthy gestures just what their intentions were. The victims didn't have to understand the language to catch the drift.

Strangely enough, they showed no traces of fear. Neither did they show anything resembling bravery or defiance. They stood in a forlorn group, eyes focussed dumbly before them in woeful resignation, but at least they didn't wail or mutter a word of protest. If we were going to eat them now, why eat them we would. There was nothing they could do about it. Even Wasbus standing staunchly in their midst warning off would-be executioners, meant little to them. He was just guarding his own so he could have the fun of killing them off himself, thereby getting first claim on such choice morsels as their brains and penises.

When I broke up the death dance, the prisoners' faces showed the first trace of hope I had seen. To have transported them alive was rare enough, but not to have eaten them immediately upon reaching camp was unheard of. Maybe this strange white person *was* different. Maybe those strange sounds he made, and those strange, friendly gestures, did mean he meant peace. At least there was no harm in living to see. They kept on living, but not talking.

I talked them over with Leona. Together we went over the bows and arrows, the few other articles the hunters had in their possession when we surprised them. Both of us agreed we had seen nothing to match them in workmanship or style. They were enough different from anything we had seen to come from an entirely different country. The bone knives alone were enough to mark them as a race apart. The more we handled the stuff the more excited we became.

Tentatively I pulled on the thick, rattan string of one of the bows. It felt like it was stretched between a couple of trees. I yanked again, this time succeeding in pulling it back a couple of inches. Vexed, I got to my feet and put the pressure on. Straining until I was red in the face and my shirt ripped over my shoulder muscles, I managed to get the bow string back to firing position. Twang! I let her go. As if by magic the skin on my bow arm vanished from an area six inches long. The course string had whipped across it like a file. An 85-pound pull if it was an ounce, and I had taken the brunt of it on my bare wrist. My respect for the lost race was increasing by leaps and bounds.

The task of winning the confidence of my compulsory guests looked like an endless one. The first day I worked on them I got nothing but the stony silence they had maintained ever since we caught them. The second day I was rewarded by a few grunts. On the third day of continued good treatment, augmented by the gift of a few shells and some red hair ribbons, my efforts to establish communication met with some co-operation. I had singled out the most intelligent looking individual, one with a necklace of crocodile teeth indicating hunting skill, and suddenly he broke into a torrent of speech.

I stepped back aghast. After all my work, I had wasted my time on a man who was not only tongue-tied but a stutterer as well. In despair I looked at the rest of the bunch. They were watching me with childish grins on their faces as though expecting me to burst into applause at the eloquence of their leader. "Nuts," I said at last in disgust.

It was as good a word as any to start them off. They all began talking at once. It had been four days since they had enjoyed a good talk, and apparently they had a lot to get off their chests. It might have made sense, but to me it sounded like they had mouths full of yeast cakes that kept swelling up faster than they could spit it out.

I saw at once I was going to get nowhere on a conversational basis. I switched to the sign language. Pointing to myself and then to the south, I tried to get across the idea that that was where I came from. And where did they come from? They huddled together and spluttered. They came out of the huddle blankly. They didn't get the idea. I repeated my performance. I became as eloquent as an orchestra conductor winding up Schubert's Unfinished Symphony. I threw in variations. Once more they pooled their collective brains. This time they came out with an idea and a word. The word cannot be voluntarily repeated by a member of the white race. It can be duplicated only with the aid of a red-hot spoonful of mush. The explosive ejection of the mush from the mouth under such circumstances will closely rival the word "Sspphshphoooop."

It was my turn to look dumb. My college professors would have recognised the expression. In desperation I grabbed old Crocodile Necklace by the arms and began pumping them. A great grin spread across his face. His betel-nut stained teeth fairly gleamed in the reflected glory of his own brilliance.

Immediately he flew into a perfect frenzy of gestures, the central motif of which seemed to be a motion toward the northwest. I had it. Once the ice was broken, the rest came easy. By nightfall I had learned that the village was a large one, outnumbering in population our own party three to one. In a bit of inspired interpretation, I even learned that the name of the village, or it might have been the tribe, my inspiration wasn't exactly clear on that point, was Kirrirri. Correctly pronounced, it sounds like the chattering of a squirrel with a mouthful of acorns. The leader of the group, old Crocodile Teeth, gave me his name as Wroo.

It took a little more time to learn the attitude of the tribe in the matter of strangers. Anything as intangible as friendship or hate is hard to pin down with signs, but finally I gathered that as long as there were a hundred of us, all well armed, and since we were further supported by thunder sticks, we would be welcome. It was my pistol that cinched our welcome. In the four days they had been with us they had seen it in action several times, and while it no longer acted as a cathartic, its deadly effectiveness was black magic of the first water. Yes, we would be welcome.

Accordingly we started off for the village of the lost tribe, bearing northwest instead of straight west as we had originally planned. The few miles extra would make little difference on our itinerary anyway. As long as we reached Tannah-Tinggi, we would be doing all right. If everything ran on schedule, Schultz would be waiting for us there with our steam launch.

Our way ran along the southern slope of the Sterren mountains, just above the heavy timber line. It would have made easier going if we could have gone higher, where we would have been free of the trees entirely, but this my boys could not stand. It looked too cold up there. After a day walking along the slope I felt as lop-sided as my launch. For once my sandals were going back on me. I kept slipping out on the down-hill side. I finally had to put on my shoes, which added not a bit to my comfort. I felt like a school kid forced into shoes after a bare-foot summer, and this discomfort was further amplified by the fact that I had to dig the edges of my soles into the soft soil to keep from skidding down grade. At the end of the second day everybody was moaning. The carriers were warped out of shape by the added burden thrown upon their right shoulders when their loads insisted upon shifting to the down-hill side. Their feet were sore and bleeding from sliding on razor-edged grass so tough they could not dig into it for a foot-hold. Leona complained that she felt like the Arkansas mule whose legs were shorter on the uphill side from grazing in circles around the bluff. On the whole, we were not happy.

If, in the course of the two days, we could have hit a level spot, or better yet, a northern slope, the monotony would have been broken, and our bones would have had a chance to re-align themselves. But that was not to be. Even in plunging into and climbing out of gulches we did so on the bias. The total distance covered was fifteen miles. I thought it was 1,500. It has always seemed to me so unnecessary to make it tough on us explorers after we get back into the interior. A hundred miles of impassable jungle is fair enough. That serves to build up the romantic angle and discourage new recruits, but after we get behind the scenes the going should be easier.

When we finally caught sight of the outskirts of the village my relief at seeing the end of our journey overcame my amazement at the real estate development. The first indication we had that we were nearing our destination came when we encountered an irrigation ditch angling gently down the slope. A few minutes later we were walking single file down the middle of the ditch in ankle-deep cold water. I could almost see the steam rising from my suffering feet, and even Wasbus welcomed the cooling freshness on his prodigious dogs. That is conclusive evidence that our slope-sided journey was a tough one. Hating water under any circumstances, and cold water in particular, only the most desperate straits could induce him to take to the creek voluntarily, even willingly.

After a few minutes of enjoying the luxury of soft silt oozing up between my bare toes while once more walking on an even

Digoel Head Hunter

With Flourishes

With the end lopped off this curved calabash serves as a receptacle for arrow heads, tinder and betel nut

Fashion Plate

*From public shell to woven grass head-dress, this Jei-Anim warrior
is sartorially perfect. Note rattan wrist guard*

keel it suddenly dawned on me that irrigation ditches represented a tremendous amount of labour even in a civilised
community. In this remnant of a backward Stone-Age the
work involved must have required super-human effort. I looked
at the man-made creek sharply, but could see no clue to its
construction. It was a mystery I would have to solve later.

In the meantime we were approaching thatched huts as
neatly laid out in the centre of a meadow as a Javanese village.
Fenced in fields of sweet potatoes, tobacco, sugar cane, gourds,
cucumbers, *kladi* and egg plants flanked the irrigation ditch
on both sides. Definitely the scene had no place in New Guinea,
but as long as it was there, there wasn't much I could do about
it. Besides, I had to solve a little problem in social consciousness
rising out of the flock of savages swarming out of their huts,
armed with all manner of painful looking weapons. They had
seen us coming from afar and had deserted their fields to
prepare our reception.

H

CHAPTER X

JUNGLE TANKS

WROO turned to me with a wide grin as his tribesmen scooted for strategic positions from which to knock us off. My own crew strung out for a couple of hundred yards along the irrigation ditch were all for declaring peace in the only way they knew, by killing off the enemy. This I couldn't permit. Those Kirrirris might be deadly enemies, but they were also rare specimens. I would look silly coming home with a few hundred feet of film on a lost race, and showing nothing but corpses.

I couldn't understand Wroo. He was enjoying himself hugely, glancing expectantly from me to his brethren now diving for concealment in the vegetable gardens. Just as I was beginning to reflect bitterly that I had come through 300 miles of jungle just to get shot at from a patch of sweet potatoes, I suddenly noticed that it was not me that was exciting Wroo so much as the pistol I unconsciously clutched in my hand. Then I had to laugh myself. Remembering what had happened to his bowels the first time he heard the thing go off, he couldn't wait to see what would happen to the whole village when I let her go. Just to accommodate him, he was a pretty good egg even if I couldn't understand him, I fired three shots into the air.

The purge was complete. Even the village was evacuated. One concerted rush for parts unknown and we had before us a ghost town. Wroo could not contain his glee. He rolled on the ground in violent spasms of mirth which might have taken a serious turn had not a sudden convulsion pitched him into the creek. The ice water brought him around in quick order, and seeing how effective it was, Wasbus tossed in the other five to still their ghastly chortles. Wasbus was a handy man to have around.

We moved into the deserted village without more ado. It

gave us a distinct advantage I had not counted on. Now, when the Kirrirris began to trickle back, we would be the gracious hosts extending a hospitable hand to the wanderers of the brush instead of vice versa. As the first step in my benevolent rule, I had Wroo send his five aids into the jungle to bid the fugitives welcome to their own huts.

Not until camp was pitched and everything organised did the first, and bravest, villagers appear. On my behalf Wroo welcomed them cordially. I could only follow the conversation by watching the child-like changes of expression on the faces of my guests, but of one thing I was certain: I was the big-shot. And they thought it was mighty considerate of me to let them board and room in my village. For nothing.

It was a ludicrous situation. For the first time in my life I was the chief of a village, even if I had to go back 20,000 years to make the grade. But having once established myself, I carried off the role in grand style. Seated on my camp stool throne in front of the tent, and with Leona by my side, I held court for all and sundry. For the most part our rule consisted of being minutely inspected by each new arrival, and looking silly for the benefit of the awe-struck crowd.

If there was any doubt of my power it was dispelled after sundown when I had the gasoline storm lantern hoisted on a stout pole. Anybody who could bring back the sun after it had gone away was mighty powerful medicine. And when they discovered that our sun not only shed plenty of light but roasted beetles as well our prestige knew no bounds. We were it, and no mistake.

That storm lantern was worth its weight in gold. Without it our equipment would have vanished piece by piece just as certainly as absent-minded natives forget to return items they find in their hands, after dark. Among such items could be included our heads. While the lantern's illumination was invaluable in the pursuit of nocturnal duties, its greatest value lay in discouraging raiders. No tribe no matter how powerful, dared attack us while the camp was bathed in its magic white light. This was true whether we were sleeping in villages or in the jungle. In fact, it was even truer inside villages than outside. Our hosts were always delighted with the lantern's brilliance, but the chances were ten to one they would have been more delighted by its absence. A hundred strange heads were mighty tempting morsels under the best of circumstances, and total darkness was not the best. I much preferred to keep my hosts delighted with light than overjoyed with heads.

That night we really stretched out and slept. After hiking for two days, one foot up, other foot down, on the steep slopes, it was a relief to lie flat and let our warped bones resume their normal length. It would have been better if we could have slept late in the morning, but as king and queen we had to be up and doing, what with three hundred or so natives squatting expectantly on their haunches around our tent.

It is an invigorating experience to eat breakfast in the great outdoors just as the sun lifts over distant peaks, the cool, crisp air completely bogged down by the odour of hundreds of natives. Every spoonful we ate was watched intently by 300 pairs of eyes from the time the spoon left the bowl until it reached the mouth. Then 300 throats swallowed in unison. If Leona swallowed ahead of me, then our audience had to swallow in double-time in order to get the benefit of my spoonful.

In the fore-front of our appreciative gallery I noticed a woe-begone figure in dejected conversation with Wroo. I didn't need a second glace to realise that here was the dispossessed chief. I let him suffer. After all, it wasn't every day that I could be chief.

Finishing a second cup of Wirio's excellent coffee, I swung around imperiously and beckoned Wroo to bring his companion forward. The chief immediately began to shake with an audible clatter. His knees knocked together so hard they threatened to crack the joints. Achmed had to come to his assistance or he would have collapsed on the spot. As king I was getting off to a flying start.

Then began fifteen minutes of futile sign language in which I got exactly nowhere. Neither did anyone else, so everything was all right. Just to show there were no hard feeling I had Achmed string the cover of a coffee can on a red ribbon, and this I hung over the neck of the chief with suitable gestures. After the receipt of that glorious medal there was no holding the man down. A mere chief before our arrival, now he was a super-super. In fact, he was my assistant, and beyond that he knew no man could hope to aspire. He said as much to his subjects. They giggled like excited ducks, and rubbed their feet bashfully in the dust when they encountered my gaze. Taken as a whole, they were a high class lot. They appreciated me.

As was their custom whenever within the confines of a strange village, my boys stuck close together, refusing to mingle with the local gentry until they were sure of their ground. They had no more confidence in their fellow-natives than I had in them, and this suspicion was not misplaced. There were four boys from my original party whose absence was unaccounted for, but whose heads I have every reason to believe are decorating the lodge poles of some of our amiable hosts.

This aloofness on the part of my warriors held true only as far as the male sex was concerned. When it came to the women they were an experimental lot. They conducted their experiments in broad daylight and without benefit of privacy. By noon it was obvious that their tentative passes were not being made in vain. Couples locked in carnal embrace could be found all over the place, much to the delight of the Kirrirri males. They were gratified that their women should find such favour in the eyes of so powerful a bunch of warriors.

As usual Wasbus was right in there. He had picked out a sly little minx, light brown in colour and with a shape that would have compared favourably with hollywood standards. Her jet black hair was combed straight back, coquettishly augmented with grease, clay and switches of braided grass that fell in rope-like strands to her slender waist. There they were gathered beneath a rattan G-string, her only article of apparel. Her smooth body glistened beneath an application of coconut oil that brought out every ripple of her sleek muscles so enticingly that Wasbus was falling over his big feet as he pursued her around the village square. As she passed I caught an aura reminiscent of oiled sardines as enchanting to native nostrils as attar of roses.

Leona and I watched the primitive love scene with interest. Wasbus was growing warm as his voluable protestations of devotion met with a flashing smile of even, black, betel-nut stained teeth and nothing more. The girl kept about six paces ahead, and when Wasbus made a sudden dash she was off like a kangaroo. The giant black shook his head in bewilderment. He wasn't used to having his advances thus repulsed. Suddenly a look of sly cunning crossed his terrifying face. Hastily removing an inch-round bamboo plug from his nose, he fitted it over the point of an arrow. From a discreet distance the girl watched his actions with interest. When he had finished, the strange pursuit began again. Once more Wasbus made his sudden dash. Again the girl eluded him. Stopping in his tracks the ardent lover fitted the blunted arrow with one swift motion.

ZZing! Right in the plump buttocks the arrow caught her. She went up in the air like a sky rocket. When she came down she landed running, but all her speed was gone. That arrow packed the wallop of a sledge hammer, putting a serious crimp in her style. Wasbus caught her within ten paces, and thereafter the love-match proceeded along lines more to his liking.

We didn't have a chance to shoot any pictures the first couple of days we were in the village. We were too much of a novelty to move more than three steps without collecting a crowd of curious subjects. Our colour was as much a source of amazement as our clothing. Hands were always reaching out unexpectedly to touch our garments. At first I thought they were trying to find out what kind of stuff cloth was, but finally I became convinced they were trying to see what colour I was underneath. To settle the question once and for all I staged a strip-tease that for drama and public appreciation has seldom been equalled on the legitimate stage.

Standing in the centre of the village I removed a garment at a time to the accompaniment of tremendous gasps of awe. Off came my shirt. "Ooooh!" Open-mouthed wonder.

Off came my pants.

"Ooooooh!" The gasp was longer drawn out. Underneath it I caught a stifled giggle. My wife was not appreciating the solemnity of the occasion.

As a shirt and pants were all I wore, the show was over. Hastily I donned my garments, and though the Kirrirris seemed deeply impressed, my satisfaction was marred by Leona's giggle. I could never be sure after that that the show was a hundred per cent success. Maybe the natives felt like laughing too, but were too polite to show it.

The longer we remained in the village the more impressed we were with the evidences of civilisation. Although the rectangular huts followed the same general pattern of those found along the Merauke river, they were of infinitely better workmanship. Not only were they actually rain-proof, but some went so far as to stand straight with nary a sag to left or right. The bachelor hut was a regular palace, large enough to shelter a hundred bucks without crowding, and containing several architectural flourishes such as eaves, air vents, and patches of different coloured thatch worked into rude patterns. The huts alone were sufficient testimony to the industriousness of the Kirrirris, but it was left to the gardens to supply the conclusive evidence.

The gardens were located on the edge of the jungle in that strange zone between the tropics and the snow line. It was a perpetual springtime, the temperature hovering in the eighties, and never varying more than ten degrees year in and year out as far as I was able to determine. Incidentally, if you want to tackle a job in sign language, select a six-year-old youngster whose tongue is foreign to you and pump him for the weather reports for the past year. Unless you are a patient man, you will give up after three or four days.

In a setting like that, anything would grow, and everything did. Weeds took to the fertile soil as eagerly as the plants, and insects of all kinds thrived on both. Thus scarcely an inch was wasted. It was a good thing, too, because there weren't many more square inches to each plot than was absolutely necessary.

Like a lord surveying his estates, I had myself conveyed to the rural area. It was laid out like a checkerboard, each square enclosed by a three-foot fence of bamboo posts and rattan wire. The fences were to keep the kangaroos out while they were out but if one or two did get in, the fences were to keep them there. Each morning the farmers approached their plots with a feeling of expectancy, wondering if they were still raising vegetables, or pasturing kangaroos. If the latter it meant fresh meat in camp, because, according to the rules of the game, the kangaroo could not jump more than one square at a time, and if he had more than three squares to jump, they usually got him as he topped the last fence. In Australia, the kangaroos are regarded as a scourge, but the Kirrirris gratefully take them as they come, and eat them. The kangaroos eat their gardens, they eat the kangaroos, and so get back not only their vegetable produce but some choice steaks as well.

The same atittude holds true in regard to insects. The farmers go over their sweet potato patches with a fine tooth-comb, turning up each leaf in search of parasites. It's when they don't find them that they are disappointed. The bugs are a delicious by-product, hunted not because they destroy the gardens but because they are good to eat. Though 20,000 years old, it is the best solution of the pest problem I have encountered. Now if American entomologists could start breeding grasshoppers, potato bugs and fruit flies for flavour, farmers would get the Kirrirri slant on the insect scourges. Instead of bemoaning their fate at the arrival of a winged plague, they would be out with their harvesting machines, gleefully reaping the benefits bestowed by a bountiful nature.

It took me a longer time to figure out the advantages of the weeds, but once I saw the light I was surprised that the idea was not wider spread. In the first place, weeds serve to conceal the plants, and more than one kangaroo has lost his life to expert marksmen after feasting all night on nothing more valuable than weeds. In the second place, when the time comes to dig the potatoes, it is a simple matter to yank out a huge clump of weeds, and up come the tubers, tangled in the roots. In the third place to plough the fields it is only necessary to pull up the deep-rooted plants and grasses, beat the earth out of the roots by knocking the clumps together, and leave behind a field of soft, well-pulverised soil. By the time it is necessary to plough again, another crop of weeds has grown. In the fourth place the weeds shelter more delicate vegetables such as the cucumber from twelve hours of sun. This keeps them from ripening too fast, and stretches out the bearing period. It is futile to argue that the weeds starve out the vegetables. The vegetables are there and they don't look starved. But they could be bigger? The natives only look puzzled at this. There is more than enough to eat. Why should they be bigger?

Weeds furnished the answer on tilling the soil, but they couldn't account for the irrigation ditches. These criss-crossed all over the place, fed by a mountain stream diverted into the meadow from its natural bed nearly half-a-mile away. The main ditch itself was an achievement comparable to the Panama Canal when one considers that these brown hill-billies and their stone clubs were stacked up against some of the finest engineering brains in the world, backed up by the most efficient machinery of the time.

I was fortunate in catching a branch line of the canal under construction. It looked more like a mud fight than an irrigation project, but the boys meant well even if their efforts were a little misdirected. Standing knee deep in water in the main ditch, they were attacking the bank with shovels of coconut palm. The shovels were made by yanking a huge frond out of the crown of the palm tree, chopping off the leafy part and letting the stem dry in the sun until hard. That part of the stem that joins the crown is thin and scoop-shaped, like the base of a blade pulled out of a ripe pineapple. The stem is round and hard, like a pitch-fork handle once the thorns along the edges have been removed. It makes an ideal shovel. If you work too hard or try to take too big a load, it breaks. The natives are careful about this. The ones I caught with my camera would take out two or three scoops of mud and then wait for the water to soften up the next few shovelsful. It might take fifteen minutes before they deemed the soil suffi-ciently saturated to be removed. I couldn't waste film on their rests so I had to spend three hours getting together a sequence with enough action in it to convey the idea. I remember this vividly, because of the jarring note it produced on me when I finally ran the film off in a London projection booth. There on the screen before me I saw Kirrirris industriously shovelling mud out of their new irrigation ditch, the soil practically melting away in front of them. It struck me as funny as some of the fast-motion chases we used to film for the old Mack Sennett comedies, until I recalled that the action on the screen was composed of thirty-second shots taken over a period of three hours. It was the only phoney note in the whole film. The idea of natives working hard.

I was beginning to think highly of these squirrel-chattering, agriculturally-minded brown boys by the time I had finished my tour of inspection. The pastoral scene, so different from anything I had expected to find in the interior, had so influenced me I was almost willing to dismiss some of my meaner suspicions. Leona, however, had a stronger story.

In all the villages at which we stopped, it was Leona who asked the questions, made the friends, and jotted down all the facts. There were several reasons for this. In the first place, I was a white man, the most powerful being the natives had ever gazed upon. If I went around asking questions about things of which even two year old native kids knew the answer, I would lose prestige so rapidly I wouldn't be able to get a hundred miles. If I became too friendly, the natives would think I was not much better than they were. If I talked too much, got my words wrong or mispronounced them, they would again have reason to suspect I was not infallible. Foolish in speech, foolish in war—knock him off—pow! For that reason I never tried shooting a native bow while the natives were around. If they saw me pull back the bow, take aim, and then miss my target by about three feet, they might not laugh in my face, but they would have designs on my head. With Leona it was different. Women are not expected to know much, and they excused her ignorance on account of her sex. She could ask all the questions she wanted, sure of a quick, courteous answer. The answers came quickly, partly because she was white, partly because she was my wife, and partly because she was always accompanied by her Malay bodyguard and a couple of *klewang*-armed chain-gangers. The latter were reminders of the former.

While I was on my tour of inspection Leona had been taking in the village, accompanied by Wroo and her bodyguard. It was a pleasant morning, not too warm and not too cool. Here and there men and women were loafing in the sun or oiling themselves up with coconut oil to relieve the itching of their dried-up scaly skins. For this purpose they sat on banana fronds so that what oil dripped from their bodies might be caught and saved for future use. Women were heating stones for cooking, kneading out sago dough, fighting and otherwise pursuing a normal every-day existence. Down at the far end of the village, near the bachelor lodge, a small crowd had gathered, but it seemed to be just the usual crowd, attracted by anything the least bit out of the ordinary. As she neared the lodge she thought she heard the crying of a baby, but as the sound was not repeated, she dismissed it from her mind.

Attracted by a native woman husking a coconut, she wandered over to see how it was done. The woman, not more than fifteen years of age, and with a sleeping baby carried in a rattan sling across her back, was pounding the bulky nut upon the point of what at first glance appeared to be the last two feet of a huge elephant tusk or the horn of a rhinoceros. Whatever it was, it made an excellent coconut de-husker. Feeling thirsty, Leona broke open a coconut herself, thereby making a warm friend of the girl whose hospitality she shared. At this point Leona was introduced to another use for the oil the natives applied to their skins. The baby rolled over in his net, wet profusely and at great length down his mother's back. The water rolled off as though she was a duck.

By signs, the girl conveyed the idea that while the coconut was good, down where the crowd was gathering was something that soon would be much better to eat. Just how good it was, was expressed by licking the chops and then grinning to the point of lock-jaw. Leona went along, not because she would have eaten anything native-prepared, but because she wanted to see what manner of delicacy could be so highly regarded.

She was just in time to round the corner of the lodge as the witch-doctor came out carrying a two-year-old baby by the heels. The baby was dead, all too obviously killed by a blow on the head. Stopping by a collection of rocks he swung the child's corpse over them until all were liberally sprinkled with blood. Then he moved on the the next pile, repeating the performance. Leona was sick, she was still sick when she told me about it, but she couldn't show it in front of all those natives.

She followed along to the irrigation ditch flowing along the edge of the village. There the tiny corpse was plastered with clay until it was just one big block. By the time they returned to the lodge a huge fire had been kindled. Into it was tossed the baby. The roasting process being a long one, Leona managed to break away without attracting undue attention.

I was not shocked by the story as Leona told it to me, but I was curious. The whole island was cannibalistic, but the roasting of babies was generally regarded as a waste of time when there was larger meat to barbecue. There must be some meaning behind the ceremony, and what it was I resolved to find out.

We had the girl who had acted as Leona's guide brought to us, and between her and Wroo we managed to get the whole revolting story.

The baby came from a far village, captured in a raid and saved for just such a moment as this. After getting that far in sign language we were stuck. Wroo suddenly had a bright idea. Beckoning us to a hut he motioned us inside. In the dank gloom we made out the figure of a woman going through the agonies of childbirth, made more agonising still by the fact that she was surrounded by rocks, the same rocks upon which the witch-doctor had sprinkled blood, and every time she rolled or tossed she encountered their rough edges. The witch-doctor was there, surrounded by a corps of mid-wives whose sole assistance seemed to be poking the expectant mother in the stomach.

It was now apparent to me that the blood-stained stones were to aid the mother in giving birth, and to insure their efficacy, the witch-doctor was stroking a small wooden idol. At first I couldn't believe it was a real idol. As far as I knew, Dutch New Guinea was about the only place in the world without idols as such, but here was a witch-doctor stroking one and murmuring incantations for all the world like a voodoo doctor. For a moment my amazement at this discovery nearly threw me off my original investigation.

Wroo by this time was plucking at my sleeve. It was all right for him to bring me into the hut, but he didn't want to stick around while any baby was being born. That was no place for a male. Outside he made the motions of eating, and then led us on a tour of the village, gleefully pointing out each pregnant woman as though he alone was responsible. At each one he made the gesture of eating, so I gathered that the baby still cooking in the fire was to be fed to all the expectant mothers, probably to supply them directly with enough already-made baby to meet the needs of their about-to-become babies.

We were at the far end of the village when a sudden commotion at the combination bachelor and ceremonial lodge announced that the feast was ready. Women not already at the fire came streaking out of their huts like so many dogs and in a moment they were packed together in a fighting mass that would put to shame any sale in a Broadway bargain basement. I hustled Leona into our tent before she became violently sick, but the noise coming through the thin walls damaged her stomach almost as much as the sights. I came out just in time to head off Leona's little girl-friend with the efficient-kidneyed baby. She was clutching a chunk of steaming, pale white meat, "for the white lady." I told her she could have it for herself, and she went away happy.

While the women were busy insuring their fertility by eating baby-meat, I hunted around for the elephant tusk Leona said she had seen. I found not one but several, and they weren't elephant tusks. What they were I couldn't tell, but whatever had raised them was something big. Tremendous would be a better word.

The tusks, if that was what they were, were composed of a substance resembling horn, applied in cone-shaped layers like a nest of conical paper drinking cups, gradually diminishing in size until the top one came to a sharp point. The tusks were about eighteen inches in length and about six inches through at the base. There was a small, cone-shaped hollow in the bottom, but even so they must have weighed about twenty pounds apiece. I couldn't make them out.

I called in Wroo, who by this time was becoming invaluable. "What is it?" I asked in my eloquent sign language. I pointed to my teeth and then to the horn. That wasn't it. I tried it on my head. That wasn't it either. Finally Wroo, aided by two or three volunteers, drew a lizard-like figure in the sand. It had a long neck, a huge, bulging, hump-backed body terminating in a long tail. At the end of the tail, Wroo indicated, the horn fitted like a cap. I had them draw it over, fearing I hadn't understood. That horn never came off the tail of a lizard, even a ten-foot iguana.

This time they drew it over with addition. The neck now had a flaring hood behind the head, with huge triangular scales jutting out of the back just as shown on re-constructions of dinosaurs in the museums back home.

"How big?" I asked increduously, measuring off six feet with my arms.

Wroo grinned hugely and shook his head. Marking a line in the dust with his toe, he started pacing off ten feet, twenty and then thirty. He stopped and looked back, estimating the distance he had come. It wasn't enough. He paced off ten more feet. Forty feet in all. Then I made a mistake. I laughed. Instantly the Kirrirris froze into statues of offended dignity. No native can stand ridicule, and I had touched them on a sore spot.

I looked at the horn again. One side of the thing looked as though it might have been worn down by being dragged along the ground. Whatever had worn it must have been plenty big. Maybe forty feet wasn't too long. Just because I had never heard of the creature before didn't mean it didn't exist. I had never heard of the Kirrirris before, and they existed. Things managed to exist in other parts of the world without my knowledge, so maybe they could do it here. That's a thing a white man has to watch out for in the jungle. After running around looked up to as a god by everyone he meets, he is apt to feel he is omnipotent and begin to believe his own publicity.

The natives were quick to sense my change of attitude. When I asked where the creature might be found, they pointed, not down into the jungle as I had expected, but up into the hills to the northwest.

"How far?"

Two, three days. Not very far.

Would they take me to them?

This question required some discussion. There was much snarling and showing of teeth, accompanied by clawing gestures and a gnashing at each others' bodies. By that they meant the beast was tough, and plenty tough, too. Wroo threw back his head and howled, "Rooow, Rooow, rrrow, row!"

The imitation may not have been a good one, but it was enough to send the shivers down my back. It was as close to a hiss as a roar could be, and as close to a roar as a hiss could be. But having heard of the beast I had to see it. If such a monster existed, and I could photograph it, the value of my film, to science would double. I patted my pistol assuringly, informing the natives that if the thing got rough I would turn my magic gun on it. They didn't want to look too doubtful to my face, but I could see that if it came to betting on my gun or their *row*, as they called the monster, they would put their money on the *row*. Still, they agreed to show me one, and more than that I could not ask. I set the hour for departure at dawn the next day.

When my boys heard I was going to leave them in camp for four or five days while I went on a hunting trip with the Kirrirris there was a howl of protest. Such loyalty touched me, but I pointed out we would be travelling fast and light, that we would be stalking elusive quarry, and that a group of more than twenty, including my five Malays and a couple of chain-gang marksmen would do more harm than good. Then they got down to the real reason for not wanting to be left in camp. They had seen plenty of signs, a lot more than I had, that the Kirrirris like to take heads and eat human meat, preferring it to kangaroo.

Wasbus was lugubrious as he pointed out the vast quantity of steak packed in his long legs. "They are good shots, tuan," he pleaded. "They have better bows (I knew Wasbus admired their bows. He had stolen two of them and asked me to hide them for him in my duffle) they have better arrows, and there are three of them for every one of us. If you go there will be three hundred of them for one of us. We will all be dead." He ended up on a wail.

I was firm in my refusal to take more on my trip. On the other hand, I recognised that their fears were not as groundless as they should have been. So that night I gave shot guns to four chain-gangers and had them give a demonstration of their magic marksmanship in the village square, shooting out candles. As each candle was snuffed out in a roar of hell-fire, the village population shrank in size, until the final round when there was no one left. My hunting guides were gone too. It took me an hour to get them back.

The next day we got another dose of the one-foot-up, one-foot-down hiking, angling across the foot hills, but this time it was worse because we were climbing. By nightfall we had reached a high plateau where we camped. It was a good thing we did, because by that time I wouldn't have known how to walk on level ground. It was cool up there though we were still a couple of days below the snow line. Leona and I welcomed blankets, but the Kirrirris took it raw. Remember, these were the same boys we had caught hunting Dutch New Guinea ptarmigan above the snow line dressed in their altogether.

The next day, instead of cutting across the plateau, we followed along the edge, heading straight west. The farther we went the more precipitous became the slope falling away below us until at last it amounted to a cliff almost vertical the last fifty feet. Up where we were the vegetation was sparse, a few clumps of grey heather, a little bunch-grass, and some brown brush was about all there was. It was like finding a section of Texas desert stuck down in New Guinea except that there were no stones in the hard, dry soil.

The plateau, as flat as a table, reached for ten miles on our right before there began the final rise to the snow capped peaks shimmering pinkly on the horizon. Behind us it seemed to extend indefinitely. I recall crossing a mile-wide stretch on my previous dash to the snow line, but ahead I could see we were rapidly approaching the end. The Kirrirris could see it too, for now they were keeping us well back from the rim of the cliff, sending a scout over from time to time for inspection. There was a feeling of tenseness in the air hard to describe, but there were times when I could have cut it out in chunks

We reached the western lip of the plateau and headed north. At length Wroo decided we had gone far enough. He gave me a sign for extra caution. I got down on my hands and knees and crawled with him for a peep over the side. What I saw surprised me. While we were travelling across what amounted to a desert, below us the country had changed into a regular swamp, bogged down between our plateau and another one that began farther on and at a lower level. The swamp, tri-

Amiable Head Hunters

More superb specimens of manhood, than these boys from the Upper
Merauke River, would be hard to find

Drummer Boys

Cannibals of the most treacherous order are the two drummers shown here. They are members of a Jei-Anim tribe dwelling far into the interior of Dutch New Guinea

All Greased Up

A Kaya-Kaya ' onim ha ' or dandy

angular in shape, covered about forty acres and formed a sort of delta between the two plateaus. At the narrow end on the mountain side a thin stream trickled in, vanishing almost at once in high yellow reeds. There was no outlet on the southern side that I could see. But abruptly I stopped looking. I saw the reeds move.

I have been scared many times in my life. Several times I have sampled death. But never in my life was I paralysed with fear. But I was paralysed now. My camera was in my left hand, my gun in my right, but they might as well have been miles away. I couldn't reach them.

How long I froze there, waiting for the reeds to move again, I'll never know. Leona says she saw me tighten up fifteen minutes before she started to crawl toward my side, but I can't depend upon her figures. She saw the thing too, and after that you can't be sure of anything.

Leona reached me on her hands and knees just as the reeds parted and a head rose up like something out of the *Lost World* or *King Kong*. Except that those were phantasies, and this monster was real. Leona gave a soft sigh and collapsed on the ground. I thought she had fainted and managed to turn my head to look. She was staring wild-eyed at the earth below her face, clutching at a clump of grass with both hands as though to keep her grip on reality. Her shock was enough to partially restore my own senses. I couldn't stay paralysed with her so much more helpless than me.

"It's all right," I whispered.

Her gaze remained fixed on the earth. She gave no indication of having heard

Slowly, as though I were directing each muscle from some distant control tower. I moved my camera into line. As if in obedience to my wishes, the colossal remnant of the age of dinosaurs stalked across the swamp. Once its tail lashed out of the grass so far behind its head I thought it must be another beast. For one brief second I saw the horny point. I heard it · hiss—Roooow—Roooow—Rooow. I licked my dry lips, suddenly aware that I had not started my camera.

The spring was already wound for a hundred feet. I pressed the release. To my ears the whirring gears sounded like a threshing machine. Sweat rolled down my face. Ice cold sweat. The *row* seemed to catch the sound for it suddenly stopped, reared up on its hind legs, its small forelegs hanging limp, and shot its snaky neck in our direction. It was a full quarter mile away, it couldn't possibly hear the camera, but I found myself cowering back as though that snapping-turtle shaped beak would lash out and nab me. I gasped with relief when the creature settled back.

Up to that time the only thing I had noticed photographically was the *row*. Now I was noticing other things. That the monster was a light brown yellow in colour, almost the identical hue of the reeds through which it was passing. I noticed that it was covered with scales laid on like armour plate, that the plates were uneven, almost as though they were designed for camouflage. I looked at my filter indecisively, then left it on. It was giving me as good a contrast as anything. There was no filter in the world that could separate two matching colours, and if I filtered out the grass I would lose my *row* so I left it on. Twice more the *row* reared up, giving me a good view of the bony flange around its head and the projecting plates along its backbone. Then with a click my camera ran out just as the *row* slithered behind a growth of dwarf eucalyptus.

"It's gone!" The words in a low whisper almost in my ear nearly caused me to jump out of my skin. In that one jump I left the Pleistocene age for the present and lived to tell the tale. For a second I didn't think I was going to do it. Then my heart started beating again.

"Yes," I finally stated, except that no words came. Leona looked at me curiously.

"You're scared."

I nodded. "Let's get out of here," I finally managed to whisper.

"I can't," she confessed. "My legs won't move."

I found mine wouldn't either, at first. They were as though asleep. Gradually some strength flowed back into our bodies. We managed to wriggle back on our stomachs, about as helpless as a couple of snakes with broken backs. Our guides and our Malays followed, also on their stomachs. I don't know if they were too scared to stand up like we were or if they just wriggled because I was setting the pattern. At any rate, I finally decided we couldn't crawl on our stomachs all the way back to camp so I made an effort to stand.

Not until I got to my feet did I realise I was soaking wet. My shirt, I was relieved to notice, was just as wet as my pants. I like to think it was all sweat.

Once I got to my feet I was all set for heading back. So was Leona. So was everybody else. Behind us there was a *row*. According to Wroo, there were a lot more where that one came from. And there weren't any cages between us and them. Against a beast like that, our rifles were about as useful as citronella. No sir, it was time for us to go back.

CHAPTER XI

SUNRISE CURFEW

IF I had had my way, we would have kept moving all night, but on that point my way and the way of the jungle differed.

While we were on the plateau we could travel in the dark, guiding our steps by the black silhouettes of brush looming up ahead, but once we plunged over the lip, with the horizon lost below us in a black void, we could walk wide-eyed into a tree without seeing it. Overhead were millions of stars, as absolutely devoid of light as dead white specks painted on a field of black.

Of necessity we camped, but that didn't mean we slept. Smoke whirling up from our blazing camp-fire assumed fantastic shapes, the most recurring one being the long neck and head of a *row*. There were times when it took a distinct effort on my part to repress a sudden mad desire to fire wildly into the twisting column. In a way it was comforting to feel like that. As long as I felt like swinging into fierce action, I could be sure no row was present. If one did show up, I knew darn well I would be as petrified as a toad in front of a hungry snake.

We were up before dawn and on our way after the briefest of breakfasts. It's one of the tragedies of mountain travel that on the way up there is not a single down-grade, and on the way down there are nothing but up-grades. I swear we climbed more hills getting down to the village than we did getting up on the plateau. By the time we got back my straw sandals were so thin I burned my foot stomping out a cigarette.

We were not expected back so soon. My boys looked guilty, like pups caught in a sheep-fold. They circled uneasily to get in back of me where they would not encounter my gaze The Kirrirris, on the other hand, looked puzzled, like hosts whose hospitality has been spurned. I sniffed the air, then sent Leona to the tent. The meat I smelled roasting never came from a kangaroo. Too many times before I had encountered the sickening odour to fail to recognise it now. A little innocent cannibalism had been going on during our absence.

Wroo and his men plunged eagerly forward. Achmed and Wirio looked disgusted. My Javanese were indifferent, and the rest of the party who had been with me on the plateau looked mildly disappointed. No one of them would have admitted a yen for human flesh, but all knew friends who would eat it. And with those boys, one's best friend is himself.

I thought the time was ripe for a tongue lashing, and I gave them one. I called my whole crew together and waded into them, verbally and physically. It was the first serious disciplining I had given them, and they took it, knowing full well it was deserved. Achmed aided by his four brethren, wielded bamboo rods indiscriminately, missing some and whaling others twice, but when they got through the boys knew they had been punished. Wasbus had welts all over him. He was so big he couldn't be missed. I think all five Malays gave him a going over, accidentally, of course. No resentment was shown against the Malays for the punishment meted out, but if I had appointed natives to whip their fellows they wouldn't live long to enjoy their satisfaction. To the childish minds of the Kaya-Kayas a superior can do no wrong, but they refuse to recognise any fellow-native as a superior. Retaliation is quick and sure, and usually means death.

After the wholesale punishment was over and the boys had slunk off to compare welts, and shame to those who had only little ones, Wasbus came cringing around, about as abject as an elephant.

"We were tempted, tuan," he offered at last.

I didn't answer. I just stared gravely ahead as though in deep meditation.

"It was for our strength," he said after a long pause.

Still I didn't reply.

"We go now to fierce country." He was determined to clear himself and began to talk rapidly to get in as much as he could before I cut him off. "We must fight, and to fight we must have warrior strength and warrior cunning. One day ago a sago tree fell on a warrior. He was cutting it down," and here Wasbus stopped to re-enact the scene. "It fell. He ran. He fell down. Whoosh!" Wasbus fell on his face and shivered spasmodically. He stopped abruptly and lay still. "Dead."

"I don't think he was dead," I said grimly. "A sago palm is hardly big enough to kill a man."

Wasbus got up and scratched the ground with his toe, abashed. "His arm dead," he said at last, flapping his own loosely. "No good as fighter anymore. Head man hit him with a club."

"So you ate him," I said harshly.

The big black was genuinely surprised. "Of course, tuan. What else was there to do?"

"You know what else there is to do. All your life you have been taught it is wrong to eat human flesh."

"That was in Merauke," he quickly explained. "Here we are here, and things are different. Here we must be brave so we eat warriors to get their bravery. In Merauke the white soldiers are brave for us so we do not need to eat warriors. Oh no, tuan, in Merauke I would not eat a man, or a woman, or even a little child. We always go a long way off, and when we are a long way off the white soldiers are not there to be brave for us, so we have to be brave for ourselves, and to do that we . . ."

"Get out!" I shouted, and Wasbus got.

I knew the futility of arguing with a native on cannibalism. The white man's arguments against it are so much weaker than the native's defence it is useless to try to bring the issue to a conclusion on the basis of logic. The only reason to be put forth that carries any weight at all is the stern admonishment, "Don't do it, because if you do we'll punish you for it." Thus it is only natural that when the fear of punishment is removed, the native will fall back upon his old habits. If the native's conscience should prick him, which it wouldn't, he can persuade himself easily enough that the white man doesn't know what he is talking about. To his mind he is not desecrating the dead by devouring the corpse. On the contrary, he is honouring the victim, giving him a second-hand life by means of the digestive process through which the victim imparts his strength and intelligence to all who partake of him. He lives on in the bodies of those who have eaten him, and the better the man he was, the better will be the successors to his tissues. The native can further argue that human meat is good to eat, easy to cook, and easy to digest. He can claim for it certain properties for the soothing of ghosts and demas, the curing of certain illnesses, and in the case of males, the bolstering of masculine virility. In the case of females, certain portions of the feminine body are infallible remedies for barrenness, other portions ease the pains of childbirth and still other portions will insure an abundant milk supply. Where else can a meat be obtained so rich in beneficial properties? The white man is great, and good, and wise, certainly, but gods make mistakes and surely it is foolish to consign so much goodness to the ground, where the ants and worms will desecrate it.

The boys were a strangely chastened lot the next morning when the time came to pick up their packs and hit the trail leading south. As closely as I could figure it, we had about eighty miles to go before we reached Tannah-Tinggi on the Digoel River where Schultz would be waiting for us with the steam launch. There were no charts, no trails, no nothing but the assurance that the going would be tough. A few miles of open forest, a few miles of savannas and then once more the Rain Forest. A month's work if it was a day's, and the boys knew it. Feeling low mentally from the punishment of the day before, and low physically because of the depressing prospect of hard work, it was nearly noon before they had assembled all the odds and ends and were ready to step.

In the meantime I had uncovered another amazing custom of our strange hosts, the Kirrirris. Arising at dawn as was my habit I was standing before the tent enjoying the freshness the air possesses before the natives begin to sweat when a frightful hissing broke out in the hut across the way. Exercising my prerogative as chief I sauntered over and peered in.

Backed into the corner, the picture of embarrassment was a young warrior and a girl I recognised as a member of the household. Keeping him cornered was a circle of women engaged in hissing at the young buck and shaming the girl. As I stuck my head through the doorway, some of the women turned to see what was causing the interruption. Instantly the buck made a dash for liberty, streaking by me like a brown phantom. Not knowing what was up, I thrust out a foot, and the boy ploughed dirt with his nose for a dozen feet. Before he could arise he was at the bottom of a pile of screaming women.

I was about to take my life in my hands and go to his rescue when I noticed the father of the girl and a dozen or so more men watching the scene with intense amusement. Apparently whatever was going on was not serious, at least as far as they were concerned. What the young man might think was a different matter and of no consequence. Try as I would, I couldn't get a satisfactory answer to my questions put in sign language. The young man was picked up, some the worse for wear, and hustled back into the hut. The women crowded after him, followed by more and more until the inside was packed to the bulging point. Whatever the hapless youth felt I knew he wasn't comfortable.

It took me until noon, counting time out for packing interruptions to get to the bottom of the strange affair at dawn. But when I finally got the answer, it was worth the effort. Once more the Kirrirris had demonstrated the soundness of their social structure. Knives of bone, splendid weapons, irrigated farms, painted idols, benevolent leadership and well-built houses all indicated the superiority of the race, but it was left to this incident to prove that their civilisation was destined to last through the ages. I had witnessed a betrothal.

Boiled down to its essentials, the affair was simplicity itself Unlike adolescent members of the Marind-Anim tribes who must spend each night in the bachelor lodge, the young bucks of the Kirrirris have the run of the village just so long as they do not sleep in the hut of their parents and report back to the bachelor lodge before sunrise. If a youngster desires to spend the night with the girl of his choice he may do so, sure that he will not be molested by the girl's parents, even though his presence may crowd the sleeping quarters a little. But he must be up and away before sunrise.

This is a fine state of affairs. A young Romeo has his choice of sleeping quarters, and there is scarce a damsel in the village that would bid him nay. Love 'em and leave 'em at dawn is his policy. And when you consider that his profligacy has the full consent of all concerned, you can realise what an admirable paradise the young man is living in. He is free of responsibility; the girl's father must support her and any off-spring that may result from his casual encounters, and he is left to go his way undisturbed by economic pressure. What inducement there is for him to pick out a single woman and settle down into a respectable, hard-working husband is not evident at first glance.

But there is a catch to it, a catch that is so successful there is no possibility of any able-bodied man remaining long a bachelor. Out of 100 marriageables, 100 get married, a 100 per cent record few civilisations can boast of. As a general rule the more profligate the lovers, the lower the marriage rate, but not so here. And the catch was as simple a thing as the sunrise.

Before dawn man's powers of resistance are at their lowest ebb. But that is the hour at which he must get out of a warm bed from beside a desirable sleeping companion, and go out into the cold mists and dark, dank wetness and go home to sleep. Sooner or later he is going to find a bed so comfortable, or a sleeping partner so thoroughly warming he is not going to want to get up and brave the chill pre-dawn breezes. Maybe he had a hard day the day before, or maybe he has a hangover, but the time is bound to come when dawn finds hims sound asleep beside his inamorata.

And when that happens, the girl's long suffering mother pounces on him. He has brought shame upon the house. Her screams, artfully simulated, bring in other women. More screams. The girl alternately beams and screams. The young man suffers, but there is nothing he can do. He is married. He got that way by sleeping with his love while the sun lifted above the horizon. Simpler marriage rites have yet to be found.

Of course celebrations always follow in which the young couple are subjected to further humiliations and congratulations to clinch the marriage, but they follow only because it is the nature of the native to celebrate anything and everything. They are the result of the marriage, not a part of it. And the young men know it and know the futility of trying to escape the immutable law. They accept their fate with resignation and thereafter make good husbands. They can trifle on the side all they want, constancy being an unknown quality, but they can't avoid their family responsibilities. Public pressure will see to that.

I was glad to get out of there. Some of my boys were hard sleepers, Wasbus in particular, and I needed carriers more than the village belles needed husbands. I gave the word and we headed south. Toward home.

CHAPTER XII

MRS. MILLER'S STONE-AGE COOK BOOK

SOMEWHERE south of Kirrirri land and east of the Digoel river on the northern edge of the Rain Forest, we stumbled onto a small village of the Marind-Anim tribe, one of those outcast villages whose sole purpose in life seems to be the raising of heads for stronger tribes to crop. As Marind-Anim's go, they weren't a bad looking lot, but in comparison to the Kirrirris they looked pretty seedy. Their huts were dilapidated, their weapons were second-rate, and for their living they depended entirely on the jungle. No cultivated plants of any kind were in evidence. In spite of this I would say they were more advanced than the pigmies or the river natives at Bara. Being on the edge of the Rain Forest, they had not been retarded by the full weight of the oppressive jungle.

We did not spend much time with them, but we did pick up one important piece of information. On the bank of the Digoel river, just two days to the west of us, there was located a large village rich in canoes. Yes, they were members of the Marind Anim tribe. That was all I wanted to know. If they were Marind-Anims, they were blood-brothers of mine, and if they had canoes, I could rent them. And with canoes I could thumb my nose at the Rain Forest while gliding down the Digoel river in style.

The next morning, after a suitable distribution of gifts, we changed our course for the west.

"Just follow the trail," the chief advised. You will come to a lake in a few hours, but we have built there a tree walk.

"A tree walk?" I asked in some surprise. Bridge-building was an art of which I thought Dutch New Guinea natives knew nothing.

"Yes, tuan," the chief nodded vigorously. "Trees we have put there so when the Digoel warriors attack us, we can run to the large village for protection."

I was sceptical but willing to be convinced. And when the chief volunteered to lead a party to show us where this bridge was located I assented eagerly.

We had no trouble finding the lake. The trail was clearly marked and easily followed. Apparently the villagers had had frequent cause to flee over it to escape marauders.

A more beautiful spot than this lake would be hard to find. Fringed by drooping palms and giant ferns framed against a darker background of ebony and eucalyptus, the water mirrored every passing cloud with a depth and colouring that surpassed the sky itself. Thousands of water fowl, from the statuesque pink flamingoes guarding the shallows to the tiny hell-divers scooting over the surface like water bugs gave the sanctuary the appearance of an over-stocked aviary.

In the jungle one hears wild life on all sides but seldom sees it, a fact which made this sudden glimpse all the more amazing. Even as we watched, from behind a point of reeds came a battalion of black ducks, their necks rippling in unison as they swam in close formation before us. In size they were slightly smaller than Canadian geese, and as they passed solemnly quacking like black-robed mourners in a funeral procession, the chief who was acting as our guide pointed at them ecstatically: "*Tamu winingapa*" (good eating), he grunted, his mouth watering.

It didn't seem fitting to turn loose a blast in this paradise, but we had to eat. Achmed and I lined up our shotguns and blazed away with both barrels.

The echoes of the report never had a chance to get started. From the lake came such a quacking, squawking, clattering hub-hub I thought I would go deaf before I could drop the gun and get my hands over my ears. Thousands upon thousands of birds lashed the lake to foam as they took off. Every stalk of marsh grass must have concealed a dozen ducks, and when they flew out I thought they were going to take the lake with them. The worst of it was, they didn't associate us with the sound, and the clouds circling above us were just as thick as anywhere else. And the stuff that was splattering us and the leaves around us wasn't all water shaken from their wings. We dived for cover beneath the palms, smelling like individual chicken coops.

One thing out of this turmoil startled me more than anything else. The black ducks at which we had fired had taken off for the tall timber and were now roosting in the trees all around us. Such unorthodox behaviour for a duck was upsetting. As soon as it was safe to look up, and this wasn't for ten or more minutes, I studied the situation. Seen from below my ducks looked different. Their breasts and bottoms were white as snow, and they hopped from limb to limb as nimbly as crows.

Wasbus came up then with an armful of dead ones, and I could inspect one at close range. It was a duck all right, if the flat bill and oily feathers meant anything, but the feet were as free of webs as a chicken's. After an hour's puzzling over the matter, the only ornithological conclusion I could come to was that they were mighty good eating.

In the meantime calm had been restored to the lake. The armies of water fowl were pursuing their normal existence as though nothing had happened, and it was time for us to hunt up the bridge.

I turned to the chief. "Where is the *Koi* walk?"

He looked surprised. "Here."

I looked at the rippling water blankly. The butt of a coconut palm resting on the shoreline was all I could see, that and the dim outline of its trunk wavering beneath the surface.

"What happened? Did it fall in?" I could see ourselves walking for miles around the lake and the swamp that bogged it in at both ends.

"Oh no, tuan," he said brightly. "This is it."

I still couldn't figure it out. I hadn't expected much in the way of a bridge, but at least I expected to find a few trunks of trees strung end-to-end on piles of some kind. Here there was nothing.

The chief explained patiently. The trees were there. They were under the water, resting on the bottom, all the way across. All you had to do was wade to the end, feel around with your toes for the next one, and wade on. The lake, at its deepest point, came only to the waist, he said.

Leona looked at me. "I can't make it," she said at last. "I can't walk a tight-rope, and I can't walk those slimy tree trunks. What would happen if I fell off in that awful mud? I'd just sink out of sight, that's what would happen." Already she saw herself vanishing forever in a primeval quagmire.

I asked a few more questions, and when these were answered to my satisfaction, and the chief had waded out a hundred yards to show me the bridge actually existed, I decided to chance it.

"I 'll have Wasbus and one of his partners carry you across on a litter," I advised Leona. "We can cut a couple of bamboo poles and make a seat that will get you across in great shape."

She was doubtful but willing. Two stout poles were cut and a rude seat quickly made of rattan. Wasbus shouldered the front end and another tall black took his position in back.

"Just sit on top and keep your feet up," I said. "I 'll be right behind if you fall in."

"I hope you think that makes me feel better," she retorted as her perch began to wobble under the uneven strides of her bearers. I didn't envy her the half-mile stretch of water she had to negotiate from that unstable position. Even with her feet braced on the cross-piece and her hands gripped tightly behind, she bounced and swayed on the springy poles like something about to be cast out of a sling.

By the time we reached the middle of the lake I appreciated the ingenuity of the engineers who had designed the bridge. Theirs was not a problem of bridging the water; they had to bridge the bottomless mud. From the thousands of palms overhanging the water they had selected those most easily toppled and pushed them in. The roots were then clubbed off, the fronds beaten down, and the trunks, not quite buoyant enough to float and not too heavy to be supported, were pushed into position. There they slowly settled to the bottom, end-to-end links in the submarine bridge.

The trunks were as slippery as greased poles, but my warnings of what would happen to anybody who fell in and wet my equipment were strong enough to keep the boys upright. Leona was the only casualty. When the water went up around our armpits the give to her litter poles was a little too much for comfort. She was high and dry on the up-swing; it was on the down-beat that the sagging bottom of the litter slapped water with a gentle pat-pat as of waves against a drifting canoe, and it was Leona who composed the principal part of the sagging bottom.

I was grateful to the lake for one thing, however. Without it I would have had to wait for a heavy rain to rinse off my boys. They had smelled strong enough before we reached the lake, but after the deluge of bird droppings they would have been impossible without a quick wash. Now we were all fresh and clean and raring to go.

The friendly chief and his crew left us once we had safely crossed the lake. They were richer by a half-dozen shells apiece, some red ribbon and a handful of beads. I felt guilty in giving them so much. When word of that concentrated wealth spread through the jungle some avaricious tribe or other was only too likely to pay a social call on the village, departing only when all gifts had been collected down to the last bead, and no village was left.

We had no difficulty finding the unnamed village on the bank of the Digoel river. We had our trail and we stuck to it. There was no other alternative. The jungle wall on either side was so thick and so tough we had about as much chance getting off the trail as a cow changing course in a cattle chute.

We were expected. We knew no runners had been sent ahead. We had heard no drums. Just the same we were expected. When I entered the village at the head of a picked crew, leaving Leona in the jungle guarded by her Malays, one of the first things I was asked was where was the white lady. And when I finally deemed it safe to bring her forth there was no sudden rush of the curious. Rather they looked at her as if for confirmation of what they already knew. I don't attempt to account for this prescience on the part of ignorant savages; I am merely stating it as a fact. I have seen it evidenced too many times to doubt it.

Our welcome was a warm one. My boys were greeted like long lost brothers, supplied with food, drink and women. Such an air of hospitality pervaded the place I became suspicious. It was not good. Ordinarily, my boys remained haughtily aloof, putting on airs over their backwoods brethren, but by evening under the warmth of their hosts' admiration they became expansive and relaxed with condescending camaraderie.

Such an attitude was dangerous. Not that I expected a wholesale attack once my boys' suspicions were lulled to sleep. There were too many of us to risk a stunt like that, but what I did expect was the sly singling out of unsuspecting individuals, a sudden ganging up and a quick murder in a quiet spot. I had no reason to feel as I did, but I could feel something was wrong too strongly to ignore the hunch. I decided to give the chief and his witch-doctor a lesson right then and there.

My glaring storm lantern had attracted the usual crowd of awe-stricken natives and under its white light I had soon collected the entire population. My own boys, expecting a good show, crowded in with the rest. I singled out the chief and his witch-doctor side-kick, and summoned them to my side. I told them what a powerful man and dema I was, demonstrating my powers at the same time. I snapped on my cigarette lighter, put my flashlight in my mouth and turned it on, causing my cheeks to glow redly; I lighted matches and let the chief burn his fingers on the glowing stubs, and finally fired my revolver. Strangely enough the revolver did not have the purgative effect I expected. They had heard of the thing, and while they were scared they weren't paralysed.

My grand finale being thus dampened, I tried another. I produced a couple of fire crackers. These looked harmless enough and the bright red paper covers were fascinating. The wicked-looking chief and the witch-doctor accepted them eagerly. I placed their fingers on the butts just so, directed them to hold them high so everyone could see, and then touched my cigarette to the fuses. As a shower of sparks descended the chief and his compatriot in devilment grew nervous but I calmed them momentarily.

BOOM! BOOM!

The chief stood like a statue. The witch-doctor dropped like a log. The show was over but nobody moved. They just stood there, their mouths wide open, eyes popping. Gradually the outer fringes of the crowd melted away. As those in closer felt their rear guard vanish they too were moved to disappear. Soon there was left only the chief, the unconscious witch-doctor and myself. The chief's arm was still rigidly extended upward. His eyes were fixed straight ahead in an unseeing stare. Presently he began to shake. Then a rush of sweat bathed his face and ran down his oily body. His bowels relaxed.

"You can go to sleep now," I said soothingly.

He turned his head slowly.

"Go to sleep," I repeated.

He stumbled off with nary a glance to the left or right. I roused the witch-doctor with a few slaps. He too wandered off, staggering like a man stunned by banshees.

The gas light overhead hissed on. Achmed and his Malays on guard around the tent smiled inscrutably as I passed inside. I didn't expect any further trouble.

As long as I had the villagers so thoroughly impressed, I yielded the next morning to Leona's request that we stay over for a couple of days to enable her to complete her notes on the culinary arts of the Kaya-Kayas. Her notes were already voluminous, but here was a spot as ideally representative of the Stone-Age as could be found. No white man had ever penetrated this far back. The cooking utensils, menus and methods, were exactly as they had been for thousands of years.

What started out to be two days of research lasted two weeks, due to an unexpected emergency to be mentioned later, with results best described by Mrs. Miller herself.

The only utensils a young couple has to acquire to set up housekeeping in Dutch New Guinea are a couple of cooking stones, as flat as top on possible, and a few coconut shells. The rocks are the hard part. As scarce as hen's teeth, they are jealously guarded by all good housewives, and it takes a good thief to get away with one. In fact women are quicker to recognise their cooking stones than their children. Many a young couple has had to start out in life equipped with nothing more than a couple of fire-baked clay balls, slightly flattened on top, hoping the meanwhile for the great day when they will be able to take part in a raid upon a distant village to steal some stones.

Of coconuts there is plenty, but it takes considerable skill to crack out a dish without splitting the shell. While still full of meat the coconut is up-ended on the ground and the segment between the three eyes tapped out with a stone club. Then with gentle strokes the edges are chipped away a little at a time until the top quarter is knocked off, leaving a nice round bowl of slightly less than a pint in capacity. And that is the extent of the kitchen ware. There are no clay bowls, no wooden dishes, no pottery of any kind. Just rocks and coconut shells.

Sago is the staff of life. It is at once bread, vegetable, meat and drink. The sago palm itself is common all over New Guinea, growing thickest along the banks of streams or around the edges of lakes and swamps. The palm is from sixteen to twenty feet in height, crowned by wide, drooping fronds. The rough trunk is hard and stringy on the outside, but the pale grey inside is soft and pulpy and can be easily scooped out with a shell or flat edged stick.

Because of the vast amoung of food stored in the trunk of a sago palm, one tree will do for several families, and the preparation of the meal calls for a regular little festival on the order of a husking bee. The tree is cut down by the men who attack it with their stone axes. Once it has fallen a layer of the rough exterior is stripped off and thereafter the work is turned over to the women.

They begin by scooping out the pulp with shells, sticks or split bamboo, tossing the moist chunks on the ground where other women pick them up and carry them to the sluice boxes of palm leaves, which have been erected to separate the meal from the fibrous pulp. The sluice boxes are ingenious affairs. A huge palm frond with a stem anywhere up to eight inches wide is laid trough side up with the butt end on a stump or bamboo post and the leafy side resting on the ground. At intervals down the V-shaped stem piles of coconut fibre are tied to serve as strainers. A chunk of sago is now laid on the wide butt of the frond, a woman pulverises it with an ebony stick on the order of a baseball bat while children empty coconut shells of water over the mass. The water mixes with the sago and pretty soon a milky stream begins to trickle down the trough, flowing through the strainers but leaving all strings and lumps behind. when it reaches the bottom the white sediment begins to settle, sometimes in the leaf itself, sometimes in a basket of bamboo serving as a settling tank at the end of the trough. It is this sediment that makes the sago meal.

All day women scoop sago and mash it. Small boys and girls

form a constant chain, running to the stream with their empty coconut shells and returning with the full ones to dump into the sluice boxes. Other children run howling around, getting in every one's way and having a grand time. When the sediment in the trough threatens to run over, the muddy mess is dumped into a sack made of plaited palm leaves and hung in a tree to drain. This is repeated until sundown when the women collect all the dripping sacks and return to the village in gay triumph, and with food for another month.

Sometimes the sago is dried right in the sack, sometimes it is stored in sections of bamboo, and sometimes it is moulded into cakes and set on the rafters to dry. When dry it is as hard as a ball of clay and about as imperishable.

So far everything has been conducted in a fairly sanitary manner. Aside from the dirt on the ground and the mud in the water, the sago has come through in pretty clean shape. But when it comes to cooking it, that is a different matter. Sago can be cooked straight, with bananas, with meat, birds or fish. If straight the cake of meal is pulverised with an ebony *saker*, best described as a Stone-Age rolling pin, mixed with water until it is a doughy mass, and then tossed on hot stones or into the open fire to bake. This is only done when in a hurry.

The more elaborate and most popular way is to mix the sago flour with coconut water. This is done by tapping the coconut with a boar tusk, taking a healthy swig of the water and spraying it out of the mouth as necessary while the dough is being kneaded. Next chunks of coconut meat are chewed up nice and fine and expectorated into the pasty mass. For variety bananas are masticated to meet a similar fate. When the loaf has reached the proper consistency it is slapped on stones previously heated and left to bake. The ashes and dirt on the stone add flavour. For festive occasions when huge loaves of sago are baked it is the custom for the women to pool their stones, raking them together in a huge flat bed often six feet wide and up to fifteen feet long. The women line up around the edge and at a given signal each woman tosses on her contribution of dough, spitting furiously and resorting to frequent swigs of coconut water to keep the mass moist as she pats and spreads it to meet her neighbours on both sides and opposite.

The dough hisses and spits on the hot stones. Steam rises up and the heat is tremendous. The women are dripping with sweat from the moment they start, and this sweat forms the only salt in the loaf.

When the dough has been spread out evenly over the stones and no gaps are in evidence, whatever meat is handy is tossed on top. If the men have been fortunate in fishing, the fish are spread on whole, unscaled and uncleaned. Palm leaves or strips of fragrant *kajoe poeti* (eucalyptus) bark are spread over the whole and it is left to bake and steam until done. It is easy to tell when it is done when fish are included. As they cook through they fill up with steam, and when they explode the sago is done. Wild boar is another favourite top dressing for sago bread. The boar is cut up in small chunks and scattered around, hair, filth and all. Not even the rich odour of roasting *kajoe poeti* bark can squelch the smell when wild boar and sago are on the hot stones. And it usually takes from sundown to sundown for the stuff to cook through. I don't know what it tastes like. I couldn't force myself to eat it after watching it prepared. Taste and smell being closely related, however, I'd say the sago tastes like sour yeast and the meat tastes like something left too long in the hot sun. That goes for the fish, too.

Meat and fowl are cooked in the simplest way. Chunks of kangaroo or wild pig are just tossed on the fire, unskinned. The hair will burn off, and it gives the meat flavour. If it burns too much the charred surface is gnawed off until the edible portion is reached. If underdone, the cooked portion is chewed off and the rest tossed back on the fire for further broiling. Fowl are tossed on whole. When the feathers have burned off and the intestines have exploded from pent-up steam the bird is cooked.

Bananas, plantains, wild sweet potatoes and bread-fruit are all cooked by being tossed into the fire. Another item highly regarded by the natives is a greyish clay speckled with little brown flakes resembling rust. This clay is found only in the high savanna country, and hence is regarded as a rare delicacy in the Rain Forest. Natives eat it until their bellies sag under the weight of the stuff.

For drink the men have *wati* and *sagoware*. The former is made of a root so bitter a lump of alum tastes like rock candy in comparison. It, too, must be chewed by the women before it is ready for consumption. The women gather the roots and then sit together, chewing grimly, their faces puckered out of shape as they spit their production into coconut bowls. The bitterness of the root induces a rapid flow of saliva so when they get through they have a liquid of which less than fifty per cent is the juice of the root. It ferments within the space of a few hours. Stuff set out in the sun at noon packs the wallop of straight alcohol by evening. Even when taken fresh from the brewery it is mighty potent stuff, judging by the lethal results I have seen it produce. Natives seldom get viciously drunk on the stuff. They pass out unconscious before they can get violent.

Unfortunately, such is not the case with *sagoware*. *Sagoware* is the nut brown ale of the jungle. No brew masters are needed to guide the slop through the various stages of fermentation. Chunks of raw sago pulp simply are tossed into a section of bamboo until the jungle keg is about half full. Water is added, the stuff is mashed around a little, and left to ferment. This may take anywhere from three hours to a week, depending upon the need for refreshments. Sagoware is never too green to drink, and never too rotten. A higher class of brew is made by substituting coconut water for plain water. This beer is not only sweeter to drink but it packs a high alcoholic content.

The big advantage of sagoware over wati is that the natives can get drunk and still remain conscious. And when they get drunk, their inhibitions are removed, and without inhibitions the Kaya-Kayas hit bottom. To say they are bestial would be the grossest of understatements. Fratricide, matricide, murder, pillage and rape may be indulged in by a single native within the space of a few minutes once he goes berserk on sagoware. Nor are any restraining hands laid on him. Everybody else is drunk too, and when they are drunk decency is the only thing not tolerated.

Another product of the woman's mouth is coconut oil. The rendering of this valuable product is a social affair about on par with the American institution of the Thursday Afternoon

Women's Bridge Club. The village gossips get together over a pile of coconuts and then spend the afternoon cracking shells with a stone club and chewing over the contents along with the gossip. The white meat is masticated into a juicy paste which is spat into a coconut shell. The bowl is then passed to the next woman and she relieves her mouth of its burden. Round and round go the bowls, the women chewing, spitting and gabbing. Full bowls are set aside and empty ones brought up until the coconuts and the women are exhausted. Three or four days later a film of oil has risen to the top, and this is skimmed off from time to time until every drop has been squeezed out. The oil is the one solace for itching skin, and the one ointment for dressing wounds.

Except for the Kirrirris and the pigmies who cultivate their own fruits and vegetables, the natives are entirely dependent upon the jungle for their food supply. Fruits, nuts, vegetables and tobacco are gathered daily, or as the need arises, but so bountiful is nature in this respect it is seldom necessary to go more than a hundred yards from the village to find whatever is needed.

The meat supply is a different problem. Game learns to shun the villages, a regrettable circumstance which makes it necessary for the warriors to go out and hunt for it. There are three angles to every hunting expedition and it is hard to tell which is the most important. First is the cause of it all, the securing of sufficient meat to last the village for a week or so; second is the ever-hoped-for possibility of encountering another but smaller hunting party with the resultant taking of heads and human meat; and third the ever-dreaded possibility of encountering another, but larger, hunting party, with the resultant loss of heads and shanks. It is a matter of complete indifference if the hunting parties come from villages friendly to each other, unless by chance both parties are of equal size. In that case they pool their strength and proceed their merry way. After a time they decide it is a shame to have so many fighting men together and not do anything about it so they head for the nearest little village and lift a few heads. But when the forces are of unequal strength, the larger falls upon the smaller, kills as many as can be caught, and feels sorry for the mistake later, if ever. To their minds it is far better to feel sorry for having the heads and have them than to feel sorry for not having the heads, and not have them.

In the event the hunting expedition turns into a human massacre, there is no delay in rushing home the meat. It is eaten at once even though the supply be so huge as to keep the entire village feasting for days. Human meat, however, is recognised as a superior product and is accorded special condiments and processes not wasted on ordinary flesh. As a concession to humanity, arms and legs are never tossed on the open flames. They are carefully wrapped in green palm fronds along with a strip or two of *kajoe poeti* bark for flavouring, and placed on glowing coals where they are allowed to steam until done. Hearts are wrapped in clay and baked, and testicles, those highly valued preservers of virility, are just stuck on a stick and roasted. Heads though are of great ceremonial value and are prepared under the direct supervision of the witch-doctor and the chief. They are not for the common herd. The ceremonial aspects of cannibalism are so multiple they will have to be taken up later.

Kangaroo meat is the best all-around provider the jungle affords. Wild boar is the most prized in spite of the fact it is ninety per cent bone and the rest muscle. Like man, wild boar is best when eaten fresh. Kangaroo, however, is practically cured on the hoof. Those lean, cast-iron muscled, double-gauge jack rabbits are very toothsome fresh, but dried kangaroo, on the other hand, fringes on the borderline between food and a geological formation.

The drying of meat is not an art. Kangaroo haunches are cut into chips the size of a piece of sole leather strung on rattan, and hung up to petrify. The only reason they are hung up and not tossed on the ground is because of the hungry dogs who will gnaw on anything. In the event of a couple of days of rain, the meat will putrefy, raising the general smell of the village about three notches, something I would have said to be impossible if I hadn't smelled it with my own nose. This does not mean that the meat is spoiled. Sooner or later the sun will come out and the drying process will be resumed. The altered flavour is all to the good. These chips are strung on arm bands and worn as part of the costume. In that position they collect sweat and dirt, becoming that much more palatable.

It will be seen from the foregoing that the Kaya-Kayas are gluttons but not gourmets. The only pleasure they get out of eating is the sagging sensation of a full belly. In this respect a few pounds of grey clay is every bit as satisfactory as a few pounds of banana-flavoured sago or a dozen pork chops. Being more interested in a full belly than in food, they have no set time for meals. Whenever they get hungry they eat, and as they are hungry most of the time, the dinner hour lasts twenty-four hours a day, there is no need for breaking up the menu into breakfast, dinner and supper. In the morning they just start eating where they left off the night before, adding to it such varieties as come in during the course of the day.

That the stomach may be permitted a few hours of rest, all Kaya-Kayas are ardent betel-nut chewers and pipe smokers. Betel-nut is the chewing gum of the Orient, and though the habit may have been introduced into New Guinea, there is little resemblance between the Kaya-Kaya method of mastication and the Oriental. In Java, Ceylon, Singapore, etc., it is the custom to wrap the nut of the betel palm in a leaf of a climbing plant called the betel vine, the sharp, spicy tasting leaf blending perfectly with the acrid, bitter nut. In New Guinea there is a bastard betel palm. Instead of using the nut which grows in date-like clusters on the palm, the Kaya-Kayas use the pulpy, fibrous meat surrounding the nut like an olive surrounds its pit. In fact, the betel nut is much like a green olive in colour and texture. The pulp having been scraped from the nut, it is wrapped in a green tobacco leaf, along with a few pinches of white chalk if available, to lend bulk. The whole wad, about the size of a ten-cent plug of chewing tobacco, is crammed into the mouth and the work begins. After about fifteen minutes the cud has been fairly well worked over. The green betel nut pulp has turned red, whipping up the flow of saliva. It is time to spit. Now I don't want this to be confused with anything meagre like the expectoration of a lumberjack who has been mulling over a plug of Mule Harness Super Burley, with molasses. The Dutch have a word "*kwalster*" meaning a jellyfish, scarlet in colour and about the size of a coffee cup. This word has been applied to the output of a Kaya-Kaya betel nut muncher, and it fills the bill. The chewer works his jaws, contorts his face, bobs his Adam's apple a couple of times and—Slooop—s s s Splop! A brilliant red puddle the diameter of a saucer flames in the dust, shimmers brightly for a moment and settles slowly into mud. It seems to be a rule that the expectorant be discharged in a single ball. Drizzlers in spitting are frowned upon, although it is fitting and proper to drizzle over the chin and chest as much as desired before launching a *kwalster*. But once launched it has to be a clean-cut affair.

Betel nut stains the teeth red, and chalk added to it keeps the teeth brightly polished. In those rare instances when one encounters a good-looking woman, the effect is not displeasing, but on the whole the red and black fangs displayed by most of the Kaya-Kayas are no improvement.

Smoking being such a universal habit, it is not surprising to find it flourishing even in the furthermost hinterlands of Dutch New Guinea. The Kirrirris and pigmies raise their own tobacco, but they are the only tribes who do. The rest are dependent upon such plants as they find in the wild state in the jungle. While not rare, neither are the plants common, so a certain amount of economomy is exercised in indulging in this popular vice.

That there be no waste, the natives smoke pipes, air-cooled and with scientifically designed filters. A pipe is made of a section of bamboo about two feet long and two inches in diameter, the joint at the far end being left closed. Near the far joint a hole and a half-inch in diameter is drilled with a boar tusk. The filter consisting of coconut fibres packed in a loose ball, is inserted in the open mouth piece. So much for the stem. The bowl consists of a single green tobacco leaf, rolled into a cone with the pointed end fitting into the hole drilled in the bamboo stem. Into the bowl is wadded dry, crumbled tobacco leaves, about a cupful in all. A live coal is dropped on this brushpile and the ensuing bonfire is inhaled with great delight. It is like smoking a saxophone loaded with dry weeds, but the natives can inhale a blast of smoke that would choke a good-sized flue.

The nicotine content of the tobacco is terrific, and being

improperly cured it is augmented by tar and other forms of oily residue. This stuff, plus the moisture in the green bowl, is caught by the filter. Caught but not wasted. When the last whiff of smoke has been dragged out of the tobacco, the stinking, nicotine impregnated filter is tenderly removed and plopped into the mouth where it is chewed with great appreciation. In a land where waste is the order of the day, this bit of conservation is touching.

By the time these gustatory sidelights had been dutifully recorded on my film and in Leona's notebook we were ready to go. I had previously made several overtures in the way of lining up the canoes to take us down the Digoel, but so far had come to no definite bargain. The old chief was wily. In spite of the scare I had thrown into him with fire crackers he had not come around as rapidly as I had expected. He had something in the back of his mind. Just as I was playing a slow game working him out of his canoes he was playing a slow game in broaching whatever was bothering him. I decided the time was ready for a show down.

CHAPTER XIII

CANNIBAL CARAVAN

I FOUND the Chief seated on a banana frond in front of his hut enjoying the sun in oily splendour. The wily black rascal was at his smoothest. He rose respectfully at my approach, something I always insisted upon, and his manner was ingratiating.

"The great white tuan does me honour," he said.

"I 've got more honour for you," I said bluntly. I am leaving in the morning, but I like your company so well I am going to pay you to take me down the river in your canoes."

"Yes, tuan," he agreed, "but first the tuan can do me a great help."

"What?" I asked shortly. I had previously tried diplomacy on him and found it didn't work. Now I was going to try abruptness.

"We are close here to the fierce Digoels," he whined. "Many are the times they have raided us for heads, and we are so weak. But now, with the magic of the great white tuan, and his mighty fire-bows of thunder, and all his brave warriors we are strong. We could raid all the villages, and kill all the men."

"No," My shout brought the witch-doctor sidling up.

"Think of all the heads," wheedled the chief.

"And all the good medicine," implored the witch-doctor. "Much brains to fight off the evil demas. Much strength for everyone."

"No." This time my negative answer carried the chill of ice. Both men cringed, but their attitude did not change.

"We can leave in the morning," continued the chief. "My men are ready." He pointed and as I followed his motion I saw a group of warriors emerge from the bachelor lodge, their faces daubed with grey clay, the Imo sign of a headhunt. One glance showed they were drunk.

"Who told you to let them paint up?" I demanded sharply.

The chief shrugged. I glared at him, about to take sudden action at this affront, when cutting through the stench of his oily body I caught the odour of sagoware. He was drunk too.

The situation now confronting me was an appalling one. The white man's hold over the savages is a slender one at best, but when they get drunk this hold becomes so intangible as to be practically non-existent. I glanced sharply about for some of my own men. The first one I saw was Wasbus, reeling unsteadily across the square, his face streaked with grey clay, his prized boar's tusks replacing the everyday bamboo plugs in his nose. While I was out with Leona taking in the preparation of sago, the chief had smoothly outwitted me by getting my own men drunk.

My heart stepped up to double-time. I was scared, and it was the kind of fear that accumulates in waves, building up like an incoming tide driven before a hurricane.

I set a grim guard on my emotions and turned an impassive face on the chief, "Tell them to wash off the clay.

He raised his hand protestingly. "I can 't."

I pulled my gun. It might have been suicide, but that chief was going to obey me if it was the last thing he did and I did. If he ever lorded it over me even a little bit, my life wouldn 't have been worth a nickel anyway. He glared at me. I glared at him. A drum began to thrum. Others boomed in. Still we glared at each other. I raised my gun slowly, holding his gaze locked in mine until I was staring at him over the barrel of my revolver. With an almost imperceptible nod of my head and a slight flick of my gun I indicated the dancers beginning the first few steps around the drums.

"Make them stop."

"I can 't." His voice started out defiantly, but broke in the middle. With head bent he shuffled off to obey my commands. I followed. I didn 't trust that boy five feet.

As the chief approached the drumming stopped. He turned to me appealingly but I motioned him on. He coughed nervously, suddenly scared sober. He knew far better than I what he was up against. But at least he tried.

At the first few words there was a deathly silence, the calm before the storm. The next moment there was a crash of drums almost drowned out in the roar of protest. From all corners of the village warriors came running up. A spark of indignation was fanned into a roaring conflagration within three seconds. Here was no longer a well-organised tribe. Here was a mob, as fierce, as primitive, as absolutely without reason as any mob civilisation can produce. Because they were closer to the primitive, they became a mob faster but no more viciously than mobs I have witnessed in so-called centres of culture during the World War.

I knew without being told what to expect next. In another second the howls would be replaced by action, and after that a bloody shamble. Even as I stepped out an arrow whizzed through the air, aimed in our general direction. A huge fellow I had noticed before hurled himself between me and the mob. In the midst of this bedlam he had time to flash one gigantic smile, then his war club was out and circling his head in whistling arcs. Good boy, I thought.

From now on it was up to me. I knew I couldn't lead that bunch of blood-thirsty cannibals my way, but I could lead them their way. Lead them one way, or lead them another, the main thing for a white man to remember is that he must lead them.

I checked the noise with a shot from my pistol. Another shot brought silence, but I could see I would have to speak fast or my speaking days were over. I spoke. I told them about all the heads we were about to get. How the mighty white tuan was going to lead them to victory. How defeat was impossible, as I would use my magic guns. To that tune they were willing to listen. I hoped, as long as I had them quiet, to lead them around to a peaceful mood, but the Marind-Anim language is a language of action, not well designed for oratory. Either you do something or you don't. There were no words to effect a transition between going head hunting and staying home for a feast.

When I finished my speech I was not only committed irrevocably to going head hunting, but I was committed to lead it. However, I was still alive, and still leader, two things I wouldn't have been otherwise.

The big buck who had sprung to my assistance was still hovering attentively near me, apparently acting as my self-appointed bodyguard. Everything had happened so swiftly none of my personal protectors were around. The Malays, of course, were with Leona, and with her I saw that they stayed. I gave him a friendly grin and he came over.

"*To igese*" ("What's your name?") I asked. This is the formal greeting of the Marind-Anims when encountering friendly strangers.

"I am Weepal," he said, flashing betel-nut stained teeth at me. He was a handsome brute in spite of the disfiguring nose plugs. His head had been shaved half way back, and the rest of his hair, heavily oiled, was worked into a protective ball over the base of his skull. His features were clean-cut, his eyes wide-set and intelligent. Light brown in colour he looked more like an Arab than a Kaya-Kaya. I was impressed by his personality and doubly impressed by his size and obvious strength. He must have measured six-foot four, with the smooth muscular build of a Greek god. He was proud of his appearance, I could see that. All hair had been plucked from his face by the painful process of seizing each hair between two clam shells and yanking it out, and only the aristocrats take such pains with their appearance.

"Weepal is not good enough for you," I said. "You 're Herman."

He beamed. "Yaah." He beamed some more in gaping wonder at being thus honoured. "Yaah. I 'm Herman." He kept repeating the word in silent ecstasy. "Herman, Herman." The name agreed with him.

We didn 't have much time for conversation. "Stick with me, Herman," I ordered, "we 've got a lot to do."

"Yaah." No questions. Just dog-like obedience. For the first time in my life I had encountered a native whom I felt I could trust in any extremity. It was a strange feeling, but I had it and knew that I was right.

The drums were once more rolling. Wati was going around, and so was sagoware. Here and there I could see women busy chewing up wati roots and spitting the stuff into bowls that were seized and drunk by thirsty warriors before they were half full. Dancing was getting into full swing. There was no special significance to the dance other than a manner of letting off steam. Ceremonial dancing always follows a headhunt but seldom precedes it. There is another ceremony, far grimmer than dancing, that precedes a head hunt. It takes place the evening before the dawn on which the raid is launched.

I turned everything over to the chief and his witch-doctor aid. He was glad to get back into control, to square himself with his men after his apparent desertion of their cause.

I took my newly acquired bodyguard back to the tent where I had left Leona.

"Things look tough," I said as reassuringly as I could.

She was surprisingly calm. "What is it?" she asked. "I heard all the shouting and the drums."

"Just a headhunt."

She blanched. "We're just getting out in time."

I shook my head. "We aren't getting out. You're staying here. I'm going along."

She thought this over a long time. "It's absolutely necessary, I suppose."

I nodded.

"In that case you had better let me have that spare .45 to go with my .22 pistol. I can't aim the .45 but it makes more noise." Thus calmly did she take it.

"You'll have Achmed, and Wirio and the rest, of course. And the chain gang. I'll give them all klewangs. You'll be just as safe as if you were at home."

"Of course," she agreed. "Are all the other boys going?"

"Most of them I guess. They are all drunk and dancing their heads off out there."

"Can you keep them under control when they are like that?"

I laughed to the best of my ability. "We'll know more about that later, but I'm guessing there won't be any trouble. Right now I've got to follow developments. I'll post the boys and be back as soon as I can."

"Be careful," she called as I stepped out of the tent.

Achmed moved aside as I raised the flap, stepping back immediately once I was outside.

"Got lots of ammunition?" I asked.

He grinned, the light of anticipation in his eyes. "Yes, tuan."

"And all the rest of the boys have plenty of ammunition?"

"Yes, tuan."

"Good. Keep the usual formation, one boy at each corner and you at the door. Get the chain gang boys to put up a rope fence around the tent, and don't let anybody inside the ropes. Shoot them if they try it."

"Oh, tuan, yes. That will be fine."

"I'll put the chain gang crew outside the ropes with klewangs."

"That won't be necessary. We'll shoot, tuan."

"You're just a killer, Achmed."

"Thank you, tuan."

"Come on, Herman."

Herman stepped up smartly, in imitation of Achmed, and we set out for the bachelor lodge where the warriors were already beginning to congregate. The sun was just setting, blood red. A faint mist hung over the jungle, a mist that picked up the red rays and spread them thinly until the whole sky from east to west seemed stained with blood. By the time we reached the lodge it was dark.

Inside was a frightful stench, almost overpowering in its acridity. It took me a moment before my eyes became accustomed to the darkness, relieved only by a smouldering fire before a low platform at the front of the lodge. When at last I could see I made out the dim outlines of the warriors squatting on their haunches, row on row of them packed closely together in semi-circles, all facing the platform in hushed expectancy. The suppressed excitement was as evident as the smell. As I forced my way through more than once my feet encountered the prone body of some warrior who had passed out from too much wati. My presence added to the excitement. A whisper of anticipation passed over the assemblage like a wave. In this darkness, where no face was recognisable I was grateful for the presence of Herman so close to me he trod upon my heels.

Outside I could hear, as though from a great distance, the eerie moaning of bamboo whistles calling the warriors to the meeting. The weird sound was the product of a round cylinder of bamboo, plugged at one end and blown across the top like a small boy blows on a bottle or a cartridge case, but even knowing this I could not dismiss the thought of banshees from my mind.

Warriors in the front row silently made way for me as I squatted in their midst, Herman by my side. Evidently my bodyguard was a man of some standing in the village, for no protest was made at his taking a select position.

We waited. The glowing logs cast a red light over the oily faces of the living and over the dead, for as my eyes became accustomed to the awful gloom I could see we were gathered in the presence of scores of heads, detached embodiments of death. They hung from the roof on ropes of rattan like clusters of coconuts. They were lined up on bamboo shelves along the walls, ghostly spectators awaiting in hushed expectancy the grim drama about to take place. A few heads presided from the platform, and these dried relices were decked in flaring head-dresses made of the gorgeous plumage of birds of paradise. Plainly these were the leering heads of chiefs and mighty warriors whose ghosts were expected to take a major part in the coming raid.

I checked a shudder, but I could not control the goose-flesh that was creeping over my body like the pricking of a thousand tattoo needles. The whistles outside had ceased, leaving a silence even more pregnant with menace than the unearthly moans. Inside could be heard only the heavy breathing of the closely packed savages, punctuated from time to time by sharp, explosive gasps as some tense warrior released his pent-up breath. Movements were not made individually but in waves. When one warrior shuddered, the tremor passed from one end of the lodge to the other like the ripples of a stone cast into a black pond. So fraught with terrifying suspense was the long wait young men to whom this was a new experience fainted in twos and threes. They were left where they fell. I could feel it myself—a sensation of having a heavy black curtain just above and not quite within range of my eyes that threatened at any moment to descend and close me off in oblivion. I blinked my eyes to banish the phantom curtain. When I once more looked up, the platform was occupied by two figures. A gasp of awe and horror swept the assembly at the sudden manifestation of the apparitions.

L

Of course I knew that beneath the towering head-dress of feathers, human hair, bones and reeds, surmounted by a dried head, was the stinking, pot-bellied chief. I knew it in spite of the white, skull-shaped mask, and his weird grotesque make-up; I knew it, but like the rest I was enveloped in a wave of mass hysteria that rocked me back thousands of years. I was afraid, just as were the savages on all sides of me. The second figure, no less terrifying than the first, was crowned with a head-dress topped with the open-jawed head of a boar, tusks gleaming as though stained with blood in the ghastly light of the dying embers. Drummers, unnoticed in the dark shadows, began a throbbing dirge. The head-hunting ceremony of the dread Imo was underway.

A nudge brought me around. Without a word a coconut bowl was placed in my hands, a bowl filled with grey clay. I did as indicated, smearing the stuff thickly over my face. The cool moisture felt good. I passed it on to Herman. Now the witch-doctor was beginning his long address to the demas who watched over all undertakings. The friendly demas were praised, the evil demas flattered. He paused. The roll of drums rose to a roar. Abruptly they stopped.

Then began the most horrifying part of the whole barbaric ceremony, the roll-call of the dead. Before setting out on a *karawarie* or head hunt, the ghosts of all those warriors killed in the last raid or who have died since then must be appeased, and the only appeasement worthy of a departed brave is blood, blood and the companionship of the soul, liberated by the sacrifice.

The chief thrust forth his hands. In the one he clutched a stone axe, in the other a bamboo knife.

"Labum," he called, his voice echoing hollowly inside his masking head-dress.

A thin, high-pitched wail swept over the assembly. Behind me a boy who had fainted cried out in fear with the return of consciousness.

The witch-doctor had disappeared behind a crude curtain of woven fronds. It was this drapery which I thought to be a part of the back wall, that had enabled the diabolical couple to make their first appearance so suddenly. Now he re-appeared dragging by one withered, crippled arm a small, terrified boy. The youth's eyes were wild with fright. His mouth opened and closed, the cords on his neck strained in effort, but no sound came.

"Labum." This time it was the witch-doctor who repeated the name of the dead warrior. .

Without more ceremony, the chief raised his club and brought it down with stunning force on the back of the crippled child's head. The blow was not calculated to kill. A fatal wound would have enabled the soul to escape. Rather, the blow was intended to render the boy unconscious that his stunned spirit might flow out unresistingly with the blood, to lie quietly in the bowl when caught and not to return to consciousness until resting safely in the stomachs of the warriors who sipped of the blood. Thus the boy's unearthly spirit would be in the spirit world with Labum, and his body spirit would be absorbed by the warriors who drank the blood, forming a brotherly spiritual alliance with the departed but still powerful Labum.

Before my horrified eyes the chief made a quick slash across the boy's throat. Blood spurted, but even before it could reach the floor the witch-doctor caught the flow in a coconut bowl. The bowl filled and ran over. A moan escaped the assemblage. The sight of hot blood robbed them of the last vestiges of humanity. They were beasts, held in check only by the awfulness of the ceremony.

Ten times was murder committed on the platform that night. Ten warriors had died; ten helpless cripples, the blind and halt and sick of the village were sacrificed. Then times bowls of blood were passed into the mass of sweating warriors, to be sipped avidly and passed on to the next. Mechanically I went though the motions, and once a shudder of revulsion caused the bowl to splash over and I tasted the warm, sticky saltiness on my lips and saw the dark stain spread on my shirt. I was sick, horribly shaken, but grimly fought down the nausea that threatened to betray me as a weakling.

At last, it must have been after midnight, the ceremony was over. The witch-doctor announced that the spirits were appeased, that the signs were favourable, and that all those wearing the clay on their faces would start at sunrise for the west. Silently we filed out. As I reached the doorway I turned back. The witch-doctor and the chief, like two ghouls in the fitful light were busy beheading the corpses of the sacrifice victims. They would keep the heads to divide the wisdom therein. On the morrow the villagers who remained behind would have the meat. Nothing was wasted, not even the souls.

The fresh air was like a tonic to me physically, but nothing could calm the mental turmoil through which my mind was struggling. I staggered to my tent like one drunk, to keep Leona awake all night with my sleepless groaning and tossing. At every moment when it looked like at last I might drop off to sleep, a fresh outburst of yelling in the village would bring me starting to my feet. All night the howling and drumming continued as warriors and women worked over fresh bow strings, pointed new arrows and split new knives out of bamboo. Dried meats were brought in and rationed out for the trip, but by dawn most of it had been eaten by the celebrators. Loudest of all were the young men about to take part in their first raid. It was their great day, for if they returned successful, with heads of their own taking, they would be allowed to leave the bachelor lodge and marry.

I refused to permit Leona to leave the tent to witness our daybreak departure. Exacting only her promise to remain in the tent for forty-eight hours to give the excited villagers a chance to calm down, I plunged out with the briefest of good-byes.

Most of the warriors were already on the west bank of the river. Willing paddlers ferried me across the oily-smooth stream, and as our canoes cut through the early morning mist and came within sight of those on shore a great shout went up. The great white tuan was here. The raid could go on.

I was surprised at the number of women present. At first I thought they were just seeing their men off, but as the morning wore on and the village lay farther and farther behind they made no move to leave. I asked Herman about it.

"Of course they come, tuan," he said. "They carry for us, they cook for us, and on the way home they carry the meat and the heads."

At noon we reached a small stream and stopped for lunch. I

took advantage of the pause to take stock of our force. We were about 250 strong, of which number probably 75 were women and 60 were men from my party. Wasbus was there, studiously avoiding me after the tongue lashing I had given him for getting drunk during my absence. In his home village of Merauke, Wasbus was regarded by his fellow natives as a good natured buffoon, but here among strangers he was posing as a great fighter, a man of prodious strength, bravery and cunning. He wasn't wanting me to give him another dressing down that might cause him to lose face.

No fires were permitted during the daylight hours, so those who had eaten their supply of dried meat on the preceding night had to content themselves with fruits. Late that afternoon we came to a small clearing in the jungle in which could be detected several droves of kangaroo. Immediately the word passed down the line, and a few seconds later the men were in position and began closing in on the game from three sides. The fourth side was left open, not so much to let the kangaroos escape as to give the hunters at least one direction in which they could shoot without killing each other. That the kangaroos weren't exterminated can be laid to the inaccuracy of the natives, and that the natives got any meat at all can be laid to the dumbness of the kangaroos. Shot at from one side, the *sahams* would jump for the other. A blast of arrows would turn them to the third side where they would be caught in another flight of arrows. About one beast in ten had enough sense or luck to try the unguarded fourth side. Given three chances at each flying streak of grey, the native managed to bag fifty out of a possible 500. This low score was not encouraging to me. If these men weren't any better shots than that, our chances weren't so good if we ran into a tribe of expert bowmen.

Not all the fault could be laid to the marksmen. Their arrows hastily tossed together for the head hunt, were of all shapes and sizes. Some were straight but unbalanced to such an extent they actually turned over in mid-air. Others were so badly bent their flight resembled that of a boomerang more than anything else. But the natives did not seem depressed. They had killed fifty kangaroos, and that was more than they could eat in two days. Certainly no more than that could be expected of anyone.

That night fires were lighted, bellies were filled and boastful talk ran high. Enough extra meat was put aside for the next day. This was cut into flakes and tied to the arm bands where it would be out of the way yet convenient to reach. For some reason meat was seldom packed in the carrying-bags, without which no native could appear, probably because it might grease up cherished feathers, bits of ribbon and other valued objects, always to be found in the bags, though this desire for cleanliness was seldom evidenced elsewhere.

For five days we worked our way west, studiously avoiding two large villages that lay in our path but which were regarded as too tough to attack. From time to time we stopped to hunt or fish. Everyone was gay and happy, a holiday spirit pervading everything that was done. It was hard to realise that the ultimate objective was the gathering of human heads and flesh.

Then abruptly, on the morning of the sixth day, the attitude of the party underwent a complete change. We were nearing our destination. Loud talking and laughing ceased. We moved forward cautiously, only the light swishing of brush marking our progress. A halt was called shortly after noon. Scouts were sent out in bands of five. The witch-doctor brought out his kit and began to don his regalia. I looked to my pistols and waited.

It was sundown when the first band of scouts returned. They were in a state of intense excitement. They had located the village without difficulty and found it to be ideally suited for our purposes. Not more than a hundred warriors in the whole village. Judging by the sleepy appearance of the village square, their selected victims were entirely unaware of our presence. The witch-doctor took the credit for this, claiming his magic had blinded their eyes to danger. Maybe it did.

It was estimated we were within three miles of the village, too close to permit the lighting of fires. Not that there was much danger of the smoke or flames being seen through the dense jungle, but in the moist, heavy air of a tropic night the odour of smouldering wood might carry for miles.

The plan of attack was simple. Under cover of darkness we would move forward to surround the village, approaching within a hundred yards of the huts on all sides. The witch-doctor's whistle was to be the signal for the drums to sound, launching the charge. After that it was every man for himself. Just one precaution was taken. In order that our men be able to recognise each other in the heat of battle our heads and faces were smeared with grey clay. This had a double purpose. Not only did it serve to make the black heads of the victims conspicuous in comparison, but it also made everybody in our army look alike, a little feature not without its advantages. A massacre provides an admirable opportunity to settle personal grudges between members of the same tribe, and many a grudge would be settled with a stone club from behind, if the grudgee only could recognise his sworn enemy. Those boys are like that.

By the time the last band of scouts had returned, we were ready to advance. A half-moon had risen to give us the ghostliest of illumination. In its thin light black shadows assumed the solidity of limbs and vines and I spent half my time clawing through nothing more substantial than empty air, all the while the actual obstructions casting the shadows were tearing at my face and clothes. To these difficulties of travel I was grateful. They kept my mind off the dreadful prospect ahead.

It might have been my imagination, it might have been the dank miasmic mist rising from the jungle floor, it might have been a score of things, but I am convinced those stinking savages with whom I travelled exuded the odour of death. We were sweating furiously, all of us, but the stench was not the normal scent of carefree natives on the trail. There was a heavy overtone to the effluvium that reeked of the charnel house. During all those long hours in which we slunk through the jungle like beasts it was this oppressive odour that grated most on my nerves.

It was with relief that I caught the redolence of burning eucalyptus bark, strong and close by. The column stopped while the chief and the witch-doctor conferred briefly with the scouts. Then came the order to spread out on both sides, in two wide-spaced columns that were to come together on the far side of the village immediately before us.

I took my place with the chief and the witch-doctor as the men slipped by like phantoms, one to the left, one to the right until there were fewer than twenty men in the main column behind us. Then abruptly the two side columns stopped. The village was surrounded. The chief turned to me.

"You go first with the magic thunder bow," he suggested.

"Nothing doing," I replied firmly. "I follow you."

His eyes narrowed, his mask of grey clay crinkling eerily in the pale light. His hand, I noticed, was gripped tightly over his stone axe. I placed my hands on my guns significantly. "I follow," I repeated.

The chief turned away, but not before I caught the gleam of a snarl on his black teeth. "I 'll have to watch him," I thought.

A deathly silence settled over the jungle as we began the long wait for dawn. The drip of condensing moisture sounded like hail as it splashed upon heavy fronds as resonant as drum heads.

Suddenly there was a brief scuffle behind me. I was shoved back by a heavy body, and as I threw myself clear a huge figure hurtled over me to fall upon another figure struggling on the ground. Not a sound was uttered, but the silence was electric with terrific force. Abruptly, the struggle ceased.

"I am sorry, sombe-onim," I heard a hoarse whisper I recognised as belonging to Herman. I wondered vaguely where he had come from.

The chief rose, spitting angrily, "What are you doing here?" he snarled.

"I 'm guarding the white brother."

"What 's the trouble?" I broke in harshly.

"I thought the sombe-onim was an enemy," lied Herman. "I did not know the sombe-onim would be behind the white brother with an axe."

In a flash I had the whole picture. Herman, unbeknownst to me, had been sticking to my heels like a faithful dog all evening. And when the treacherous chief had tried to get behind me Herman had simply picked him up and tossed him out of the way. I saw also that the chief had no intention of my returning to the village in one piece. The episode of the fire-crackers was not forgotten nor forgiven.

"You belong on the other side of the village," retorted the chief furiously.

"Be silent," I said. "He belongs with me. If you want to keep a whole skin you will leave him and me alone."

At that moment the air was split by the shrill blast of the witch-doctor's whistle. I was suddenly aware that the darkness was yielding to grey, that the outlines of trees were distinct. After that my impressions were vivid splashes interspersed with long periods of blankness. I recall hearing the rumble of a score of drums and thinking how odd and flat they sounded with the drum heads slack from moisture. Then I recall the stinging slash of a saw-edged coconut frond across my face as I was swept forward with the charge. The din was frightful. The very ferocity of the shrieks and howls of the rushing warriors was enough to paralyse the sleep-muddled villagers. I was yelling myself, yelling in a voice I could not recognise as my own. Then at the very edge of the clearing I saw my chance and plunged headlong into a dense growth of lianas. The blood-crazed horde swept by.

Like packs of wolves bursting upon their kill the head hunters swarmed across the clearing in a mad rush, yelling like demons. There was no circling of the huts to gain entrance through the doorway. Swinging their stone clubs like battering rams they crashed their way through the fragile walls like avenging furies. The hut directly in front of me went down like a pile of straw. To the yells of the attackers were now added the screams of the terrified villagers, screams that rose high and piercingly, to be cut off sharply in the middle as death struck here, there and everywhere at once.

The attack swept through the huts practically without opposition and rolled out into the square. Through the gap left by the demolished hut I could see a wall of resistance suddenly pile up as the survivors of the first rush found themselves forced into knot in the centre of the square. Hard pressed from all sides and with no loophole for escape, they fought like demons. The surprise over, their minds cleared of sleep, they began demonstrating that the ferocity of the Digoels was not over-estimated.

Our men were utterly insane with blood-lust. Their only impulse was to fall upon the circle of survivors and destroy them tooth and nail. They could not stand off and fight. They had to get in there, clawing, biting, hammering. Kill, kill, kill. Back to back, the Digoels beat down each wave of maddened Marind-Anims with their stone clubs. No formed square of soldiers ever showed greater resistance, or fought back with more telling effect. The pile of dead grew until the Marind-Anims were fighting over the bodies of their own brothers.

If any commands were shouted, they were lost in the bedlam of screams, but suddenly our men fell back. A wild scramble for bows dropped in the excitement of club warfare, and the next second the air whined with flight after flight of arrows aimed into the densely packed mass of Digoels. They couldn't take it. Screaming with pain and fear they broke, scattering every way possible. It was a chance for our men to cut them down practically without resistance, but by now this was no army of organised fighters. It was each man for himself, and as the desperate villagers plunged for freedom the Marind-Anims fell back in terror.

And now it was my turn to feel the full horror of the raid. Bearing down on my clump of lianas came a group of Digoels, their eyes wild with fear, their stone clubs whirling in murderous circles. The line of Marind-Anims between me and them was cut through as though blown down by the wind. So close to me was the fighting I could hear the crush of skulls as the stone clubs rose and fell. The next moment I was on my feet, both guns blazing.

In that pandemonium the roar of my guns meant nothing. Fear was already so overpowering there was no adding to it. A cannon fired in their midst would have gone unnoticed. Nothing short of death would stop them. With less than twelve feet separating us I began cutting them down. I was back in the World War now, coldly killing with the mechanical efficiency of a trained soldier.

My guns were bucking in my hands when the first wave

rolled over me. I never relaxed my grip. I started slugging, the gun in each hand lending crushing force to my blows. The stench of bodies struggling against me infuriated me. A stone club striking a crushing blow on my left shoulder dropped me in a tangle of vines, but I was so beside myself with rage I fought my way back to my feet unconscious of the pain. Three times I swung my injured arm in jolting haymakers that cleared a circle around me. I turned to the right, but pulled my punch. I recognised the clay-whitened head of one of our own men. Other clay-daubed heads were in the brush with me.

Another rush of Digoels carried us still further into the jungle. I had not time to reload my pistols. I could only fight with the clubbed butts. But in brush fighting I held the advantage. I needed only a straight shot to score a knock-out; the natives must swing their clubs from the shoulder, a feat nearly impossible with lianas clinging to every move. I went berserk. The stab of a bamboo knife in my chest brought me swinging around in a whirl of fury. I saw a face close to mine saw it flatten beneath my gun butt, saw the body fall. I saw other bodies on the ground, and still others coming up. I saw all this clearly, but what I did about it seemed to be done by somebody else. I remember seeing a club whirl toward me, and remember the start of surprise I felt when I found that it was my right arm that was holding the native off, that it was my gun that came up stained with blood after the native dropped.

Suddenly there was no one left to fight. I stood upright, swaying on my feet, punch-drunk. Around me I could hear groans, subdued blows, painful gasps for breath indicating the fighting was still going on, but I seemed to be alone save for the dead and unconscious that lay in grotesque heaps. I drew a long, shuddering breath. As I did so a rattan vine resting against my cheek quivered like a jerked rope. Without thinking, I threw myself flat. This instinctive re-action saved my life. A stone axe whistled down so close it smashed a first aid kit on my belt. I twisted on my back and lashed up with both feet. I caught a clay daubed figure squarely in the mid-riff, hurling it back six feet where it hung on a liana like a knocked-out boxer on the ropes.

I had no time to scramble to my feet before a giant burst between us like a whirlwind of death. Hack-slash rose his club. There was a horrible crunching sound, and the next second the victim of my kick was battered to the ground, his head a shapeless pulp. I looked up into the contorted, almost unrecognisable face of Herman. His chest was rising and falling in great, laboured gasps. The cords of his neck were swelled like ropes. His heavy blood-stained club twitched in his mighty hand like a twig. It was a full minute before he could control himself to speak. In the meantime I lay on my back like a broken doll, too surprised to move.

"The *sombe-onim*," he said at last. He was suddenly terrified at what he had done.

"The *sombe-onim*," I repeated incredulously.

Herman nodded. I climbed shakily to my feet and peered at the corpse. There was no identifying the face, but the body and trappings were certainly that of the chief. I laughed weakly.

"Herman, you're a good boy," I managed to get out. Small praise, but I could see it was all Herman needed. He gave the body a kick with his foot.

"He would eat his own mother," he said in what amounted to the acme of cannibal humour. "He was no good."

We had no time to read obituary notices over the dead chief. Already screams of agony and shouts of crazed warriors in the village announced that the head hunt had entered the second phase. Again I wished to avoid any participation in the inhuman activities but again I was forced to take part against my wishes. Warriors returning from the pursuit of the fleeing Digoels swept us back into the village.

If the raid had been brutal and ferocious beyond description, the aftermath was more so. Everywhere the ground was strewn with bodies, but it is the nature of primitive warfare that the wounded greatly outnumber the dead. A stone club is a stunning, bone-crushing weapon, but unless the blow falls squarely on the head it is not necessarily fatal. For every corpse there were a dozen groaning, screaming men with shattered shoulders, crushed ribs, broken backs and arms and legs. Some were pierced through with round-pointed arrows, the shafts protruding from the wounds and plugging the flow of blood, thereby prolonging life for additional tortures.

These things I saw first because they were the most obvious. But not the most horrifying. In the huts, emptied of warriors in the first rush, still remained the women and children, cowering under mats or the litter of demolished walls. These were now being dragged out by the hair or the feet, whatever part of the body presented itself first. Babies were just swung by the heels against a tree or the hard packed earth. Children of six or older were tossed into an empty hut to be taken back to the village as captives. The women and girls were temporarily spared.

By this time the sun was just breaking through the trees. Not a half hour had passed since the drums had first sounded their roll of death. Yet in that brief time an entire village had been wiped out. But our men had not come just to wipe out a village. They had come for heads. And they were getting them. All over the village the ghoulish business was going on, not systematically but with inhuman ferocity.

The young men who had to bring home a head before they could assume the status of warriors fought over the dead and the dying like starving vultures. They had killed to get the heads; they were ready to kill to keep them. The older warriors were no less determined to go home with trophies, and with two survivors for every corpse, the only way to even the score was to kill each other. This they were apparently set on doing. More than once that morning fights over heads ended fatally, a circumstance that was not regretted provided the new head was not bashed in.

In cases where the victim was already dead, the ceremony was brief. A quick slash across the throat with a bamboo knife, and then a deep cut to the spinal column as close to the shoulders as possible. When all the neck muscles were cut the head was seized in a hammer-lock and given a sharp wrench that snapped the vertebrae with a report like a pistol shot. Clawing in the crowd surrounding each decapitation would be the favourite woman of the knife wielder, and to her would be tossed the head. She would clasp it to her bosom with both arms, and nothing short of death would get her to release her hold.

Victims still unconscious or sorely wounded were accorded a slightly different treatment. Before they were separated from their skulls they had to produce some sound more intelligible than a moan. The last sound made would be used as a name. If it were a young man who laid claim to an unconscious Digoel, he would grimly fight off all contenders, in the meantime doing everything possible to restore his prize to consciousness. If the wait was not too long for his short-lived patience, he would be rewarded by groans and mumblings as his victim showed signs of coming to life. As soon as two coherent syllables were pronounced, the young man would repeat them in a loud voice, and slit his victim's throat. Thereafter the youthful warrior would drop the name used during his adolescence, and be known by the name born of blood. Older warriors would use the same process to secure names for their offspring, these names to be used until such a time as the off-spring would grow up and carve out names for themselves.

The work of harvesting the heads lasted little more than half an hour. By that time the odour of blood hung heavy on the air, an overpowering odour that drugged the mind and drove the senses mad. Reason had fled with the first drum beat but now followed an exhibition of violent, mass insanity so utterly revolting not even the ruthlessness of modern civilisation in a fanatic mood or the beastliness of the lowest of scavenging animals could match it. Absolutely berserk, men and women fell upon the corpses in an abandonment of perverted lust. They grovelled in blood-soaked mud, hacked the bodies with bamboo knives to rub their arms and legs in the freshly opened wounds, smeared themselves from head to foot with gory filth, and rolled on the ground in incontrollable convulsions, drunk on the powerful stimulant of mass-murder.

The place became an abbatoir gone mad. Arms and legs were cut through and wrenched off by brute strength, Hearts and livers were yanked forth and tossed in a pile with the rest of the meat that was to be taken home for the feast. Spinal columns were battered free of the ribs with stone axes to take their place on the growing heap. And when the dead were disposed of, the lust-crazed natives turned their attention to the living.

The third phase was the most repulsive of all. As though at a given signal the women were dragged from the hut in which they had been confined, thrown to the ground and attacked. Rape only whetted the perverted instincts of these savages. Every form of sadism, flagellation, and related sexual abnormalities were evidenced on all sides. The men out-numbered the women five to one, and, as in the case of the heads, the fighting over who was to get who was appalling. Sometimes these fights were settled in favour of the woman, that is, she would be killed on the spot. Even so her body would be horribly violated, not once but several times. It was mid-afternoon before the orgy came to a close. What few women who survived were despatched by women of our own party. They had kept discreetly to the background during the carnal riot, but now came slinking forth to secure such portions of meat as would aid them in their own child bearing.

During all this time I had remained at the edge of the village, my two guns ready for whatever might turn up. There was no telling what these bucks might do in their insane frenzy. Right before my eyes I had seen father kill son for possession of a head and brother kill brother for a woman. That they might, in their inflamed condition, try to add my head to the pile was not only possible but entirely probable. Herman, Wasbus, and a few loyal men of my own crew stuck with me, though the temptation to join into the festivities was almost over-whelming. Once early in the morning, Herman had slipped away to return a few moments later with a head which he placed at my feet.

"Yours," he said, and pointed to my guns.

"You can have it," I said as firmly as I could.

He grinned widely and retrieved the head from the dust. He was still clutching it fondly under his arm when a curious thing happened. Over the screaming, shrieking bedlam sudden-ly fell a silence as abrupt and complete as to be stunning in its force. Natives rolling on the ground staggered to their feet, staring about them fearfully. Others stood stock still, listening for something that was not to be heard outside their own minds. The voice of fear. Uneasily they began to sidle toward me, aware for the first time that something was missing. Somebody called for the chief in a terrified voice. There was no answer. Panic rippled through the crowd in a perceptible wave. That was what was missing, leadership.

It was time for me to step in before the panic bacame a riot.

"The *sombe-onim* is dead," I stated loudly, my voice echoing against the silent walls of the clearing. "I am your *sombe-onim* (chief)."

This had the desired effect. The milling around stopped, but their was no lifting the weight of terror with words. Those boys knew what they had done, knew what they could expect in retaliation if the few Digoel warriors who had escaped in the morning returned with an armed force from neighbouring villages.

"Collect your weapons," was my next order. "We're going home."

Without a word I turned and led the way into the jungle, preceded by Herman and closely guarded in the rear by Wasbus and his men. There was no excited hub-bub as the men and women shouldered the heads, and the meat. Just an apprehensive silence. I set a fast pace, but soon the panic-stricken natives were crowding on the heels of my men, urging a faster get-away. I held them back, knowing full well that if I increased the pace they would want still more speed until at last the retreat would become a disorganised stampede.

However, I did not hold them to a snail's pace. I was only too well aware that their unconcealed terror was not without foundation. Too many Digoels had managed to break away to leave the situation entirely re-assuring. Once they got on our trail, they would be after us faster than wolves on the scent. Then would come a dawn, and the morning's events would be repeated, with us on the receiving side.

We ate on the march, plucking fruit as we passed. Bananas make good travelling food. If any meat was eaten, it was human meat, and if it was human meat it was eaten raw. We built no fires. At night we stopped sleeping where we fell. Guards were posted at the head and tail of the column, though what good they were I could not tell. They refused to leave the main body more than ten feet, and as an attacking force always approached silently to within a hundred yards and then

Imo Killer

Beau Brummel of
Frederik Hendrik Island

Fishing Trap

*When a fish is sighted in shallow water it takes but a
second to slap this conical shaped trap over it*

Dead Child

Her face painted with white clay, this Koembe River mother mourns the passing of her child. She holds the baby thus for days so its first spirit won't get lonely in the new world

Debs and Sub-debs

Those at the foot are the village trouble-makers

announced its charge in no uncertain terms, the best the guards could do was announce our doom about three seconds after it was sealed.

The trip that had taken five days going was accomplished in two returning. On the morning of the second day I let five of the fastest men go ahead to announce our return. This would serve a double purpose. If they got through all right the women would have the fires going and the stones heating in preparation for the feast by the time we arrived. If they didn't get through we would hear sounds of conflict and know there was an ambush ahead. They got through, for which I was greatly relieved.

M

CHAPTER XIV

SKYSCRAPERS AND DEBUTANTES

ALL the way back fear had kept our force pretty well in line, but once we were safe in our own village the lid was off. The boys were home, with meat, and with heads. If a few were missing, they could be mourned for later. Right now the main thing on the programme was a celebration. For this the women were already prepared. Bamboo containers of sagoware made with coconut water had been brewing ever since we left. Coconut shells of wati lined the shelves of every hut, and on the hot stones was a huge loaf of sago covering nearly fifty square feet.

I was the chief, and as such I had no time to waste on women on so great an occasion. Beyond one fleeting glance that assured me that Leona was all right, and a shouted instruction to Achmed to keep her out of this, I stayed with my mob. I had far more influence by staying with them than I would have trying to handle them by remote control from my tent. As long as I was in direct contact, I could stop anything before it got started, but once I dropped my leadership, even for a moment, there was no telling what might happen. I was sure of only one thing, if something did start, the chances of stopping it were nil. Inflamed as these boys were, we could wipe out half the tribe, but the other half would get us.

The men who took part in the raid played out after about three rounds of wati, but the ones who had remained at home took up the torch with all the revolting ferocity that had marked the second phase of the head hunt. With the arrival of darkness a hint of organisation crept into the festivities. It was like a madhouse under the directorship of the most violent of the patients, but at least under directorship.

A never-ending procession of women and old men plied the fires with dried fronds until the flames threatened to destroy the huts. At one end of the village a hastily erected bamboo platform twenty feet high formed a stage upon which was performed the *nanoa zi* (dance of the skulls), with young bucks cavorting crazily about the edge to the accompaniment of a furious beating of drums, waving the fresh heads by the hair. When the platform crashed, severely injuring three boys, they were butchered on the spot and their meat passed on to the women who were in charge of the feast.

The dance was now resumed on the ground. There was no pattern to it, no attempt to follow the beat of the drums. In fact there was no rhythm to the drum beats. Each drummer banged away at his own discretion, and as long as he banged hard and fast there was no complaint. Men and women alike took part in the dance, a preliminary get-together in preparation for the sex-orgy to follow. For this was not the festival of the *wemanuwe*. This was just the first round, the warming up period. The meat would not be cooked for another twenty-four hours.

I snatched my sleep while I could get it, protected by Herman on one side and Wasbus on the other. They were never separated from me more than three feet during the three days when lust ruled the village. To this fact I owe my life. Without their loyalty I would have been a dead duck. Wasbus stuck by me because he was jealous of Herman; Herman stuck by me because he was loyal, the only native in Dutch New Guinea whom I could trust absolutely.

The dance was still going on the next morning. It never stopped for seventy-two hours, a primitive marathon dance in which exhausted revellers were relieved by fresh recruits who needed the exercise to pack down the food already eaten to make room for more. By this time the odour of cooking flesh permeated the air, heightening the anticipation of the events of the evening.

There was one task yet to be done before the celebration would be officially underway. That was the dressing of the heads. This had to be done in the presence of myself as *sombe-onim* and the witch-doctor. Herman didn't like the witch-doctor. Two or three times he broached plans for getting rid of him, but there was a lot I didn't know about the magic profession and I preferred to keep an old hand around where I could keep an eye on him.

The heads, there were sixty of them, were piled up in a hideous mess. Seizing one as casually as he would select a coconut, the witch-doctor made a quick incision up the back of the neck and half-way up the scalp. The two edges were then pried loose, the flaps seized with both hands, and the skin was peeled off like a butcher skins a rabbit. The ears were cut off whole. No particular attention was paid to the eyes, nose and mouth as these holes would be sewed up with rattan after the skin had dried.

With the skin off, the flesh was carefully scraped from the skull and the brains dug out. These parts were the choicest on the body and were reserved for the bravest warriors, the chief and the witch-doctor. It was believed that great wisdom would follow the eating of such selected viands. The skulls were then placed in the sun to be picked clean by the ants, and the skins were stretched over balls of grass to dry. The curing process lasts about a week, after which time the dry skins are soaked in water until pliant, then pulled over the skulls from which they were removed. If they get mixed up a little, that's all right. The back flaps are laced shut, the neck skin pulled tight across the base of the skull, and the nose, mouth and eyes sewed up. With this completed, the head is above a smouldering fire where it is smoke-cured and dried. In that condition it will keep indefinitely.

By the time the first steps in this gruesome business was completed, the villagers were ready for the real festival of the *wemanuwe*, or the eating of human flesh. The warriors were decked out in their gaudiest of head-dresses. Huge piles of birds of paradise feathers, gorgeous plumes of egrets, colourful leaves, flowers, butterflies, anything with brilliant colours was collected and worked into their crowning glories. The witch-doctor out-did everyone else. His head-dress was nearly seven feet tall, and so heavy it had to be supported by his shoulders as well as his head. Much of the weight could be attributed to the human bones and dried heads he had fitted into the design.

I won't go into the details of that second night. They were repulsive beyond description. Three times we had to beat down impulsive young bucks, drunk on blood, who sought to bring themselves great glory by adding my head to the pile. One curious thing I noticed. The backbones that had been so laboriously carried back from the raid were strung up all over the place, festive streamers to add a gay note to the feast. That was their only purpose. The Japanese use lanterns, the Europeans use flags, the Americans use bunting and crepe paper, and the Marind-Anims use backbones. Each man to his own tastes.

By the third night of continuous drunken revelry, the villagers began to show signs of the strain. Fewer dancers were circling the fires, more men were sick in their huts, the wati and sagoware were exhausted and food was running low. That is the one sure thing to stop a festival, the absence of food and drink. But still I dared not call the thing quits. I waited until the last drum beat died away, and the drummer had fallen asleep over his instrument before giving the sign to Herman and Wasbus that all was over, that they could get some sleep. All three of us had been on the absolute peak of nervous tension for forty-eight hours, and the let-down was terrific.

I staggered into my tent like a drunken man just as the third dawn since my return began to tint the sky. I hadn't spoken to Leona for ten days, and I couldn't speak now. I just collapsed. I don't know now whether I fell asleep or dropped unconscious. I think it must have been the latter, because after witnessing the things I had, sleep should have been impossible.

It took three days for the festival to run its course, and it took five days to recover from it, five days in which I learned what a poor little rich girl could do amongst savages when she got around to it. Scarcely an hour went by without some woman coming in to my wife for treatment for herself or an ailing child. Men, too, came to have their ailments treated, and all of them evidenced the greatest of confidence and respect. It soon became clear that in that village Leona was chief, witch-doctor, good spirit and everything else. What she said went, and though her only prescription was castor oil or quinine tablets, she got results.

One thing really established her and that was the delivery of a child from a mother who heretofore had lost every infant at birth. Responding to cleanliness and careful treatment, the child was still alive at this late date, a miracle if there ever was one for the belief was generally established that the woman was possessed of an evil spirit who prevented her from having living babies.

Leona's triumph was not only a physical victory but a spiritual one as well, and when one is powerful in both planes at once there is no stopping her.

There was no longer any question of our getting all the canoes we needed, what with me being chief of the village, and Leona outranking me in influence, but there was one other serious obstacle. When we pulled out, we would be leaving a village leaderless and with only a witch-doctor in whom they no longer had much confidence. I decided to settle the matter by making Herman chief, a position he was eminently fitted to fill. I couldn't help thinking at the same time that with Herman in the chief's hut, the fate of the witch-doctor would not remain long in doubt.

To instal him properly and lastingly, to establish his position beyond all peradventure of a doubt I decided to put on a little show. The witch-doctor, aware of the way the wind was blowing, had come out the night before with one of his dreams, a dream, he claimed that come to him as the result of eating a lot of new heads, always a powerful magic. In this dream he saw Herman as a dead man within a week. He had every intention of seeing that this dream came true, too, I could tell that. So I came out with a dream of my own.

When a crowd had assembled I pointed out that my departure would leave them chiefless. "However," I said, "I have had a dream in which I saw Herman as your leader, shrewd, a great hunter and a greater warrior. Under him I saw this village become powerful and have many heads."

The witch-doctor was plainly shaken by this statement, and I saw him exchange glances with some of his henchmen. "There was a sign by which you would know him as your chief," I continued. "I am going to call this sign to appear before you now."

The natives were open-mouthed in awe. By the time my preparations were completed, every soul in the village was gathered in a hard-packed knot around me. Before me, enclosed in a circle drawn in the dust, was a small pile of kindling, but concealed beneath the wood was about a hundred feet of highly inflammable film. I beckoned to the witch-doctor.

"Get water and pour it over this wood."

He went, not too happy about it, and fetched a coconut shell full of water. "Pour it on," I commanded, "And get more. Lots of it."

When the pile of kindling had been thoroughly drenched I turned to the witch-doctor. "Will that burn now?"

He agreed that it would not burn.

"It will burn," I stated. "It will burn because that is a sign that Herman will be a good chief." Herman looked pretty glum at this. He saw his chances going glimmering. The rest of the natives looked incredulous.

I snapped on my cigarette lighter, potent magic in itself. Just as I was ready to apply it to the film a drop of water fell on the flame, putting it out for good. Herman's face dropped a foot. Not daunted, I struck a match. This time I was successful. The film caught, flashed up in a sheet of flame that burned all the hair of my arm, and launched Herman on an inauguration ceremony unequalled in the history of Dutch New Guinea. He was one great man after that.

There was nothing for it but he would himself conduct us down the river as far as the next village where we could get more canoes to take us to the next, and so on from village to village down to Tannah Tinggi, approximately sixty miles away. The head hunt and ensuing ceremonies had delayed us about two weeks, and I could see Schultz stewing around wondering what had happened to us. I knew if we didn't show up pretty soon he was apt to turn the country upside down on a little head hunt of his own.

It was good to be back in a canoe again with Wasbus and his crew of giants, minus one who vanished during the head hunt. I selected another big buck to take the place of the missing one, and began then and there to put them through a period of intensive training. I knew Schultz would be waiting to match his boys with mine, and I knew he wasn't training them on strained fruit juices.

We were travelling through dangerous country now, Digoel territory. However, I had the assurance of Herman that the first couple of villages were little ones. That being the case, I knew our show of force was enough to compel peace in the first village. After that we could send Digoel messengers ahead with presents for the chiefs of the larger village and thus buy peaceful passage.

We made the first village by evening. There was some alarm, but my peaceful overtures soon restored order. The language was different from that of the Marind-Anims but the distinction lay mainly in the suffixes, most words having common roots. The big difficulty lay in the speech itself. The Digoels clacked. They talked as though their tongues were steel springs against which a certain amount of pressure had to be placed before they snapped. Eight words were about all we needed to make our wants known, and with those eight I was content. I never could learn to snap my tongue around any more words even if I did find out what they were.

The next morning Herman and I parted, and I must confess he was one native I was sorry to see go. He had twenty men with him, two men to each big war canoe, and they were making the water fly. I remained in the village for two hours after he left, just to make sure none of the Digoels started out in pursuit. At last, sure that if Herman kept up the pace he had started out with he would never be overtaken, I gave the word and we started out into unknown country.

The river began to widen shortly after we left, and soon we were cruising through the flat lowlands of the Rain Forest. At noon we saw our first stilt village, but we did not stop. The village was a small one of two or three huts set on bamboo poles about fifteen feet high to allow for flood waters.

That afternoon, however, we arrived at a real stilt village. There were a dozen huts visible, each of them large enough to be a regular community lodge. And they were really up in the air. The lowest one was thirty feet above the ground, and the highest was a good forty. The height of a three-storey building.

In spite of the gifts I had sent in advance, and our obviously peaceful intentions, my boys and the villagers had to sniff around each other like stray dogs for about fifteen minutes before we were accepted. Once we were accepted, however, we were practically forgotten. At least it looked like we were, but that was just a ruse. Those Digoels are the cleverest thieves this side of a Singapore pickpocket, and their indifference was just an attempt to get as close to our goods as they could without attracting attention. They got away with it too. In spite of the strictest guard, I quickly learned that the only way I could be sure I had everything when I left a Digoel village was to ransack every hut immediately before departure. They were good thieves, but the only place they could hide their loot was in their huts lest some of their own tribesmen steal it from them if they carted it off into the jungle.

The skyscraper huts fascinated me. I had to get them on my film, and I didn't see how I was going to do it. The river was wide enough at this point, but the far shore was filled with mangroves that waded halfway across the stream, making shooting between the trunks impossible. Even with a wide-angle lens the best I could do was get in about half the bamboo posts. Of course I could pan up, but that was not satisfactory as it would not show the huts in relationship to the ground. I finally decided the only way I could make it was to cut a swath through the jungle for a hundred yards or so and then climb a tree with my camera. This was done, but not without protest. The Digoels did not want that swath. It would provide too nice an avenue down which might sweep an attacking party. a few shells and some beads soon convinced them the opening was not as bad as they had at first figured on.

While my men were busy with the axes, I made a close examination of the huts. Some of the largest, I noticed, were built in the crown of a tree, bolstered around the edges with giant bamboo, six to eight inches in diameter at the base and tapering but slightly all the way up. The huts creaked and groaned and swayed with each passing breeze, but just how much they swayed I could not tell from the ground.

I walked over to another house, noting the meanwhile the curious little mounds of clay, shaped like beehives, between the forest of poles supporting each hut. Two men were at work replacing a corner post, the corner above sagging dangerously over thin air as they worked. Their post hole digger was an ingenious affair, consisting of a hollow butt of bamboo the exact size of the post they were going to insert in the hole. The end had been charred in a fire until the edges were sharp and fire-hardened. This was slammed into the ground with full force, penetrating about three inches with each stroke. The digger would then be pulled up, the disk of earth knocked out and the process repeated until a hole about five feet deep was dug. Into this the corner post, forty feet high but weighing less than a hundred pounds, was snuggly fitted. The men swarmed up the polished shaft like monkeys, strained a little to raise the sagging corner as near to level as possible, and lashed the corner joists fast with wet rattan. Not a nail or a peg in the whole place.

Noticing the centre post was equipped with cross pieces to provide easy access for women loaded down with food or firewood, I started up. After a couple of rungs gave way, I began to have less confidence in my ladder. Thirty feet up and the ground began to look a long way away. Another ten feet and I felt like a sailor climbing the foremast in the midst of a hurricane with the shrouds blown away. The whole structure was swaying back and forth so violently I couldn't tell if the groans were coming from me or from the creaking bamboo. Closing my eyes, and me an aviator of twenty years standing, I made the last ten feet in what amounted to a rush. I burst through the hole in the floor with a gasp of relief, but it was about five minutes before I regained my breath.

When I stood up I learned another thing about these aeries. You had to ride them. Everyone is familiar with the whip of a bamboo pole. Now figure out what the effect would be if you uprighted a dozen of them and stuck a bushel basket on top. The slightest wind would set that basket to swaying around in the wildest of gyrations, and that is just the way these huts re-acted, on an enlarged scale. More than once, clinging to a pole and peering through the hole, I saw us sway out beyond the base of the outside poles. And just when I was getting my sea legs adjusted to a side roll the wind would veer and I would be bucking a pitch and a roll that was something to behold. A ship has to wallow around a little before coming out of a trough, but these huts just snap back as though nothing had happened. And when they snap they aren't fooling. They can get in three dives, a roll and a couple of pitches in the time it would take a ship to nose over the crest of a single wave.

Now this would be bad enough if I had solid decks beneath me but there is nothing solid in the whole house. Solidity requires weight, and weight is one thing these houses aren't built for. The floors are made of split bamboo, round side up, and if there are three or four inches of space between the floorboards, that just means you aren't supposed to walk in those places. The idea is to curl your toes around the planking, determine where you want to go and wait for the house to list in the right direction. When you get your slant you just let yourself go and unless the wind suddenly changes, you should make it. It's a sort of combination tight-rope walking and log-rolling conducted on high seas.

Under such circumstances the danger of fire is great, especially as a great deal of the cooking is done in the house. However, this is provided for by a swinging fireplace built over a four-foot hole in the floor. No matter what angle the house may assume, the fireplace is always level. The hearth consists of a flat table of bamboo liberally covered with clay and slung at each corner by a rope of rattan. In the event of sudden flames endangering the dry thatched roof, the ropes are hurriedly slashed and the whole works drop through the hole in the floor. It is the occasional flashes of cleverness like this that enable us to see how our ancestors managed to pull through the Stone-Age. Judging by what I had already seen I was ready to admit that the prospect for the human race of 20,000 years ago were pretty slim, but then something like this comes along and changes my whole opinion.

There was nothing for it but Leona had to see the inside of one of these huts for herself. Climbing was out of the question. A rope sling was the next best bet, and this we tried. What I overlooked in permitting this method of ascent was the sway of the hut. With a deep groan the structure would lean out over empty space. Leona would start to swing out, but before she could complete her arc the hut would snap to the opposite side. Stopped short, Leona would swing back, to bang up against a post before starting in another direction. The natives overhead were pulling like mad, and with every hoist they shortened the arc and speeded up the pendulum. Leona was about to be battered to a pulp on the posts when a woman slid down a pole to her rescue. She caught Leona in mid-air as she swung by, steadied her and then shinnied up the pole along side, keeping pace with the hoisters. Leona never did like those houses after that. She was bruised and sore from her contacts with the posts, but where she was really sore was where the woman had a hold of her shoulder. That native girl had a grip like a pair of ice tongs, and where her fingers dug in there were black and blue spots for days.

Back on the ground again, Leona was content to call it a day. I busied myself shooting a few hundred feet of film, mostly head shots showing distinguishing characteristics between the Digoels and the Marind-Anims. Even while I was shooting it I had to keep one eye on the finder and the other on the natives lest they steal the film out of the camera while I was still grinding. A few more shots of samples of craftsmanship and I was through until the boys finished clearing out enough trees to enable me to shoot the skyscrapers. In the meantime my curiosity was again aroused by the peculiar beeless hives under the huts.

Putting my sign language to the acid test, I endeavoured to find out what purpose they served, if any. I was getting nowhere fast when a young buck, decidedly lighter in colour than the Digoels, spoke to me in the dialect of the Marind-Anims. He was, I soon learned, a member of a Marind-Anim tribe. Kidnapped at an early age during a raid on his village, he had been brought up by his captors and was now accepted as an equal in the village.

The beehives, he told me, were graves. Whenever a member of a household died, he was buried beneath his hut, half in the ground, half above ground. The bodies were planted head first. There was a curious reason for this. The head was believed to be the seed from which anything might grow, depending upon which dema took possession of the body. The coconut dema was the most favoured because the palms grew up to yield many more heads, but any tree or plant would serve the purpose. According to this belief, the trees and plants were all growing upside down, the branches representing the arms and legs, fingers and toes, while the hair of the head became the roots. The legs of the corpse sticking above the ground were capped with a wall of clay to prevent growth while the village was still occupied. One had only to visit a deserted village and see how the trees had sprung up where the graves had crumbled away to realise the truth of these statements, my guide assured me.

I pointed out several smaller monuments of baked clay resembling short, concrete fence posts and asked their purpose.

"Those are the graves of children," I was informed. "They are wrapped in leaves, then rolled in clay and baked, They are so small they would not keep long enough to grow if they are not first baked. That would be too bad."

That was all I cared to learn about that subject. I dismissed my guide with a few beads and joined my tree choppers in the jungle. They had made good headway, most of the trees being palms whose soft trunks gave way before the sharp axes and klewangs like rotten wood. The sun was still high enough to make shooting practical by the time a pathway was cleared. Some beautiful cloud effects piled up in the northwest giving the scene a grandeur entirely out of keeping with the smell. It was worth climbing a gummy eucalyptus to get even though I had to throw away my clothes after I got down. That red, sticky gum that leaks out all over a eucalyptus like pitch out of a pine tree just won't come off.

We were off again the next morning with a fresh relay of canoes, rented at the price of a string of beads and a couple of dozen shells. We made excellent time downstream. About every ten miles we would pass a small village, but seldom were any natives in sight though we knew we were being watched from a hundred places of concealment. Shortly after noon we observed a column of smoke rising over the trees on the southern horizon. By its density I knew it had to come from a smoke-stack, and the only smokestack within 500 miles had to be on our steam launch, Captain Gustav Schultz commanding.

If you think that didn't look good, after months of jungle, you don't know what mosquitos, leeches, fleas, stinking natives and soggy mud beds can do to your opinion of what constitutes a luxury. An hour later and we were within range of Schultz's bellowing welcome, a blast of joy that scared my Digoels half to death. The second leg of our journey was over.

Celebrating ran high that night. Leona celebrated by going to sleep on an air mattress on a level cot on a level floor protected on all sides by arrow-proof wooden walls. Schultz and I celebrated by sitting on deck, a Malay on each side of us ready to anticipate our needs for fresh drinks thirty seconds before we needed them, and the natives celebrated by feasting and drinking with their new-found friends on shore. The only ones not joining in the festivities were the Digoels who had transported us there. They were somewhere upstream, paddling madly for home, speeded on their way by a blast from our whistle released by Schultz when he caught two of them below decks trying to steal the hot door off the fire-box. Those boys thought all the demas from hell were after them when that whistle broke loose.

Schultz and I talked until dawn, the aimless, rambling talk of men who have not conversed with their own kind for months. I told Schultz of Herman and his eyes lighted. "He'll be a good man to know," he said. "I'll get around to call on him one of these days." Schultz, in turn, told me of a run-in he had down the river. "At least sixty war canoes heading downstream on a raid. We just let 'em have it and came on through. They'll be waiting for us on the way back." And with that pleasant prospect, he left me to go to sleep. It was nearly dawn.

I was gratified to learn the next afternoon that in our honour the natives of a nearby *miriva* (village) were going to stage a *wahoekoe*, most important of all festivals to the women. This ceremony did for girls reaching the age of puberty what the nose-boring festival did for boys, but it was far more elaborate and richer in symbolic significance. It was the coming out party of the girls, the official announcement that they were in the market for husbands.

I was on hand with my camera before the grand march started. There were six black debutantes who were coming out, making the affair just six times more pretentious than ordinarily. They were decked from head to foot in brilliant

bird of paradise feathers, egret plumes, shell necklaces, brace-
lets of kangaroo teeth and a dozen other forms of barbaric
adornment. They positively reeked of coconut oil. So heavily
loaded down with riches were they that they could scarcely
walk.

Honorary escorts of the debs were their *ameis* (god-fathers),
tall, husky warriors fully aware of their importance on this
festive occasion. The march began at the far end of the village
to the accompaniment of the ever-present drums, but this time
the cadence was kept to a solemn steady beat. Twice around
the village the *ameis* lead their feathery beauties, followed by
the entire village population, the males carrying wati and
sagoware, the women loaded down with fruits, coconuts, sago,
sugar-cane and all kinds of fish, birds and meat.

After the second circuit the debs were placed in a widely
spaced circle around a huge loaf of sago bread baking on hot
stones in the centre of the village. The men now came forward
and placed their burdens in a circle around the girls, no
particular partiality being shown to any one of them. The
women came next and heaped their contributions up until
the girls were buried neck deep in food. If some of the fruit is
over-ripe it mashes down a little but the girls have enough
oil rubbed into their bodies to be juice-proof. Great shouting
and laughter accompies this part of the ceremony.

The tempo of the drums now increases, the gaiety becomes
more spontaneous and the girls climb to the top of their edible
mounds, shedding feathers as they climb. Once on top they
straddle the heap while the villagers dance around in wild
abandon. The food throne is the symbol of fertility, and the
wilder and more bacchanalian the dance and orgy that follows,
the more successful will be the girls in child bearing. While all
the dancing is going on the girls are not passive, They, too,
are caught up by the feeling of wild abandon. Shrieking with
laughter they pelt the circling men with ripe fruit. When their
feathers become irksome they cast them off, and soon they are
leading the festival in their all-together, dark brown nymphs,
the living personification of vital, pulsating sex.

As soon as the *wahoekoe* has run its course, which may take
anywhere from three days to a week, depending upon the

supply of food and drink, the debutantes become taboo to men until they marry but in the meantime all rules are off. They live only for the moment, and with a long, chaste period ahead of them they waste no time on ceremony that might be more profitably employed otherwise.

According to strict interpretation of the taboos, after her coming out party the young debutante must enter into the affairs of her mother's housekeeping. Where before she has been allowed to run wild with the boys, she must now learn to plait carrying baskets, weave straw, braid lavish coiffures, make sago, chew wati, and cook. She must become an expert housekeeper in preparation for the great day when some buck goes out and lops off a head, thereby becoming eligible for her hand. This she does, of course, but in the meantime there remains the problem of persuading the young buck she is the woman to marry when he lops off a head. The taboos are pretty lenient in this respect. As long as she carries on her affairs out of sight of her mother's not-too-watchful eye, the chances are there will be few objections. If any children should result from these casual mis-alliances, they are accepted into the family without question, though if the girl's father is an exceptionally lazy man he might warn her not to do it again lest he overwork himself fetching home so many ripe bananas to stuff into the growing infants.

By the time the girls have been pulled from their edible thrones, the festival had degenerated into the common brawl in which all festivals end up. Each festival starts out different and means well, but after a few hours have gone by the same three elements predominate: food, drink and sex. And when those three get together, be it it a karapau, a wemanuwe, a karawarie or a wahoekoe, there is no distinguishing between them. The ceremony is the excuse; the rest is raw nature taking its course.

Skyscraper

Only on the Digoel River can these skyscraper dwellings be found.
Floods account for part of the elevation and defence measures account
for the rest

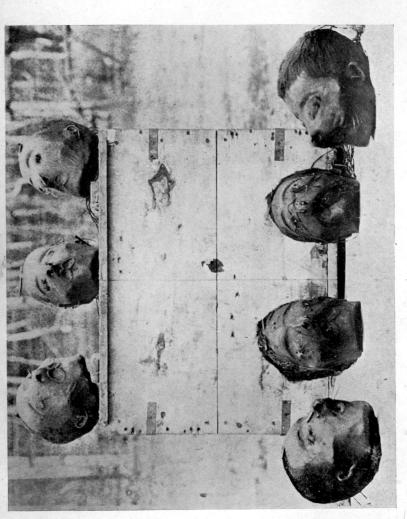

"With My Compliments"

For a favour granted a village chief, 'Cannibal' Miller was given these seven heads. To

CHAPTER XV

CHAPTER OF THE DEAD

ACCORDING to the crude chart drawn up by Schultz, Tannah-Tinggi was about 220 miles from the sea, with another 250 miles waiting for us after we reached the coast. By looking at the map and pulling a little mental arithmetic out of the air, I could see us pulling into Merauke in a little less than two weeks, our long trek over. Allowing for a speed of six miles an hour in the launch, plus a four-mile-per-hour current, we should have no difficulty averaging ten miles an hour on the river. At ten hours a day, this would put us at the mouth of the river in two days and two hours. Once we started through the Princess Marianne Straat we would lose the boost of the current, but we would still have our original 6 m.p.h's. Ten hours a day would give us 250 miles in four days and two hours, making a grand total of six days and four hours between Tannah-Tinggi and Merauke. Allowing for head winds and possible mechanical delays, we should be home in two weeks. Thus deceptive are trips plotted on maps. Somewhere on that two-weeks' journey we dropped seventy-five days. And they were tough ones.

Trouble didn't wait long to claim us. Not serious trouble, just petty, irksome trouble, but each trouble was surrounded by half a dozen of her young. Trouble begets trouble, and the period of gestation is just about instantaneous. Like the time the launch banged into a half-submerged tree, climbed half way up and hung there teetering. The first canoe in the tow was shoved into the still whirling propeller by the weight of the canoes behind it and the bow chewed off. The shrieking natives, in the ill-fated canoe, none of whom could swim, plunged overboard into water that suddenly came to life with crocodiles, while from the shore a score of savages who had been pacing us through the brush for just such a chance let fly with their entire stock of arrows. We came out of that without the loss of a single man, but Achmed, who had been below when the crash occurred, dropped our last case of gin and broke every bottle. On top of that, when we finally got the boat off the tree by moving all our firewood to the bow, the submerged tree bobbed up just as the stern settled, bending our propeller shaft at right angles to the housing. As if that were not enough, we discovered upon beaching the launch that each propeller blade had assumed a pitch of its own as the result of tangling with the canoe prow. The only substantial piece of metal in the whole propeller assembly was the sheer pin. That wasn't even nicked.

As might be expected, we did not complete our repairs in fifteen minutes. We were there all that day and the next, and never in my life have I encountered a more obstinate piece of steel than that propeller shaft. I straightened it out cold to avoid the danger of ruining the temper by heating it. Every time I hit it a lick with the back of an axe the darn thing struck back, nearly throwing me. Schultz cursed and I worked. The natives were across the river somewhere hunting for the party that had ambushed us. They had a good time bagging ten heads, but they were the only ones who enjoyed themselves. The mosquitos were something to behold, and the leeches— well, they were thick enough on the trees, but when I waded out to stand knee deep in the water fixing the propeller housing they settled on my legs so thicky anybody seeing me wade out would have sworn I had on rubber boots. Every time I entered the water I gave a transfusion. When everything was once more in order I was in need of a couple of transfusions myself.

Leona was as glad to get started as we were. All she had had to do for two days was mull over the contents of a Dutch military journal and an almanac, neither of which she could read. At the end of the first day they began to lose interest, and after that the only relief in the monotony was in watching the lumps grow out of punctures left by mosquitos tough enough to drill through a layer of citronella.

A few days later we were tied up at a village about fifty miles from the coast for more repairs. I had tied down the safety valve once too often and the head of the boiler blew off, jarring loose a few planks when it smacked against a bulkhead.

That was an emergency for which we were fully prepared, even to the packing. The repair job was one I could leave in the hands of Achmed, that wild Malay being fully qualified by past experience. While running the steam-boiler for a portable saw-mill used by the Dutch army to cut lumber for new barracks, he used to blow the head off just to see how far it would sail.

I found the villagers wallowing through an economic depression so deep, the roots of it could be traced directly to the capitals of Europe and America. For years these particular villagers had supplied thousands of dollars worth of birds of paradise feathers and egret plumes to traders from Java, in return for which they had received axes, knives, mirrors and ribbons to the value of several florins. But the demand for plumes with which to decorate milady's hats had dropped to zero, fickle fashion ceased to smile on these natives in remote New Guinea, and now they waited with a hut filled with feathers for the return of the daring trader who would make them wealthy again. They just couldn't understand his absence, a bewilderment not to be wondered at when not even the fashion experts themselves can explain it.

On top of the woe spread by the depression the natives were in a period of deep mourning or *sal* for the loss of their chief, who had died the previous month under mysterious circumstances. All of the women of his immediate family and closest female relatives were dressed in mourning garments consisting of a *kawarib*, a long grass skirt; a *soja*, a grass garment similar to the kawarib but tied above the breasts, and a *wangoe*, a grass mourning cape. Each garment overlapped the other like a thatched roof. Their faces and bodies were covered with a ghastly white clay liberally smeared with crude designs of red earth, and their hair was festooned with long white feathers thrust into the greasy braids helter-skelter. Every now and then some woman would begin an eerie wailing and soon the rest would join in a weird refrain that was unnerving to hear.

During the *sal* all dancing and all festivals are taboo. Usually the period seldom affects the village more than a day or so, and thereafter the immediate family mourns alone, but in this case Kalmoe, the witch-doctor was holding the mourning period over for a ceremony of his own. He was convinced, he told me, that Popol, the dead chief, had been murdered. He meant to keep the corpse lying in state until Popol's spirit told him who had committed the crime.

The body, daubed with white clay symbols, lay on a bier of palm fronds at the far end of the village near the bachelor lodge, and had been there for three weeks. And this was in the tropics. Now the spirit was ready to talk. I won't describe the process by which Popol's spirit was enabled to express itself. When I say it involved cannibalism, with Kalmoe as the consumer and Popol as the piece-de-resistance I am putting it far more mildly than the truth deserves.

Kalmoe did his magic and retired to sleep on it that the spirit might visit him in his dreams with the real story of the death of Popol. After Kalmoe's revolting repast, there is no doubt but what he dreamed. His sleep must have been disturbed by terrifying manifestation staged by all the fiends from hell, ptomaine-induced nightmares so vivid and startling that sanity itself must fall back appalled.

We were aroused the next morning by wails of mourning out-shrieking anything I had ever heard before. Popol had been murdered! This dream-discovery of the witch-doctor accounted for half the excitement. The other half came from the family of Japoli, the man accused of the crime. No, not accused. He was the man found guilty of the murder and already executed.

When I went ashore I found the female members of Japoli's family in deepest mourning, their faces covered with white clay, their bodies covered with the three mourning garments and their hair filled with bedraggled white feathers. Japoli himself moped beneath a tree a few paces from his hut. Death was written on his face, and in his eyes was the stunned expression of a man shot in the stomach. Only yesterday I had particularly noticed him as one of the few villagers with a perfect physique. And now, to all intents and purposes, he was dead.

I spoke to him, but aside from a terrified shifting of his eyes there was no answer. The witch-doctor had told him he had killed Popol and for that crime he would die. The verdict was final. There was no appeal. He was told he was a dead man and die he would. It might take three days, it might take a week, but the result was inevitable. No executioners were necessary to carry out the sentence. The condemned conduct their own executions, though how it is done remains a mystery. White men have been known to scoff, calling it superstitious tommy-rot, but written into the records in Java, Borneo and New Guinea are scores of instances in which white men, with all their mental superiority, have died mysteriously within incredibly short times after running afoul of the curse of some native witch-doctor. It happens, that's all, whether there's an explanation for it or not.

To me the condemnation of Japoli was a challenge. He looked like a good boy, so I decided to conduct a little investigation of my own. I found the natives willing enough to talk on almost any subject, but as soon as I introduced Japoli's name into the conversation there was an abrupt silence. I saw I was going to get nowhere that way. The living deadman would not speak, nor would any members of his family come to my assistance.

It was Leona who made the startling discovery that Japoli could not possibly have murdered Popol. Trying to console a pot-bellied, weeping youngster, she discovered that the boy's father had just returned from a long trip to the big water after shells. "He was going to take me hunting birds today," the boy wailed. "He said he would take me as soon as he got back and now he can't come." Leona understood part of it, and the rest was interpreted by Achmed.

"Why can't he?" she asked.

The boy broke into new sobs. "I don't know. He won't speak to me. They say he is dead, but I can see him over there and he isn't dead."

Leona glanced in the direction indicated by the wavering, grimy finger and saw the boy meant Japoli. It took but a second to catch the significance of the boy's statement. If Japoli had gone to the sea, and that was how she interpreted his term "big water," the chances were that Japoli wasn't even in the village when Popol died. She forgot all about the crying youngster in her rush to relay the information to me. It was the one clue I needed.

Working on the assumption that Japoli would not make so long a trip alone, I began asking around if anybody had been down to the ocean recently. I soon discovered that twenty warriors in two canoes had made the trip, returning just a few hours before we arrived.

Was Popol alive and well when they left?

Yes, he had even accompanied them for a few miles down the river.

Was Japoli with them?

At this they hedged, but I could tell by their very evasiveness that Japoli had indeed been along.

How long had they been gone?

One of the men produced a rope with thirty knots in it, each knot representing a sunrise. A month. That meant they had been gone a week before Popol died. Evidence enough that Japoli could not have committed the crime even with slow-acting poison.

I told the witch-doctor of my findings. He agreed that Japoli could not have done it in person.

"His spirit must have done it," he said at last. The man was sincere. He firmly believed that he had correctly interpreted his nightmare of the previous night, and nothing in the way of logic could persuade him otherwise. Well, if logic wouldn't do it, I had what I figured was a lot better than logic. Gunpowder.

I waited until night for my seance. I meant to have the spirit of Popol return to the village as an indication that he had left voluntarily and had not been driven out by the murderous hand of Japoli. I told the condemned man I was going to prove him innocent. A look of hope came into his eyes, but it faded almost on the instant. He slumped back against the tree.

I went through my bag of tricks: firecrackers, combustible film, gasoline that burned even when water was poured on it, red-lensed flashlight, luminous-dialed watch, storm lantern, and my guns. I was mourning the absence of Roman candles and sky-rockets and resolving that my next trip find me equipped with all manner of spectacular flares and pyrotechnical displays when suddenly I decided to make something

on that order out of what I already had. I didn't know just
how Roman candles were made, but I figured if I ran a fuse
from top to bottom in a tube of bamboo, and filled the tube
with charges of powder separated from each other by wads of
paper around the fuse, I would at least get a succession of
flashes even if I couldn't shoot out coloured balls of fire. I
packed my Roman candle on the spot, using the powder from
two .45 bullets for each charge and making a dozen wads
in all.

I made my speech that night, and if those natives had never
been scared before in their lives, they were scared then, for I
promised that not only would Popol's spirit return, but it
would return in a flash of fire that they could see for themselves.
It was bad enough for them to have spirits flying around
invisible without having to see them too. They began backing
off, their mouths open, their eyes staring, but their curiosity
was too great to let them go far. They were going to see a spirit
if it killed them. Remembering the amount of powder I had
in my home-made Roman candle, I hoped it wouldn't. Next,
I told them that the return of Popol's spirit was a sign that
Japoli was innocent, and that he would be returned to them
as a great warrior. They nodded. On those terms they were
willing to accept him back.

I turned on my red flashlight and swung it around a few
times. All eyes followed its evil-looking arcs so failing to notice
my other hand tossing firecrackers into the fire. When they
went off I lost half my audience, but I knew they would be
hovering around the edges of the huts. Next I took a pull on a
flask of gasoline, made a few mystic passes and spit the awful
tasting stuff into the fire. I made sure I spit it in one gob and
not in a stream. As it was, if I had worn a moustache I would
have singed it off in the flash that followed. By that time the
natives were ready to accept that flash as the spirit of Popol,
but I still had my Roman candle.

Under the pretence of putting more wood on the fire, I
slipped the tube of bamboo in with a handful of sticks and
stood it upright in the centre of the flames. I figured the fuse
would catch almost instantly, it couldn't help it the way the
flames were dancing all around, and the explosions should

follow in about a minute. The minute went by, then two, then five. I began to feel foolish and began waving my red flashlight.

"Get me some unexposed film," I shouted to Schultz, who was watching me sceptically. I wove the words into an incantation as it is not considered good form to communicate with mere man when one is in communion with the spirits.

I don't know how long Schultz was gone, but just as I saw him out of the corner of my eye there was a tremendous roar and a sheet of flame shot heavenward. Not just one sheet, but several dazzling flashes, each one distinct but no two in the same place. The fire was scattered all over the place, and one glowing log landed on the hut in which the birds of paradise feathers were stored. In the excitement of the blast, however, it went unnoticed. Nothing could have been done about it anyway. There wasn't a native in sight, my own men included. Even Japoli came back from the land of the dead to join in the rush. What had happened was that my Roman candle had burned through at the base, blowing the charges out the top and filling the air with loose powder that ignited in sheets of flame.

Schultz and I were hurriedly beating out the burning brands when the storehouse burst into flames. Fortunately it wasn't close to any of the other tinder-dry shacks, and the night was calm. That was the only reason the whole village didn't go up in smoke. As it was there was enough smoke for ten villages. And such smoke. Burning feathers that had dried for years. To this day when I smell burning feathers I can see lurid flames lighting up black columns of smoke and darker masses of dropping fronds in the background. In the foreground are the gleaming fronts of the huts, and always sprinting past them is the resurrected dead man, Japoli.

When the natives finally managed to overcome their fear long enough to return, it was too late to do anything for their feathers. The only thing they could do was look at the smoke and enjoy the smell. I told the witch-doctor Popol's spirit had burned the storehouse because there was no need to save the feathers any longer; the white man would not come back to buy them for a long, long time, maybe never. At any rate when he did come, he would want fresh ones. Kalmoe accepted my interpretation solemnly. He also assured me he was glad Popol had let Japoli live. Japoli was a brave warrior and a good worker. He might even become the next chief.

The next day Popol, his body painted white with fresh clay, was buried in his hut beneath the spot on which he was wont to sleep. His widow took her place upon the grave, and there she was fated to remain for months, going outside only to attend to her needs. Food was brought to her by relatives likewise dressed in mourning but not required to watch the grave. The mourning costume was worn until it dropped off. If in the meantime there should be fresh cause for mourning the new costume was put on over the old.

Each tribe and village has its own peculiar variations, but in the main mourning habits can be traced back to a common origin. Everywhere it is the custom for the women to carry on the mourning, the men going their way apparently indifferent to sorrow and certainly free of its restrictions. Coastal natives wear their widow's weeds until they fall off. Farther inland the grass garments are hung over the grave as soon as the corpse has been placed in the pit. The pit itself is left open for weeks to give the spirit a good chance to escape. In the meantime the principal mourner brings food to the grave and does daily penance until there is little left to grieve over. Then the hole is closed up. The Digoel method of burying their dead, half in the ground and half out has already been described. It is to be noticed that the farther inland one goes, the higher the scale of civilisation. Way up in Kirrirri land the dead are carefully wrapped in nepa palm leaves, and placed on a well-built platform for several days to allow the spirit to become accustomed to its new surroundings. A grave is then dug, a platform built in the bottom of it and the corpse moved to its new location. Here it remains for several more days after which time the spirit is believed to be at home in a new land and the grave can be closed.

The underlying motive which all these ceremonies have in common is to make the departed spirit happy. It is believed that the spirit undergoes a terrific shock when it is separated from the body for the first time. It returns to its body for comfort, and if no mourners are present, it gets lonely. If no food is present it gets hungry because at first it isn't ready for a spiritual diet. That is why, too, that the body is not buried for several days. If it were, the spirit would have a hard time getting back into it. This belief is also evident in cannibalism, for with the spirit haunting the body one can't partake of it without consuming part of the spirit and benefiting accordingly by the increased spiritual strength.

In the cases of small children, the mourning customs are carried to pathetic lengths. I know of one instance in which a mother sat with her dead infant in her arms for thirty days to give the wee one a chance to become familiar with its new surroundings. As the baby had never been out of the hut, the mother remained inside all that time lest the tiny spirit return and find no one present at the only spot it had ever known. In the skyscraper hut of the Digoels I saw two babies' bodies wrapped in palm leaves over on the women's side of the hut. They were being kept where they had always slept until such a time as their spirits would no longer be lonely without their bodies. After that they would be baked in clay and planted like posts beneath the hut.

There are several other instances in which other tribes bake their infant dead. Instead of being horrible, as it sounds, it is a refinement over the custom of the coastal tribes. Believing that the child's spirit will be lonesome for its mother, the coastal natives hang the tiny, clay-daubed body in a sling over its mother's bed and leave it there for a month. Within three days conditions within the hut are frightful but the mother dare not leave. Inland, where the baby is wrapped in leaves and slowly baked over a smoking fire the corpse is dehydrated and will keep indefinitely without giving offence to the nostrils. When at last the time comes for burial, the infant is buried within the hut, the mother first preserving a lock or two of hair which she carries from that time on in her carrying basket.

The ceremonies surrounding burial are as varied as there are tribes. Sometimes a week or so after a death the women will all come together in their mourning clothes, light a fire close to the grave and dance all night wailing thin songs that make sleep impossible for anyone around. In the morning they stop and by noon the departed one is forgotten by all concerned. This funeral dance, known as a *jajam*, is evident in all tribes, but not always is it as mercifully brief as this. Sometimes all the women in the village take part, stepping high and stamping their feet hard as they circle the widow or mother seated on the grave, keeping time to their moaning songs. These *jajams* might go on at intervals for months for a single person, and then again one dance might do for all the dead in the village for the past year.

So far I have only mentioned funeral arrangements for men and children. I have also mentioned that only women are involved in the mourning ceremonies. These are primitive folk, quick to give vent to their feelings, and little given to hypocrisy. They see in another woman only another rival, and certainly one is not going to moan long over the departure of a rival. The women daub their faces with white clay for a few hours, hold a cursory *jajam* over their departed sister and consign her remains to the ground. A few days later and she is forgotten, her spirit left to get along as best it can.

This care of the dead applies only to those who have died naturally, which usually means of pneumonia or malaria, the two most prominent of fatal diseases in New Guinea. Old age cannot be figured as a cause of death because in a land where survival of the fittest is the rule, there are no old. For those who have died violently in the heat of battle there is only the *wemanuwe*, the cannibal feast. And that is the only funeral in which the men take part.

CHAPTER XVI

HUMANITY'S ABSOLUTE ZERO

BY THE time Popol was appropriately interred, I was ready to leave but Achmed was having trouble threading new nuts to fit the bolts for the boiler head. He had a plentiful supply of bolts, and an even larger supply of nuts but his Oriental foresight had not extended to seeing that the two matched. He had a full set of taps and no vice. When I saw him he was patiently carving out a socket in a block of wood, the socket being the exact size and shape of the nuts. Eventually he would get around to boring a hole to take the tap, fitting a nut into the socket and tapping a new thread. In the meantime we could swat mosquitos.

Again Leona came to my rescue, and again it was through the agency of Japoli's young son.

"You know this bird hunt Japoli was going to take Wekoe on?" she asked. I could see she was greatly excited.

"Birds of paradise, wasn't it?"

"Yes, but it wasn't just a few birds. Japoli knows where they have their club house. They come there by the hundreds."

That was something else again. The spectacle of those ethereal birds coming together by the hundreds until the very jungle is aflame with their riotous colours is one which few white men have been privileged to see. I had only seen it once before myself, and I had spent sixteen years in the jungle.

Japoli was tickled to death to guide us to the spot. In fact there wasn't anything he wouldn't have done to show his gratitude for our saving his life. He was simply bubbling over with vitality and good-will. For the first time he realised that it was good to be alive. He had never had occasion to ponder over this fact before and the sudden realisation that he had been within an ace of being a dead man gave his life a brilliant lustre. It would wear off in a few days but right now he was so happy that even the over-powering odour of the feathers that were still burning was like incense in his nostrils. His little Wekoe, a precocious little brat, looked like a god to him.

We took just a small party, three Malays and five Javanese chain-gangers, just enough to insure us against a surprise attack and not too many to frighten away the birds. We left at noon and were out about three hours when Japoli, who was in the lead, motioned us to approach silently. We crept forward like snakes, burrowing under the lianas on our bellies and parting the giant twelve-foot ferns as gently as possible that the waving fronds might not betray our presence. Ahead of us was a grassy glen, not wide enough to be a clearing and yet open enough to admit sunlight, something rare on the floor of the Rain Forest. And in the centre of this glen, catching the full radiance of the sun and reflecting it with even greater glory, were five tiny huts little larger than bushel baskets, each one a veritable sunburst of colour. I heard Leona gasp in admiration. Even as we gazed a cascade of indigo poured down from the jungle crown and splashed in a pool of azure more translucent than the sky. Two blue birds of paradise had plummeted to the ground, such gorgeous creatures they could not possibly be measured by earthly standards. To say that their bodies were of the size and shape of a small dove, that their heads and beaks were like a blackbird's save for a crown which resembled that of a peacock, that their tail plumes were eighteen inches long and their wing spread was about thirty inches is about as inadequate as saying that a rainbow is a geometrical arc containing all the colours and extending from horizon to horizon. It just won't do.

The backs of the birds were a rich navy blue, and as they danced and preened in the sun, spreading their wings and tails more gracefully than fan dancers, we caught glimpses of the incredibly rich colouring of their breasts and under-surface of the wings. A luxurious violet at the tips, the wings blended into royal purple, lavender, blue, and finally, at the breast, a pale powder blue, not weak and lifeless like most light blues, but as rich and vital as the sky where it thins off to meet the desert horizon in the high wastelands of some vast plateau.

The wings were slender and gracefully tapered but it was

the tail plumes which furnished the greatest glory. The tail was forked, with enough plumes on each side to make a good rudder for a dozen ordinary birds. Completing the lavish train were two long quills, one for each side, that projected in wide graceful curves several inches beyond the plumes. Each was tipped with a vane of pure black no larger than a dime. Leona actually winced when one of the birds grovelled in a patch of clear soil, rubbing its glory into the dirt like a barnyard chicken dusting itself in the sun.

Suddenly one of the birds hopped off with a startled squawk that jolted us as much as if a ballerina were to stop in the midst of a fairy dance and let loose a string of curses. The reason for its abrupt departure was not apparent at first glance, but finally I saw a movement in the shadows of one of the flamboyant huts. A moment later a rusty individual who looked as though it once might have been a black crow before being left too long in the rain sauntered out into the sun. It was the female of the species, and a sad case she was. However he didn't seem to mind her dullness any more than males of the human race mind theirs. She just came out and began a billing and cooing with her resplendent husband that was nothing short of shocking. In a few minutes they retired to their love nest, every movement as suggestive as a bedroom scene in the era before Will Hays. It was all we could do to hold back our laughter. The other male, I noticed, had been claimed by his spouse.

I examined again the strange nests these birds had built. They were like round, open-faced lean-tos, about two feet high and three feet in diameter. The frame-work was of twigs, but the rest of it contained no such common matter. Rare, brilliantly coloured leaves, dried blossoms, rainbow-hued feathers, anything with colour to it was woven into the love-nest. The interior was as lavish as the exterior, as though the birds appreciated the beauties of love and wanted it to have the most luxurious of surroundings. I have often wondered if the female made the house beautiful to make up for her own drabness or if the vain male built it to give himself a background in keeping with his plumage. I mean to find out next time I go back.

According to Japoli we still had about two hours to go before reaching the bird of paradise club house. There we would see a different type of bird entirely from the blue ones we had just left. Instead of indigo we would have all shades of red, yellow, green, white and even black. A quick glance at the sun when we came to an open spot assured me that we had ample time to reach the spot before sundown, the congregating hour.

The jungle seemed to be engaged in setting the stage for the royal aerial ballet we were to witness. Never before had I seen so many orchids. They swung from the trees in suspended bouquets as though fairies had flitted over the jungle dropping flowers, or they clung closely to the trunks as though the hoary, moss-covered jungle monarchs had suddenly grown flippant and were sporting boutonnieres on their sombre garments. The air was filled with butterflies, great flakes of iridescent colour that flitted aimlessly like tinted petals tossed about on unfelt zephyrs. Tiny humming birds sped through the filtered green light, motes of colour weaving ephemeral patterns that lingered briefly on the air like the haze of a comet's tail. The jungle was displaying only its beautiful side that day.

For another hour we slipped silently between the trees, our steps absorbed by the soft moss underfoot. Lianas threw leafy barriers across our path, but rather than break the silence with our machetes we walked around. So successful were we that twice we came upon wild sows suckling their young, and not even the cursing parrots stopped chattering to hurl maledictions upon our heads. At last I caught an odour as familiar as the inside of a hen-house. Japoli caught it too.

"Did I not tell you?" he whispered. "Just like a bird I come straight to the clubhouse."

I nodded my head in approval. "Good boy," I said. He wriggled like a pleased puppy.

We still had half an hour before the birds would begin congregating. I spent the time investigating the site, trying to figure out a way I could get a picture in the fading light. There was nothing to mark the tree as being any different from a thousand other giants aside from the fact it had been almost stripped of leaves. It rose probably thirty feet above a heavy growth of nepa palm, but so did countless other hard wood trees. I could see by the heavy accummulation of bird droppings that I had smelled long before reaching the spot that it would not be advantageous to shoot from directly underneath, and the closest tree of equal height that I could climb was too far away to make shooting with anything less than a telephoto lens impractical. I could have spared myself my fretting. By the time the first birds arrived the sun was so far gone the best my most sensitive film would have got were a few black silhouettes. The camera might have been useless, but not our eyes.

For our position we chose a spot beneath a huge clump of fern. By peering between the fronds, we had an almost unobstructed view of the bare tree. We saw the first bird coming a long way off, a splash of orange so brilliant that a drift-wood flame would have suffered in comparison. The bird was not a graceful flier. It had to work hard to stay in the air, dipping heavily after each wing beat, but its very vigorousness made its flight all the more spectacular. Colours flashed from its fanning wings and ruddering tail like sparks from a live wire. About a hundred yards from the tree it dropped into a steep glide, wings set and tail balanced sensitively against a stall just like a pheasant coming in for a landing. He checked speed with his wings, braked his tail and came to a perfect stop on the topmost limb just as I figured he would. After watching that exhibition of his controls I could have flown him myself.

It isn't possible to describe the beauty of the scene after that. Colour after colour paraded before our dazzled eyes. Rich burgundy red, screaming scarlet, golds, browns blacks, purples, every colour in every possible shade and suggestion of a shade. Long fluttering tails; short, fan-shaped tails; slim, tapering wings; wide wings open-spaced between the feathers; anything seemed to go, the only rule being that no matter what the shape, what the colour, it had to be beautiful. The birds were not content to pose and preen. If they had been the impression they made would have been far more spiritual. But no, these transplanted bits of heaven were rowdies, clowns in royal raiment. They shrieked, cursed cackled and fought. They were all over the tree, crowing out obscenities and filling the air with unholy din and detached feathers. We watched

" Karawarie "

When the boys begin to rally round the head-hunting pole, trouble is in the offing. There is a marked resemblance here to the North American totem pole. Note human torso on top

Dead Warrior

Surrounded by gifts, this departed warrior lies in state until such a time as the witch-doctor deems suitable for burial

the glittering bedlam in complete fascination until the last flash of gold from the setting sun added a supreme touch that transcended anything on earth. Almost instantly darkness crashed down, as definite and final as though some invisible master-director had whispered, "Cut."

The show was over. Groping in the darkness, we staggered out from our shelter, suddenly aware that we were covered with mosquitos on the exposed portions of our bodies, and with leeches under our clothes. The jungle had turned off her charm and was being her natural self. We went only far enough on the back trail so that the light of our camp fire would not disturb the birds. In a small clearing we prepared for the night, first giving our bodies a thorough overhauling in search of parasites. Leona no longer squealed when she sliced off a leech. She didn't even count them. The jungle had claimed her and it hadn't taken long.

One thing made a deep impression on me as the result of our visit to the club house. That was the re-action of the natives to beauty. Even little Wekoe was profoundly impressed, and one of the last things I heard that night was him asking Japoli when they could return again so he could see the pretty birds. That might be the key to something or other, but there are other times when I am convinced that nature locked these boys away in ignorance and threw away all the keys.

The village was still enjoying its feather smudge when we got back. Schultz had about all he could stand. In desperation he had organised the Stone Age's first fire brigade, a procession of natives each loaded down with a pint-sized coconut shell which he scurried to fill at the stream and empty on the black heap of cinders within which a mass of glowing, stinking embers blinked and spit. At the rate they were going there is no doubt they would have extinguished the mass within a week but we didn't wait to find out. When Schultz saw us he let out one powerful oath of relief and began bellowing orders to the crew to get ready to pull out. Steam, I saw, was already up, and the new batch of canoes supplied by the witch-doctor was along side. Our farewells were of the briefest, but before leaving I gave Japoli a yard of calico, a box of matches and a dozen shells.

"You're rich enough to be chief now," I said. "Be a good boy."

"Yaah." His wide grin was the last thing we saw.

Just because we were clear of the village didn't mean we were free of the smell. The thick odour of burnt feathers had permeated out clothes, lockers, our bedding, even the wood of the boat itself. Three days later, when we had left the heavy mist of the jungle behind and were riding the open sea, it was like sticking our noses into a smudge pot every time we stuck our heads below decks.

At the last village at the mouth of the Digoel river we had changed to heavy sea-going canoes for our crew. These were monstrous hollowed logs forty feet long with plenty of room for thirty persons to the canoe. We had four of them in tow containing the men and women of our crew and twenty brawny savages from the village who would return the canoes when we reached the next village with boats available. The canoes were built on exactly the same lines as the smaller river boats, but the eyes gracing the prow were larger because there was no telling when a heavy fog might roll in from the sea, and anyone caught in it might have a hard time getting back to shore unless the canoe had extra big eyes to penetrate the mist.

It was pretty tough going the first twenty miles out from the mouth of the Digoel. Our little launch was hardly built for rolling seas, and every time we started down into a six-foot trough our tow rope would snub us short. We had a hundred feet of rope between canoes, but even this was not enough to take up the shock. We finally had to put the natives to work paddling their own canoes until we got into the calm waters of the Princess Marianne Straat, a strip of water between the low, flat mainland, and the lower, flatter Frederik Hendrik Island. The straat varied between five and ten miles in width, but to keep our course straight we were constantly holding our boat first on a point on one shore, then on the other according to the curves of the coast line.

To say that Frederik Hendrik Island is an island is a slight exaggeration. Actually it is little more than an ocean bottom slightly exposed to the air on which a few trees have managed to take root. That anybody might be living out there was thought to be out of the question until we saw signs of smoke. Then there was nothing to do but land to see what manner of people could exist in such a malodorous bog.

Not knowing the channels in the shallow water, we couldn't get closer than a quarter of a mile to the shore with the launch. We dropped anchor in six feet of water and twelve feet of mud and were ferried to shore in the canoes, the natives pulling us over the slimy bottom for the last hundred yards. The first thing we saw was a grove of coconut trees, the full grown nuts no larger than lemons. Other trees and shrubs were dwarfed in proportion, probably because of too much salt and an excessive amount of water in the soil.

Set back in the alleged coconut grove was the most miserable village I have ever seen in my life, and I have seen some tough ones. The huts, and the title is applied by courtesy only, consisted of a few half-rotten crooked sticks stuck upright in the ground, with a little marsh grass crammed hit-or-miss into the interstices. The roofs looked like brush piles tossed up by the wind and held aloft by sheer luck. Certainly they were not rain proof. Anyone entering one of the crude doorways had to be careful not to brush against the sides lest the whole pile come tumbling down about his head.

The village was of course deserted, the natives having taken flight long before our first canoe touched shore. The fires were still going, however, but even the flames were a pretty sorry lot. The wood was wet and mouldy, the reason being, I discovered later, that the natives have no way of cutting partially dry wood still clinging to the trees, but must pick up wood already on the ground. And wood that is already on the ground rots practically over night.

It took us about four hours to get the timid natives out of the sloughs and bogs in which they were hiding. In groups of four and five they came slinking in, drawn by the bright display of trinkets which Leona and I were offering to the apparently blank walls of the jungle. The islanders weren't pigmies by any means. They were tall enough to pass as men, but aside from their huge pot bellies they were scrawny enough to pass as skeletons. They were full size perpendicularly and pigmies laterally. And ignorant! The most brilliant mind in the lot would have required months of intensive training to pass as a moron. I am ashamed to say it but I have seen wild baboons in India whose instinct would pass for greater intelligence than those natives displayed. And even the blue birds of paradise built better huts than these so-called humans could erect. Their small, close-eyed weazened faces could master only one expression, and that was a shifty, unpleasant fear. To our efforts to enter into conversation, they responded with dumb sagging of the jaw and an uneasy shift of the feet. I passed out a few bright beads which were snatched with a sudden burst of courage, after which the recipients dashed away in fright at their own boldness. I expected any minute to see them scamper into the trees and begin chattering like monkeys.

There was only one thing to marvel about, and that was how these members of the lowest order of the human race managed to live at all. To settle this point I decided to stay over for a couple of days to see what they did in the way of making a living. Leona and I spent the rest of the day calming their fears, and gradually we came to understand the dozen words or so that seemed to be the extent of their vocabulary. Their word for meat covered all animals, and in a burst of eloquence they managed to throw in separate words for birds and fish. Then they had words for men, women, trees, water, earth and fire. Gestures took the place of verbs and adjectives. If there was any more to the language we missed it.

That night we had the first evidence of real intelligence. The village was over-run with mice, and to catch them the natives heaped up several piles of live clams over which the mice scrambled with great delight. But every now and then some mouse would stick a foot into the lips of an open shell and snap! the clam would have him. This capture would be hailed as a great victory by the natives. The clam and its squeaking captive would be held up admiringly, then tossed in the fire. In about five minutes both clam and mouse would be cooked to a turn and eaten with great relish. That was one way of catching fresh meat. The next we learned when we returned in the morning after spending the night on the boat.

On the programme was a kangaroo hunt, I having offered to help with my rifle. The natives were armed with their only vital weapon, a three-foot bamboo club. This club was to these boys what the boomerang is to the Australian bushman. It had to be secured at great risk from the mainland, no bamboo growing in their vicinity on the island. A stalk about an inch and a half in diameter was broken off about four feet above the ground, and then pulled out by the roots. This was the raw material. After securing a supply of these, the natives scurried for home, thankful for not having lost their heads to the vigorous, savage mainlanders. To make the clubs, the splintered top was thrust into the fire and burned off smooth. The roots were similarly treated, leaving only the hard, round root-neck about the size of a baseball at the base of the stalk. The club was now as nicely balanced as a drum major's baton, and those boys could really make those sticks hum. Whirled around the head a couple of times and then thrown with a snap of the wrist they would make even a crocodile wince twice if lopped in the snoot.

Our hunt began at the edge of what was more swamp than prairie. After a first glance I decided that if there were any kangaroos in there they had to have webbed feet. I was wrong. There were a lot of small 'roos concealed in the tall grass, and when they started to run they really took off. The soil was springy and the kangaroos were springy. Between the two they showed some surprising results. So did the natives. With something to stir them up, arouse their feeble interest, they came to life with a rush. They were off almost as fast as their prey, swinging their light, hard-driving clubs like a cowboy swings a lariat. Zing! A bamboo cane flashed just above the grass. Apparently there was no trajectory to it. Long after it should have been spent it kept whirling toward a wildly fleeing kangaroo. And when it finally connected, the beast went down in a heap, and no monkey business about it either. The human race was redeeming itself. The hunt now led us out of the grass and into a greasy, slime-covered salt-flat upon which the 'roos made excellent targets. The area looked like a swamp with its winding estuaries and salt-rimmed pools of water but the ground was sandy and firm. Just to make a real, never-to-be-forgotten holiday out of the hunt, I opened up with my rifle, bringing down seven 'roos with two clips of cartridges.

I was accustomed to having natives display considerable agitation upon hearing my rifle for the first time, but never before had they vanished into thin air. Yet that is exactly what happened this time. In the distance I could see the rest of the herd of kangaroos fast becoming a part of the horizon, occasional flecks of spray marking the spot where one had skimmed a pool in his mad flight, but in my immediate vicinity, where there should have been twenty hunters, there were only two of my boys and my gun bearers. The rest were gone, and there was absolutely no place for them to go. There wasn't enough cover in the whole barren flat to conceal a gull's egg.

A few minute's search finally produced one islander. He was playing frog in one of the shallow pools, his body entirely concealed by the thick slime, his hair matted with the green stuff. When he saw me he submerged completely and became as much a part of the bottom as though he had grown there. As he appeared to be determined to drown himself rather than take a chance on hearing my gun again, I sent Wirio in to pull him out. This was done, but not without a struggle. If there had been any water in the pool deeper than six inches, I am convinced the crazy savage would have slid into the depths and drowned himself like a wounded coot.

Having found one, I gave him the job of assembling his brothers. He finally managed to round up about ten slime-covered wretches, but the rest preferred to take it easy in the mud rather than take a chance on meeting a thunder demon in the flesh. It took more convincing to get them to pick up the kangaroo so miraculously slain by my rifle, it being their belief that evil spirits had aided in the work and must perforce still be in possession of the carcasses. My own boys, with wordless contempt, set an example by picking up a kangaroo each, after which the islanders, with growing delight, collected the rest. By the time we got back to the village, they were pretty big stuff. What they told the home folks I don't know, but judging by the airs they put on I don't think they were running themselves down much.

While we were hunting, Leona, who had remained in the village, had learned much of the domestic habits of the islanders.

Accompanied by her Malays, with the exception of Wirio who was with me, she had made a tour of inspection that covered about everything. She found that sago, while not unknown on the island, had to be imported from the mainland, a dangerous bit of commerce. In the first place, the natives had nothing with which to cut down a tree after they got to it. They had to pound on it with nothing more formidable than sticks, bruising the tree repeatedly in the same spot until, after a tremendous amount of labour, they finally wore a hole in the bark. The pulpy interior was then scooped out, after which it was easier to pound through the hollowed-out trunk. Even after the tree was down, there still remained the task of splitting it. This required a couple of more day's work, every minute of which was fraught with fear that a tribe of mainlanders, attracted by the pounding would descend upon them. On the whole, they preferred to make sweet potatoes take the place of sago. The sweet potatoes, fortunately, were fairly common all over the island, often growing to the size of grape fruit. On long trips, instead of carrying dried meat and sago flour, the islanders carried a couple of sweet potatoes strung on rattan and looped over the shoulder.

A couple of hundred yards from the village Leona came upon the boat yard where a twenty foot canoe was under construction. A tough old teakwood tree, apparently the victim of a sad mistake in seed migration for I saw no other teakwood in the salt-ridden vicinity, had been cut down by the simple expedient of burning it through with fire. Fire was the only tool used in shaping the exterior and hollowing out the interior, though the islanders had learned somewhere the art of scraping away the charcoal with a shell. They weren't very adept at it. Judging by the condition of the charred stump, the canoe had been under construction for all of three months and was still less than half finished.

Just beyond the boat works was the home of the kitchen ware, a gigantic ant hill. Frederik Hendrik Island being entirely destitute of stones, the natives would have had nothing to cook on had not some inspired genius such as comes along every few centuries hit upon the bright idea of making clay balls do the work of cooking stones. The only thing lacking was the clay, and this the ants, mining several feet underground, brought up to help hold their skyscraper ant hills together. As the clay balls will not hold together after being heated a few times and soaked with grease, the ants lead a hard life. They no sooner repair the damage of one assault than some other housewife needs a frying pan and chisels ten or twelve apartments out of their multiple dwelling.

Along the mid-afternoon I suddenly noticed the sky to become heavy. Not cloudy; just heavy. It seemed to sag under its own weight, to press down upon us until we had to make a distinct effort to breathe. The trees, the water, the birds, everything seemed to be affected by the strange droopiness of the air. The sun was still shining, but it was lifeless. Shadows were vague, the water had no sparkle or shimmer, the waxy leaves on the trees were as dull and unresponsive as green chalk. Within an hour the sky was low enough to be supported by a tall pole.

The sun didn't set that night. It was just erased from the sky by an invisible horizon about an hour before it was due to set. It was as though the exhausted sky had wearied of supporting the sun any longer and just let it slip into nothingness. First it became orange, then a dead white as blank and pallid as a cardboard disc. It might have been a full moon setting save that the light was unhealthy and cast no shadows. And even after the sun disappeared the eerie light persisted, glowing coldly upon a world that was dead.

The islanders stood about in dumb apathy. They figured something was wrong, but I guess they also realised that no matter what happened they couldn't be much worse off than they were now. It was a consoling sort of philosophy that didn't extend to me. I knew the best thing I could do would be to get back to the launch, and get the launch into the shelter of one of the estuaries I had discovered a few hundred yards from the village. According to the calendar the rainy monsoon was about due, and this uncanny calm probably marked the shift in the prevailing winds from southwest to northeast. If such was the case we could expect almost anything in the way of rain and tempests, for when a breeze has been accustomed to blowing steadily from the southwest for six months, it is

asking a little too much to expect it to reverse itself and blow
steadily from the northeast without first kicking up a little
fuss and that is the process through which the wind passes. Six
months from one direction, then six months from the other.
One period marked by reasonably good weather, the other by
unreasonably bad. We were entering the bad period. With
flourishes.

It was pitch dark when we finally got the launch safely tied
to a stout tree and a stern anchor out. Our crew had the
canoes pulled up on shore upside down, and as many as
possible were crowded beneath. The rest just squatted or lay
down on the bank, resigned to getting wet.

Overhead the few stars that had dared to come out were
fast disappearing. Still no clouds were evident unless the whole
sky was one thin cloud. It looked ominous to me, but even if
this were the lull before the end of the world, we were unable
to devote to it the solemn observance it deserved. The mosquitoes were too bad. I give my word, if those stars hadn't
disappeared in a cosmic void, they would have been blotted
out by the blood-thirstiest clouds of vicious mosquitoes I have
ever had the misfortune to encounter in all my life. How it
happened that my boys on shore were not sucked dry of blood
is one of the mysteries I'll never be able to understand. Below
decks, even with the air full of citronella spray plus a suffocating
smudge from Schultz's pipe they were unbearable. What they
were like on shore can only be estimated in astronomical
figures.

Suddenly there was a moaning in the jungle and then the
boat tilted under a puff of wind. I dashed out on deck. The
sky overhead was black, but in the southwest it was a lot
blacker. Then there was a flash of green lightning. It came from
the northeastern horizon. It was answered by a flash from the
southeastern. One monsoon was starting work before the other
quit, and by the looks of it they were going to meet for lunch
right overhead. But I didn't mind. The third big puff of wind
had cleared the air of mosquitoes.

We were still alive the next morning, and stranger yet, were
still afloat. The boys on shore were still alive also, but somewhat
dubious about what they had to live for. The night's storm had

been no joke, and neither were the prospects for the day. Though the wind had gone down somewhat, the rain was falling in buckets, with every indication that it would continue to do so until it got good and ready to quit.

In the not-too-optimistic hope that I might be able to arrange better shelter for them in the village, I donned a raincoat and slopped off to see what could be done. The low ground was already submerged under two inches of water. In the centre of the miserable village only a black pile marked the perpetual fire that was kept going day in and day out so that all who needed a fire might get a light without spending a day or so spinning a stick in a hardwood socket. The fire was not out, I discovered later. The natives had merely taken it to bed with them.

Sticking my head in the first hut I came to, expecting to find the residents squatting in about three inches of water, I was surprised to find them sitting on bunk-like shelves about four feet above the ground and built for just such an occasion as now. They had their fire right up there with them on a little platform of sticks and mud. The rain was falling as heavily inside as outside, but at least there were a few spots in the roof around which the rain had to detour. The islanders had been thousands of years evolving to the point where they could build shelves high enough to keep their feet out of the water. Maybe in a few more centuries they will reach the point where they can raise their whole hut out of water, like the Digoel natives do with their skyscrapers. But perhaps I expect too much.

Not finding any relief for my boys in the village, I returned to the boat, issued axes and machetes all around, and set out to build a decent village of my own. It took three solid days of working in continuous rain to do it, but when we got through we had the best looking, driest bachelor lodge in Dutch New Guinea, floor, fireplace, smoke vent and all. It was a good thing we built the hut. Once started, the rain didn't let up for more than an hour at a time for two weeks. Without the warmth and shelter of the hut some of the boys would have come down with pneumonia beyond the shadow of a doubt.

Twice during that time I went out and shot kangaroo. Their feeding meadows were under three inches of water and I guess they didn't care whether I shot them or not. At least they didn't run very far when I scared them up.

Aside from our real estate development and the two kangaroo hunts, those two weeks were the most monotonous I have ever put in. The grey sky dripped constantly, and in those brief intervals when it wasn't raining the wind leaped to hurricane proportions as though glad to be released from the weight of the water. There wasn't a spot of ground on the whole island above water except at low tide and then only in the estuaries. The raised, levee-like embankments tossed up by the incoming tide along the inlets served to keep the fresh water from draining off at low tide, thereby producing the paradoxical situation in which the only ground above water was in the ditches at low tide.

Leona and I spent most of the time developing stills in our improvised darkroom below decks, and saw that we had enough in the negatives to make me yearn to get the stuff into an enlarger. When I saw the first patch of blue sky, indicating at least a day of clear weather, I gave the order to hoist anchor and get moving. With luck we should be able to reach Merauke in a week.

Our boys were reluctant to leave their new bachelor lodge, but the islanders were anxious to move in. In fact, before we got out of the channel, the wretches were lugging their few sweet potatoes and bamboo clubs into the huge dormitory. The whole village is probably living there now if it hasn't rotted away completely. If it has three-quarters rotted away, it is still better than their original homes.

We encountered plenty of rain once we left the shelter of Frederik Hendrik Island, but by some freak of good fortune there was little wind. On those few occasions when we did have to run for shore, we employed the time spent in the shelter of the banks to good advantage in replenishing our fire wood for the boiler. Only once did we run into threatened danger. Coming around a low, marshy point, we ran smack into a fleet of fifty war canoes coming out the mouth of the Bian river. Evidently they were the same boys Schultz had encountered on the way up. Armadas of that size are not common in New Guinea.

Catching sight of the smoke pouring out of our steam launch, they turned about in confusion and headed for shore. Once in the safety of the jungle, however, their courage returned. We were wallowing along at little better than six miles an hour, giving them ample opportunity to size up our force and decide they could take us without too much difficulty. Back they came, paddling like demons and shouting like fiends. My boys cut loose from the tow and put out to sea, waiting for nothing.

There was nothing for us to do but engage in a naval battle. I gave three long pulls on the whistle cord and put about, charging headlong for the fleet. The whistle had them paralysed. The next minute Schultz opened up with the shotgun, spraying the fleet with bird shot that was twice as effectual in its impartiality as rifle fire would have been. Schultz might have killed a dozen with his rifle, but that would have meant little to that outfit. But with a hundred or so burned up with pellets that whine through the air like evil spirits after every thunderous report, they lost an awful lot of belligerence. A few of the bravest released a barrage of arrows that fell short by a hundred yards, after which their activity was limited to plying the paddles in wild retreat.

"Get the bastards," yelled Schultz, and banged away with two more barrels.

I held the launch full on for the river mouth, tooting the whistle for all it was worth but with due regard for the ailing boiler. Between the reports of Schultz's shot-gun and my whistle, the native navy was completely disorganised, so much so that we actually gained on them and that's saying plenty. They were trying to paddle in all directions at once, including straight up when some of Schultz's pellets managed to connect.

I decided to give them a thorough lesson so I kept right on going even after we entered the mouth of the river. Suddenly an amazing thing happened. Two or three natives in the rearmost canoes picked up bamboo sections and began tossing fine white dust high into the air. The stuff was so light it hung there like a smoke cloud. Within thirty seconds the river from one jungle wall to the other was obscured by the floating pall, and ahead of us, where there had been a shrieking bedlam, there was now a deathly silence. Not even the pounding of the paddle against the gunwales could be heard. We had been tricked by a modern enactment of the world's first smoke screen.

I wasted no time turning about. It was useless to try to find anything in the cloud of dust ahead, even though it was already beginning to settle and float upon the water. On the other hand, these boys might take to the brush and double back, giving us the well-known works from shore. We got out of there.

By the time we were once more at the mouth of the river our own brave boys had returned from their Odyssey out to sea and were ready to mop up on whatever corpses we had left lying around. They were just a little bit let down that our victory had been a moral one rather than a bloody one. After all, with out whistle and shotguns we should have had at least one head to our credit.

That night we tied up on shore for the last time, I hoped. Merauke was a scant twenty miles away. Our launch was running as perfectly as it ever would, and the red sunset indicated a perfect day ahead. It was true our rudder had dropped off somewhere between the Bian river and our present, un-named point, but I had carved out a long sweep with an axe, and it was doing every bit as well as the rudder. A little steam was leaking out around the boiler head, but that, too, was all to the good. It would give Achmed something to worry about and keep his mind on his business instead of on the Javanese maiden he was so soon to rejoin in Semarang.

True to my most optimistic forecast, we rounded the delta of the Merauke river shortly after noon. Just a mile away, staggering out into the river, was the sagging, wobbly pier of Merauke, as pretentious at that moment as the Statue of Liberty in New York harbour. Another five minutes and we sighted the tin roofs of the army barracks, more imposing than the New York skyline. Civilisation at last. Gin splits with ice. Sheets and a bed—with springs. White men. A radio. Even newspapers, old but good.

It was too much for Achmed. He forgot his leaky boiler.

He forgot the stubborn safety valve. He forgot his roaring fire. He forgot everything, until the boiler head blew off again. Then he was regretful. I made a quick rush for the rail. If the tide was coming in—but it wasn't. The roiled, bubbling water was going out, and taking us with it. A fine thing.

There was nothing for it but to send the boys ahead in the canoes and have them send the gasoline tender back to tow us in. Schultz looked at me and I looked at him. Here was a chance to race our canoe crews. Schultz summoned his crew. I called in Wasbus and his nine giants. While Schultz was giving verbal orders to his head man, I wrote a brief note to Captain Versteegh and gave it to Wasbus.

"And remember this," I warned. "If Schultz's men get there first, you're going to have to come back here and tow the launch in by hand." It was taking unfair advantage of Schultz, but I had to win. That threat of labour carried far greater significance to Wasbus than any threat of punishment Schultz would hold over his crew.

"Ready?" I asked Schultz.

"Ready," he said.

I fired my pistol and the boys were off. Leona joined me at the rail.

"A gin-split says that Schultz's boys beat yours," she said.

I grabbed the bet. My boys were a hundred yards to the good.

A few minutes later I saw her in conversation with Schultz, but the race was getting hotter now and I paid no attention. Wasbus was throwing up such a cloud of spray I couldn't tell who was ahead. Then there was a sudden calm. I saw Wasbus throw himself upon the dock and sprint madly for shore. I had won. Schultz's demons were defeated. I didn't care now if we floated clear out to sea. At least I had scored a great victory, and the sting of having to enter port in disgrace at the end of a tow rope was greatly salved.

"You owe me a gin-split." I informed Leona.

"Collect it from Schultz," she advised. "I bet him he would lose."

"A fine gambler you are," snorted Schultz. "Playing your bets both ways against the middle."

"That's just what you told me to do when we first started out," Leona replied sweetly. "You told me that I should never gamble in the jungle, and that if it ever came to a showdown, I should put my money on both sides at once. And that's just what I did."

Schultz nodded solemnly. "That's right. You never lose but what you win. And in the jungle you have to win when you lose because if you just lose you never get another chance to win. Or don't you get what I mean?"

"I know I've got a gin-split coming, and you can't win on that one," I said.

"Here comes the launch," said Leona.

THE END.